DESIGN
EXPERTISE

BRYAN **LAWSON**

DESIGN
EXPERTISE

KEES **DORST**

ELSEVIER

OXFORD AUCKLAND BOSTON JOHANNESBURG
MELBOURNE NEW DELHI

Architectural Press is an imprint of Elsevier

Linacre House, Jordan Hill, Oxford OX2 8DP, UK

30 Corporate Drive, Suite 400, Burlington, MA 01803, USA

British Library Cataloguing in Publication Data
A catalogue record for this book is available from the British Library

Library of Congress Cataloguing in Publication Data
A catalogue record for this book is available from the Library of Congress

ISBN: 978-1-8561-7670-5

For information on all Architectural Press publications visit our web site at
http://books.elsevier.com

Printed and bound in the United Kingdom
Book Designer: Bec Paton | www.bpicky.net

09 10 11 12 13 10 9 8 7 6 5 4 3 2 1

Working together to grow
libraries in developing countries

www.elsevier.com | www.bookaid.org | www.sabre.org

ELSEVIER   BOOK AID
            International   Sabre Foundation

CONTENTS

ACKNOWLEDGEMENTS

The authors are grateful for the time spent by many outstanding designers discussing their work and processes over a period of many years. In particular we thank:

Eliane Beyer
Santiago Calatrava
Wim Crouwel
Wim Groeneboom
Theo Groothuizen
Frans de la Haye
Herman Hertzberger
Eva Jiricna
Hella Jongerius
Jan Lucassen
Richard MacCormac
John Outram
Jeroen van Oyen
Denise Scott Brown
Robert Venturi
Michael Wilford
Ken Yeang

We thank dr. Robin Groeneveld for the quotes of the Dutch designers, they were originally part of the interviews in his PhD thesis (Groeneveld, 2006).

We also thank the research students who have worked on projects that we have relied on for data and insights, particularly:

Khairul Khaidzir
Alex Menezes
Marcia Pereira
Ishmail bin Samsuddin

We also acknowledge the efforts and insights generated by the many design students who have participated in our research studies. In particular students of the Design Academy Eindhoven, the Department of Industrial Design at Eindhoven University of Technology, and students of the Departments of Architecture, Landscape, Civil and Structural Engineering, and Mechanical Engineering, at the University of Sheffield.

Finally, we would like to thank our many colleagues, especially in the design research community, for their engaging and challenging discussions over many years of debate.

We acknowledge the following illustrations:

Figure 1.1	Professor Peter Blundell Jones
Figure 1.2	University of Sheffield
Figure 1.4	Hella Jongerius
Figure 2.1	Wim Crouwel
Figure 2.5	Theo Groothuizen
Figure 2.6	Eliane Beyer
Figure 2.9	Yorkshire ArtSpace Persistence Works (photograph Bryan Lawson)
Figure 2.11	Ken Yeang
Figure 2.12	Theo Groothuizen
Figure 4.4	John Outram
Figures 4.6–4.9	Alex Menezes
Figure 4.11	Ishmail bin Samsuddin
Figure 5.2	John Outram
Figures 5.5–5.6	Robert Venturi
Figure 6.1	Ishmail bin Samsuddin
Figure 7.3	Jeroen van Oyen
Figure 7.4	Frans de la Haye

We would like to thank our graphic designer Bec Paton, for creating the book that now lies before you.

1

JOURNEYS
THROUGH
DESIGN

The artist is not a special kind of man.
Every man is a special kind of artist.
ERIC GILL

Engineers like to solve problems. If there
are no problems handily available, they
will create their own problems.
SCOTT ADAMS

WHAT IS THIS BOOK ABOUT?

Designing is one of the most complex and sophisticated things we can do with our minds. Many of those who design for a living find it to be so addictive that when they do not have a current commission they may invent one for themselves. And yet designing remains one of the least well understood of all our cognitive powers and most difficult to teach. Part of the excitement of designing is that you never really know how good a job you can do; each project is unique and there is no comfortingly repeatable process that will guarantee success. Above all designing is creative and unpredictable. The comments on the opposite page by the British architect, Richard MacCormac summarise this duality with the feeling born of experience. This book explores the process of becoming a designer, the creation of design expertise. What knowledge, skills, attributes and experiences are necessary in order to design fluently and to good effect?

In one sense we are all designers. Many of us design parts of our homes, gardens, and workplaces. At the very least we make decisions about how to dispose and arrange items; we all make decisions about which clothes to buy and design our own appearance every day. And yet we admire, seek out and pay for the work of the world's most outstanding professional designers. There seems a huge gulf between what they do and the everyday design of ordinary people. Exactly what does it take then to become such an expert designer? What is the real nature of design expertise and how do we create and develop that expertise? Throughout the book we shall discuss these questions and offer some answers.

Implicit in much design education and criticism is the idea of the 'talented designer'. Behind this notion rests an assumption that some people have an innate ability to design and others do not and might as well give up. We shall challenge that notion throughout this book. While it may well be the case that some people design without apparent effort, we shall argue that for most of us design is, like so much other human cognitive activity, a skill. In fact we shall argue that it is a complex collection of skills.

That simple notion leads us inevitably to the consequence that these skills can be identified, learned and taught. It also suggests that there may be some ways of doing all these things that are more likely to be effective than others. Although it is possible to teach and learn sophisticated skills such as a sport or playing a musical instrument, this sadly does not mean we can all become world ranked or a virtuoso. But most of us can improve significantly if we can only find the best way for us of learning and creating expertise. So it is for design.

Fig 1.1 Fitzwilliam College Cambridge Chapel by Richard MacCormac—a fine example of his sensitive approach to university buildings

JOURNEYS THROUGH DESIGN
RICHARD MACCORMAC

 This is not a sensible way of making a living, it's completely insane. You agree to do this job with no idea really that you can come up with anything worthwhile... no idea how much it will take to do it... there has to be this big thing that you're confident you're going to find, you don't know what it is you're looking for and you hang on, it's a journey really, I mean the analogy of a journey is a very interesting one... the design process is a journey, an episodic journey towards a destination which you don't know about, which is what life is and what writing and all arts are like; a journey.

RICHARD MACCORMAC

Richard MacCormac studied architecture at Cambridge and the Bartlett School in London. He was heavily influenced by the work of Leslie Martin and Lionel March. He admits to having an 'almost obsessive interest' in the Prairie Houses of Frank Lloyd and has developed an almost equal respect for Sir John Soane. After setting up his own small practice he soon formed a partnership with Peter Jamieson and eventually also David Prichard. They became known for a series of influential low rise housing schemes including student accommodation as well as a number of academic university buildings at both Oxford and Cambridge. Richard MacCormac has written and lectured extensively on his approach to architecture, and taught architecture at Cambridge and Edinburgh Universities. He was elected president of the Royal Institute of British Architects in 1991 and championed high quality design. His presidency was celebrated by the 'Art of the Process' exhibition at the RIBA that showed the evolution of designs by a series of well-known British architects. His more recent work includes a major centre for Cable and Wireless, an underground station on the Jubilee Line and the redevelopment of Broadcasting House for the BBC.

We hope that those who are reading this book, whether they are students, practitioners, educators or researchers, will find help and inspiration here in developing their own particular way of understanding designing.

WHAT IS IN THE BOOK?

We begin in Chapter 2 by rehearsing our contemporary understanding of the nature of design problems and the activities that, taken together, constitute the act of designing. Even the most cursory examination of design reveals that it is not a simple singular activity but involves a complex array of tasks. Design is not like some physical skills such as riding a bicycle or swimming. Designing is not a matter of doing one thing but of doing many things. Designing depends not only on some clearly defined and well understood set of knowledge but also makes use of apparently remote and wide ranging ideas. Our more detailed analysis will show that design depends upon skills, knowledge and understanding. The design student then is challenged by having to acquire all three, and the educator bears the responsibility of assisting in that process. Professional designers must keep developing the skills, knowledge and understanding that make up design expertise through their professional practice.

Some of the skills that designers rely upon can be isolated and studied in their own right and this book will not dwell extensively on those. An obvious example would be the skill of drawing. There are many excellent books to help the student learn to draw and this book will not tread on their territory. However, there may well be some issues to do with drawing that impact on the more central cognitive processes and activities of designing and that will definitely be of interest to us here. Similarly, designers obviously need substantial chunks of knowledge. They need to know about the technicalities of constructing the things they are designing. They may need to know about the relative costs of different ways of manufacturing and operating the objects or systems they are designing. They will need to be able to calculate and compare some features of the technical performance of their objects, or at least work with other professionals who specialise in such matters. Again it is not the job of this book to explore, teach or research such areas. As with skills, it may be that certain ways of knowing about such matters do indeed impact on the very business of designing, and we shall be interested in that.

In Chapter 3 we shall begin to turn our attention to the issue of expertise in general. One of the key common characteristics of generic expertise models suggests that experts do not necessarily do the same things as novices. Whether we look at the playing of chess, the solving of mathematical

EXPERIENCE
RICHARD MACCORMAC

I think that my role in the practice is to initiate the design processes in all the major jobs, not so much in building types like housing where I think we have established a kind of repertoire, a typological repertoire, which is to do with density... it's sort of vernacular if you like, we do quite a lot of it for housing associations and so on... vernacular in the sense that it's a language that's the common language...

p.t.o. →

problems or the flying of aeroplanes, we find that it is not simply a case of experts working faster, more effectively or better than novices. What we find is that they operate differently. We shall explore the implications of this for design. It strongly suggests that there are several modes of designing. These modes depend upon different levels of experience and knowledge enabling designers to think in different ways. Some modes may suit some individuals better than others and some may be difficult to operate on without considerable practice and experience.

One example of this being explicitly recognised is given by Richard Mac-Cormac who tells us that his role in the design practice changes when the job involves an unfamiliar building typology. He clearly feels that he should adjust the way he relates to the design team according to the extent of their experience. Effectively MacCormac is telling us the way the design process is organised even within his own practice depends upon the level of expertise available. Designers are thus aware of the development of expertise through their practice and yet relatively little has previously been written about the nature and growth of expertise in design.

Design research is now maturing as an area of study and in recent years we have begun to understand more about this process of creating expertise. Design has been taught as a central subject in the degree courses for such disciplines as architecture, interior design, industrial design and graphics. More recently, other areas of design have become popular including urban and landscape design, theatre design, fashion and textile design, and have been joined by web and interface design. Of course there have always been those who wanted to understand and improve design but as a serious field design research is a relative newcomer. In the middle of the twentieth century there were enough people working in the field to begin to hold conferences and publish their proceedings.

Even so it would not have been possible to write this book until recently. While the output of the world's greatest designers has always been examined in the greatest detail and endlessly argued over, their processes have been relatively neglected. Around the turn of the century, a number of studies began to appear that focused specifically on outstanding designers.

In Chapter 4 we look at the start of the journey. We investigate the kinds of skills and ways of thinking and seeing that those starting out as designers need to acquire and develop. In particular, we look at the changes that take place as people are transformed from everyday designers into students of design. This is often a time of great confusion and some doubt for many design students. Not only do many of them need to develop new skills for

WRITING THIS BOOK

The first significant international conference to explore the nature of design expertise took place in Sydney in 2003 (Cross and Edmonds, 2003). This built on attempts to understand the whole idea of expertise that in turn had been driven by attempts to develop artificial expert systems and the consequent need to capture human expertise in symbolically coded digital environments. Design however remains a human activity beyond the capability of artificial intelligence and therefore poses some interesting challenges to the computational theory of mind that lies behind such work. While some have argued that it is merely a matter of time before computers will be able to design, others including the authors of this book argue that there is something essentially human about this highly creative activity.

representing design externally, such as drawing and modelling, but they also have to restructure the way they represent design in their minds. They have simultaneously to begin gathering knowledge and creating meaningful mental structures and concepts with which to evaluate and order that knowledge.

In Chapter 5 we turn our attention to the higher levels of design expertise as found in professional practice. Our model of design expertise developed in Chapter 3 will show that a graduate can normally only expect to have reached the lower levels. Design is something that has to be at least partly learned in practice. However, because of the essentially creative, experimental and unpredictable nature of design this makes learning on the job a little hit and miss. We will look at just why it takes time to acquire higher levels of design expertise and the kinds of knowledge that designers create through extended practice. We will explore the very different ways of working that are often developed by experienced designers.

In the final two chapters of the book we shall return to a more detailed investigation of design education and practice. We shall assemble together many of the questions that have been thrown up by our investigation of design expertise in order to develop a theoretical critique of current design education. One of the extraordinary features of the design education system is the consistency with which it is organised. We may look at the education of industrial designers, architects or urban designers, for example, and see remarkably similar patterns. We may travel to the continents of North and South America, Europe, Africa, Asia or Australasia and see these patterns repeated. Why is this? Has design education evolved into a well honed and highly effective system, or are there some commonly accepted practices that we have simply stopped questioning because they are so firmly embedded? We are convinced that the latter is the case, and will argue for a critical reappraisal of some of the 'sacred cows' of design education.

Finally, we shall investigate how the ideas in this book help us to understand the continuing journey that designers all make through their practice. We shall look at both individual personal development and the creation of expertise in design practices. Both here and earlier we will be informed by the words of real practicing designers who often have remarkable insights into their own practice.

Throughout the book we will continue to investigate the nature of design research. Does it cover the field well or does it have some blind spots? Have we investigated the really critical features of designing, or just those most amenable to observation and experimentation? A clue here is the rather large

Fig 1.2 Architectural design studio—University of Sheffield 1930s

Fig 1.3 Architectural design studio—University of Sheffield 2007

proportion of design research that uses students as a source of data. Could it be that we might learn new things about designing if we can study much more experienced and expert designers? Many of the issues we touch on throughout this book suggest new and interesting research questions that can only be answered by taking a more holistic approach to design expertise.

WHAT THIS BOOK IS NOT

This is not an instruction or training manual. This book cannot and will not attempt to teach a design method or process. Research in design has shown that there are many ways of designing well and successfully. Indeed, current thinking about design sees every single project as unique and special. We have come a long way since the early, rather prescriptive, ideas about design methods. We do, however, take the view that design skills can be learned, practised and improved. This book then is no more a guarantee of success than membership of a gym would guarantee to make you fit. Perhaps the ideas in this book should be seen as the equipment in the gym. If the reader takes them seriously and reflects on how they might be applied then we would expect some results.

The key here, however, is reflection. Designers all have their own unique background and collections of skills, attitudes, values and interests. Designers work on their own set of problems and circumstances. For this reason it is impossible to give some generic advice which will be uniformly helpful across all circumstances. On the other hand, it is usually accepted that being able to draw well is generally likely to help a designer to perform better. This book extends that idea and principle of identifying the things that are generally helpful for the development of design expertise. The book then provides some intellectual equipment but the reader will still have to do all the really hard work.

WHO SHOULD READ THIS BOOK?

This book is for design students and practicing designers as well as for educators and researchers.

The book is intended to help students who are trying to develop their own ways of designing. It does not offer a set of procedures which, if followed, guarantee or even promise a successful process. Rather it is a commentary on the things that more expert designers know, do and understand. One of the problems facing design students is the way that role models may be held up for them; the magazines are full of heroes. However, it may be very

Fig 1.4 'Soft Urn' by Hella Jongerius (1994)—explores the relationship between the archetypal shape of the vase, the unexpected material (soft PU) and the 'hand-made' quality of the imperfections that are carefully managed in the production process. Air bubbles in the material become decoration

IT DRIVES ME MAD
HELLA JONGERIUS

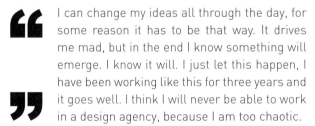

I can change my ideas all through the day, for some reason it has to be that way. It drives me mad, but in the end I know something will emerge. I know it will. I just let this happen, I have been working like this for three years and it goes well. I think I will never be able to work in a design agency, because I am too chaotic.

HELLA JONGERIUS
Hella Jongerius (1963) started her design career in the early 1990s with products for the iconic Dutch designers' collective Droog Design. She now has her own studio JongeriusLab in Rotterdam. Her work concentrates on the application of new materials within an archetypal shape language. Craftsmanship and imperfection arisen during the process of production create a new kind of decoration that is part of her aesthetic. She thus explores the boundary between mass production and the qualities of the craft object, between modernism and the decorative arts. Her works can be considered 'conversation pieces', in which she instigates discussions about the contrast between the struggle of making and the self-centred, easy process of consumption. She finds that designers don't do enough to question and explore the nature of the products they are making, and contribute to a world where the clutter of smooth and easily marketable products reduces our creativity. Her work is represented in the collections of the major museums around the world, and she has created objects for companies like Vitra and Ikea.

difficult for novice students to learn from such distinguished internationally famous exemplars. It is also often the case that what students see is not the process but the product of their role models. Simply copying the output of distinguished designers is also unlikely to guarantee a successful process, though such an exercise may have some value. This book is intended to show the stages of development through which we believe most designers progress. The developing student may find it helpful to review the book at various stages and to use it to help reflect on their own progress and the challenges that remain ahead.

One of the important lessons of this book is that it takes many years for most of us to become good professional designers. The graduate student has really only just begun the journey which must be continued into and throughout professional practice. Throughout this book we shall explore why it is that the process takes so long and there are special chapters devoted to how both students and professional designers develop their expertise through practice.

This book is also directed at those who teach and tutor design. A paradox of design education is that those involved are usually fascinated by the highly tangible outcome of the design process. It is good design that interests them and motivates them. We shall see later in the book that this is a perfectly understandable and, in many ways, highly desirable trait in tutors. However, simply showing students good design is not necessarily the most helpful way of enabling them to develop their own expertise. This book offers a resource for those who teach design to reflect upon the kinds of experiences, exercises and material that they might place in front of their students and at what stage.

Those who conduct design research should find many of the arguments in here of interest. This is not a complete theory but rather a map of the acquisition of design expertise as we currently see it. There are no doubt sections which are less well developed than others and we fully expect the design research community to help to develop them. However, a key argument in the book is that we need more research to disaggregate design expertise so that we can understand and develop it better.

HOW TO USE THIS BOOK

Throughout the book the central lines of argument will appear in the main text area on the left hand page. Interspersed with this on the right hand page the reader will find many provocations. These include examples of design thinking from students, and professional designers. Many of these quotations come from interviews with notable designers and the first time each designer is introduced the reader will also find a brief biography to set the contents into context and usually an illustration of their work. The example here from Hella Jongerius tells us that even successful designers can find the business of designing simultaneously rewarding and yet frustrating as they continue to develop their expertise. In fact, she is really confirming what Richard MacCormac told us right back at the start of this first chapter.

Also on the right hand page will be illustrations, diagrams and other items to provoke the reader into thinking more deeply. Occasionally too, we will summarise models and taxonomies that have been developed and will be central to the argument in later chapters. Some of the key models developed in the book are identified by simple diagrams or icons and these will appear whenever the model is referred to so the reader easily refers back to the place where it was first introduced and most fully discussed. However, it is important not to read these icons too literally. We have deliberately tried to make them roughly represent what we are saying and also to be memorable and recognisable. Nevertheless, these should not be taken to be completely accurate representations. In fact, we are not confident that most of the rather complex phenomena connected with designing can ever be represented by simple diagrams.

This book does not necessarily have to be read from beginning to end. The chapters are in what seems to the authors the most logical sequence. They relate to progressively more sophisticated design approaches. It may therefore suit some readers to approach the book from where they feel they are themselves. Alternatively, readers may find that as they scan through the book, items on the right hand page catch their eye and they could read selectively from there. One way of reading the book is to flip through looking for all the icons that refer to a particular model or issue and read the sections of text about it. We see the creation of design expertise as a journey. There is no one right or wrong way of taking this journey. The reader may like to see the various ideas in this book as signposts along their own personal journey through design.

REFERENCES

Cross, N. and Edmonds, E., eds (2003). **Expertise in Design: design thinking research symposium 6.** Sydney, Creativity and Cognition Studios Press.

2
UNDERSTANDING
DESIGN

Everyone designs who devises courses of action
aimed at changing existing situations into preferred
ones. The intellectual activity that produces
material artefacts is no different fundamentally
from the one that prescribes remedies for a sick
patient or the one that devises a new sales plan for
a company or a social welfare policy for a state.
HERBERT SIMON (THE SCIENCES OF THE ARTIFICIAL)

We can't solve problems by using the same kind
of thinking we used when we created them.
ALBERT EINSTEIN

INTRODUCTION

'Design' is a fundamental human activity, as well as the name of a number of quite specific professions. Since we suppose that most of our readers are practicing designers, design students or educators already involved in the field of design, we do not need to dwell on the vexed question of what would be a good definition of design. Nevertheless, we need a few words to explain what we see as the salient features of the design activity, to avoid confusion, set the stage for developing models of design and prepare to explore the creation design expertise.

DESIGN UNDEFINED

The fact that 'design' is such a confusing term, widely used and misused in common parlance, has been problematic in the development of the design professions. If we are not careful, the mere use of the word makes any discussions about design in general flawed, muddled and unproductive. We will use this chapter to put words to our understanding of what design is, and thus steer clear of this trap.

We need to establish what we mean when we say 'design'. But how can we do that? Often we tend to clarify things by defining them; that is by naming their constituent parts. But this will not do for design which is an activity and a way of thinking that is spread across many professional fields. Perhaps looking at what these fields have in common will give us an inkling of the kernel of design expertise? Yet when we look closely we see that the work of these professional fields does not necessarily exhibit one single common trait.

Their range and diversity are huge. However, these various design activities do display what Wittgenstein would call a 'family resemblance' (Wittgenstein, 1953, pp 31–32); there is a variable series of traits that some members of the family will have in common to a varying extent. Thus, within the wide range of activities one could validly call design we might see that the extremes hardly resemble each other at all, but lurking under the surface there are indeed common and characteristic traits.

To confound our problems, we have to admit that design not only encompasses a broad range of activities across many professional fields, but that these activities are also very complicated; perhaps designing is one of the most complicated things we humans do. Since we have just relied on the philosopher Wittgenstein it is worth remembering that he became very interested in architecture and expressed this complexity in a conversation in

THE FAMILY OF DESIGN

In his classic treatise, 'The Concept of Mind', Gilbert Ryle compared thinking with farming (Ryle, 1949). They are both what he called 'polymorphous concepts'. Any two farmers we meet may share almost nothing in common; one may rear sheep for wool while another may grow crops for food. And yet we have no problem seeing them both as 'farmers'. Since design is an advanced form of thinking we should not be surprised that it shares this polymorphous characteristic.

1930: 'You think philosophy is difficult enough, but I tell you it is nothing to the difficulty of being a good architect' (Wilson, 1986).

If we abandon the attempt at a direct definition of design, but we still want to distinguish some different kinds of design, we end up in trouble too. If we split design up along the lines of professional fields we might think of the fields of architecture, engineering, interior design, interaction design, software design, graphic design and product design. But if we think of these as separate categories of design practice, we miss the way the boundaries between these design disciplines are vague and tending to become more so.

For instance, in all the main design disciplines, there are branches that look very much like product design; in architecture it is the design of building systems, in mechanical engineering it is the development of small, mass-produced machines and in graphic design, the development of company logos and house styles. So, the various seemingly different strands of design just have too much in common to make a clear distinction. Often it is precisely the people who work at these crossovers in design thinking that yield the most interesting results. It is vital that any single description of design should do justice to this phenomenon. We had better leave design undefined, at least for now.

DESIGN AS...

One of the difficulties in understanding design, is its multifaceted nature. There is no one single way of looking at design that captures the 'essence' without missing some other salient aspects. Moreover, what aspects would be salient of course depends on your point of view, and your goal in trying to describe and understand design. To cater for many different points of view we will resort to describing design through a series of short paragraphs that suggest how we could see design from different viewpoints. In doing so we will be using a characteristically 'designerly' way of thinking. Conceptual design has been described as the art of seeing the design situation in multiple ways or 'seeing as'. Designers are used to performing this little dance around a problem, taking stabs at it from different sides. This may sound chaotic but if done well it allows one to build up an integrated picture in the end. So in this chapter we will be taking multiple stabs at describing design itself, and hope to end up with an integrated image of design in our minds that is strong enough to carry this understanding into the next chapters, and avoid confusion in the discussions later on.

Fig 2.1 This Dutch stamp series (1976) epitomises the 'New Sobriety' in Wim Crouwel's work. The minimalism is relieved by the friendly lower-case font and colour gradient.

WIM CROUWEL

I have to say that for me feeling and rationality are very close together. Unexplainably close. And that can bother you. I have discovered this dualism over the years. In the beginning I did not know. At the end of 1960 I was so completely convinced, that I only had one single way of working. The real discovery of dualism happened later. As I grow older, I get a sharper eye for the things I would like to do all over again, and the things I would never redo. I become more selective about my work.

WIM CROUWEL

Wim Crouwel (1928) was trained in Groningen and Amsterdam. In his long and distinguished career he was one of the founders of Total Design (1963), the leading Dutch design firm in the modernist era of the 1960s and 70s—with a portfolio that stretched from graphic design and jewelry design to product design. He is generally regarded as a leading exponent of the 'Nieuwe Zakelijkheid' (an heir to the De Stijl movement of the 1920s and 30s—the name translates as 'New Sobriety'). In all his design work he seriously pursues the adage 'Less is more', almost taking this to extremes. He integrates form and message, graphic elements and typography in subtle, deceptively simple designs of the utmost clarity. Any unnecessary elements were rigorously removed, giving his design an unassailable puritanical beauty. In addition to his work for Total Design, Wim Crouwel has been Dean and Professor of design at the Faculty of Industrial Design at Delft University of Technology, before becoming the director of the modern art museum Boymans van Beuningen in Rotterdam.

DESIGN AS...
A MIXTURE OF CREATIVITY AND ANALYSIS

It seems sensible to begin our picture gallery by describing design from the inside, as a way of thinking. In fact this is where it gets complicated straight away; design is not one way of thinking, but several. In particular it is a mix of rational, analytical thinking and creativity. This inherent schizophrenia is a defining characteristic of design, and it directly leads to the peculiar way of working that is a common trait of practice throughout the design professions. Wim Crouwel is surely alluding to this precious characteristic of designing.

This combination of thinking modes can best be illustrated in an experiment by Bryan Lawson (1979). To investigate how designers and non-designers would tackle a design-like problem, he set a series of puzzles to two groups of advanced students. One group studied science, and the others were designers (architects). And what happened? The scientists started by analysing the structure of the problem, and once they understood it, they set about solving it.

The designers, on the other hand, began by laying out high-scoring solutions and to see if they were allowed; a completely different approach. If they were not successful they modified the solutions until they found one that was permitted. Apparently, the designers were used to problems that did not lend themselves to exhaustive analysis. They were accustomed to dealing with the chaotic problems of their profession by creating high-scoring solutions, analysing those and evaluating them. Their creativity and analytical skills were focused on the solution, not on the problem. This strategy can be recognised in all design professions. In many design situations, the generation of possible solutions and their gradual improvement is the only way forward.

In the case of this experiment, the bad news is that of course there was a structure to the problem, and the way the science students went about it was far more effective and efficient if you wanted to understand that structure. Maybe one could say that designers are defined by the way they treat a problem as if it has no structure; as if it is a design problem. This does unearth a real dilemma often keenly felt in design practice; confronted with a design problem one might tackle it in either a problem-focused (analytical) or a solution-focused (creative) way. This can be a hard choice for a designer; being too analytical can lead to an unnecessary limitation of the solution space, while being too creative and generative can launch a journey into nothingness. Experienced designers often introduce constraints of their own (their own personal 'style', or their 'way of doing things') to avoid the

BRYAN LAWSON'S BLOCKS EXPERIMENT

Subjects were given a set of blocks coloured red and blue on the vertical faces and white and black on the horizontal ones. They were asked to arrange some of the blocks on a grid to create a surrounding wall that was either as blue or red as possible. But there were some hidden rules about which combinations of blocks would be allowed. The only information available was from a computer that would say whether a submitted design conformed to the rules or not.

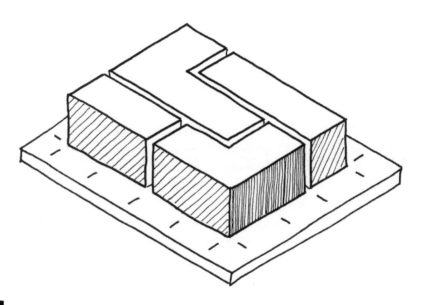

FIG 2.2 Bryan Lawson's blocks experiment

latter. Being lost in a sea of solutions is very unproductive—it is almost as bad as being stuck in a corner.

In design, we are rarely either completely free or completely bound by the problem. Designers have creatively to develop a design, but this creativity is not unrestricted. Achieving a good design is the challenge, one that solves the problems and creates value for the client and prospective user. Combining the two fundamentally different thinking styles of problem solving and creativity means that design is somewhat at odds with the normal ways in which we classify and understand the world. Traditional universities often do not have faculty structures that easily and logically accommodate design. National research funding councils are often either science or arts based. Design is an oddity. We might say it is the 'platypus' of the cognitive world. But like the platypus it is here and we had better learn to deal with it (Pirsig, 1991).

This blend of different thinking styles makes it difficult for many people to understand design. But to designers, these thinking styles are so intimately connected in a design project that they seem almost merged into one way of thinking. When steeped deeply in your design activity you just keep switching between analysis and creativity, between 'problem' and 'solution' without any effort. In practice it is often devilishly hard to distinguish between them.

This is where we should be careful not to descend into such a theoretical description and modelling of design that we lose all contact with the daily reality of life for designers. If designers do not feel a rift between these ways of thinking, then it does not help them much when the theoreticians tell them there is. The real issue resides with those of us who study design, based on the normal paradigms of science; the frameworks we normally use to describe and analyse human activities and cognitive processes ('creativity', 'problem solving', 'decision making', etc.) do not fit cleanly or easily with design.

DESIGN AS...
PROBLEM SOLVING

A recurring and dominant model of design used in design education relies on seeing design as a problem solving process. How does this work? In classical problem solving you pose the problem, search for a good solution by generating (perhaps all) possible next moves, explore the consequences, evaluate them and then choose. This process of pose-search-generate-evaluate-choose can clearly be recognised in design practice. If we observe designers working we can sometimes see them doing something remarkably similar to this. So

BREAKING OUT OF THE CONVENTIONAL STRUCTURES OF KNOWLEDGE

The Duckbilled Platypus created a real stir in the biological world when it was first discovered. It can only be found in a very small part of the world mainly along the east coast of Australia. A specimen was sent by Captain John Hunter, the second Governor of New South Wales, back to the British Museum in 1799. George Shaw, the keeper of the natural history section was suspicious. Quite simply this creature ought not to exist at all, he thought, since it did not fit into any of the existing structures of knowledge. It looked very odd with its duck-like beak, mole-like furry body and flat beaver-like tail. Its behaviour was even odder. Like a mammal it has a furry body and suckles its young, like a bird, it lays eggs, and it has almost reptilian venomous spurs on its legs.

Shaw wrote that it was 'impossible not to entertain some doubts as to the genuine nature of the animal, and to surmise that there might have been practiced some arts of deception in its structure'. Suspicions were heightened since the specimen had crossed the Indian Ocean and Chinese sailors were known for their ability in taxidermy.

The platypus was finally accepted not as a hoax but as a challenge to science when more specimens arrived. Yet the platypus was only an anomaly because the biologists made it so. It is only strange because it does not fit neatly into their preconceived view of what a mammal should be. Luckily, the duckbilled platypuses themselves do not seem to be particularly bothered by this. From their perspective, there is nothing wrong. They delight us by going about their business, happily paddling from pool to pool, in tune with their ecological niche.

Today the platypus is classified as one of only three species known as Monotremes.

Fig 2.3 A duckbilled platypus

seeing design as problem solving does capture some aspects of design. It may not be describing all of design, all the time, but capturing half of design in a model already represents some progress.

The idea that design is problem solving has led to the development of phase models of the design process, in which you first define the problem, analyse it to formulate requirements and then generate solutions. You choose between these solutions with the help of your requirements, and then implement the chosen solution. This model of design has worked tolerably well in many design professions, although it has also been criticised. Like any model, it highlights some aspects of design while neglecting others. Yet, it seems that as long as the design goals are explicit, clear and stable, and a set of comparable solutions can be generated, design can be treated very much like problem solving. This seems to occur more often in the technically-oriented design professions, like engineering, and also more in the latter parts of a design project, when many of the conceptual decisions have been taken. The sturdy problem solving model and its many accompanying methods then help to structure design work, allowing designers to tackle very complicated design problems. It also enables non-designers to understand design, albeit in a limited way, by relating to a common activity (problem solving is, after all, an incessant universal human activity).

But there is danger in thinking that we have captured all design activity in this model. There is no way in which all of design can be reduced to a problem solving activity. There are many factors in design situations that take us away from the rational high ground of 'normal' problem solving, into a much more marshy and murky area of design practice.

DESIGN AS...
LEARNING

When people first started modelling design, they tended to use the problem solving model of design as a clear and concise starting point for organising their thoughts and observations. Thus many of the early books about design tried to understand design in this manner. But the designers on the ground soon revolted against these abstractions, saying that while the problem solving models of design are particularly helpful for controlling and managing design projects, they remain remarkably silent when we want to know more about design than just how to control and structure it. This relative 'distance' from everyday experience has been a criticism voiced by practitioners of the problem solving view of design. Nigel Cross quotes Christopher Alexander, one of the early architectural design theo-

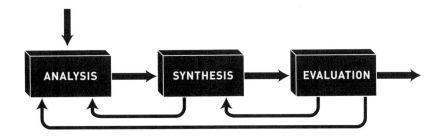

FIG 2.4 The conventional analysis synthesis evaluation model of designing

Fig 2.5 A fertiliser-spreader—Wim Groeneboom and his team at Vicon. The relationship between form and function is strong, clear and visible in this 'open' design. The subtly detailed but sturdy designs, and the consistent application of the colour scheme (yellow for non-moving parts like containers and red for mechanisms, frames and moving parts) created a strong brand image for Vicon

LEARNING FROM UNCERTAINTY
WIM GROENEBOOM

"The big disadvantage (of design methods) is that through this kind of teaching we take away the insecurity of the students. It is a way of quickly and efficiently explaining design but that is deadly. Students have to learn to deal with uncertainty, and we take that away by this kind of teaching... In the end, I would say that dealing with uncertainties is the core of our design profession.

WIM GROENEBOOM

Wim Groeneboom (1940) started his design career at the Philips Industrial Design Centre in Eindhoven and later developed his own design agency with Willem Rietveld. His major design projects include the complete development of the metro trains for the city of Amsterdam (1971) and the design of the complete product range for Vicom, a highly innovative producer of high-tech farm machinery. In his design work, he combines a classic functionalism with a strong leaning towards research-based and evidence-based design. His work is valued for its ergonomic qualities, as well as for his ability to design complicated technical objects that look elegant and deceptively simple. Wim Groeneboom has also been deeply involved in design education, being one of the founding fathers of the faculty of Industrial Design Engineering at the TUDelft, where he has continued to teach throughout his long career.

rists, as saying that 'design theorists have definitely lost the motivation for making better buildings... there is so little in what is called "design methods" that has anything useful to say about how to design buildings' (Cross, 1984). A damning remark, if there ever was one. What it does signify is that we clearly need alternative models and metaphors to capture the richness of design.

A radically different view, which tries to arrive at a much closer description of design as it is often experienced by designers, concentrates on the learning that takes place during design projects. Design can be seen as learning; as a designer, you gradually gather knowledge about the nature of the design problem and the best routes to take towards a design solution. You do this by trying out different ways of looking at the problem, and experimenting with various solution directions. You propose, experiment, and learn from the results, until you arrive at a satisfactory result. For instance, when you are designing, you sketch an idea and then look at what you have made with a critical eye. This fresh look often immediately shows you what needs changing to improve the design. So you modify and then you again look critically at what you have done. Design can be described as a process of going through many of these 'learning cycles' (propose-experiment-learn) until you have created a solution to the design problem. In this way, you explore different possibilities and learn your way towards a design solution.

This description of design was most clearly articulated by Donald Schön, in his book *The Reflective Practitioner*. He describes design and work in the other professions he studied as a process of 'framing' a problem (a form of 'seeing as'), performing 'moves' towards a solution and the 'evaluation' of these moves, that might lead to new moves or to the seeking of a new frame (Schön, 1983).

Both the problem solving and learning models are valid, in the sense that they capture a part of what design is. Since this book is about the creation of expertise it is intrinsically about learning, so we shall inevitably find ourselves making extensive use of the learning model, although we will also keep connecting to the problem solving literature.

DESIGN AS...
EVOLUTION

Creativity in the design process is often characterised by the sudden occurrence of a significant event; the so-called 'creative leap'. Sometimes such an event occurs as a sudden insight, but often it is only in retrospect that

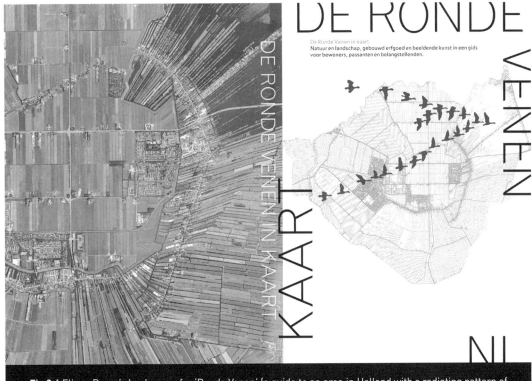

Fig 2.6 Eliane Beyer's book cover for 'Ronde Venen' (a guide to an area in Holland with a radiating pattern of Medieval polders) masterfully creates a feeling of space and suggests the continuance of the landscape beyond the surface of the book cover

ELIANE BEYER

"

Although most (of my designs) I come to intuitively, I don't just 'do something'. I start with my feeling, but then I introduce a theory. It is very hard to say how this works, but the reasoning emerges on the way. And then, when you look back, you think 'Oh, is that so?'

"

ELIANE BEYER
Eliane Beyer (1963) trained as a graphic designer at the Rietveld Academy in Amsterdam. She is part of the 'Joseph Plateau' graphic designers' collective, based in Amsterdam. She has designed several series of stamps, agendas and yearly reports for KPN Royal Dutch Post, and other major clients such as the Rijksmuseum and the Mondriaan Foundation. She has designed books and other publications for Droog Design. Joseph Plateau has received several prestigious 'best designed book of the year' awards in the last decade.

REFLECTIVE PRACTICE

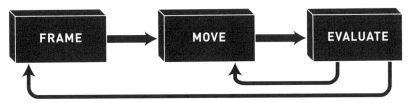

FIG 2.7 The Schönian frame-move-evaluate model of designing

a designer is able to identify a point during the design process at which the key concept began to emerge. Such reports after the fact may not be completely reliable. The idea of the creative leap suddenly illuminating the mind of its inventor dates from the middle of the nineteenth century. Of course, it is hard to say if this is truly how creativity works. There seem to be vague moments at the birth of ideas, which could be described and explained in a number of different ways. The most magical of all, the Eureka experience, is a folk psychology favourite. In retrospect, it often seems easy to imagine that an idea came to light in this sudden and unpredictable way thus confirming the theory. Often though, the evidence is either very sketchy or indeed unsupportive of the mysterious creative leap. Perhaps we are just rather attached to this romantic notion.

Observational research of designers at work has also shown that their process of solution development seldom relies on the 'Eureka' moment, but that it often is much more gradual, like an evolution. The initial ideas can be seen as the first primitive objects, evolving and becoming more subtly tuned to the design problem over the generations. But design problems are a moving target too. They are often nebulous at the beginning of the design project and as the designer acquires more knowledge about the problem and about the possibilities for solving it, the design problems become more concrete.

Jane Darke studied the way a number of architects had gone about designing award-winning public housing schemes in the UK. She noticed a common characteristic which seemed a little perverse on first examination. These architects seemed to come up with a major design idea very early in the process and certainly long before they could have really fully understood what were very complex problems. Working with Bryan Lawson for her doctorate, she was aware of his more laboratory-based research mentioned earlier which suggested that designers tended to use solution-based approaches. Together they named this phenomenon the 'primary generator', a concept which is now well embedded in the literature (Darke, 1978). These primary generators are basic ideas about how the solution might look. They are generally pretty strategic and not very detailed. They allow the designer to create a sort of hypothesis; 'what if the solution looked a bit like this?' What seemed to be happening, in the case of Darke's architects, was that in trying to develop the design along the lines suggested by the primary generator they actually discovered more about the problem. They would find ways in which this type of solution created difficulties, worked poorly or even created more problems than it solved. To use our previous way of describing design, this was truly design as learning.

THE MYSTERIOUS CREATIVE LEAP

A nice example of this mystification of the creative leap can be found in one of the greatest ideas in the history of science: Darwin's idea of natural selection as a driver for evolution. In his autobiography, Darwin claims to have created his theory of evolution and natural selection in a creative flash. He writes that the idea suddenly hit him when he was reading a treatise on human population by Malthus. Luckily for us, we can trace this moment of glory in his original diary of that time, where he dutifully reports having read Malthus. But no Eureka; just a brief entry. The next day he wrote a much longer piece on the sexual curiosity of primates. Reading Malthus was lost in a host of other books that he was browsing through at the time, and he developed many different ideas to explain the diversity of species that he had encountered in his voyage on the Beagle. If we read the diary carefully we can see that the idea of natural selection slowly dawned upon him. Darwin's creation of the theories of evolution and natural selection was a gigantic creative step. But there never was that one Eureka moment. (After Gould, 1992)

In many cases, of course, several primary generators might be tried and sometimes abandoned or eventually combined. Subsequent research has found that designers often struggle with their primary generators later on in the design project; they may be useful in the beginning, but there is a tendency to stick to them for too long, and trying to make them work no matter what. Then these primary generators can become real blockers to the development of better ideas, leading to tunnel vision and what is called 'design fixation'. Anyone extensively involved in teaching design students will be very familiar with this danger. More flexible and skilled designers, however, can often use the failings of a primary generator to enable them to reframe the problem.

Creative design then is not a matter of first fixing the problem and afterwards performing a 'creative leap' to a solution. Creative design seems more to be a matter of developing and evolving together both the formulation of a problem and ideas for a solution, with constant shuttling to-and-fro between the problem and solution. The aim of the designer is to generate a matching problem–solution pair. Design thus involves a period of exploration in which problem and solution are evolving and are very unstable, until they are (temporarily) fixed by an emergent idea which identifies a problem–solution pairing (Dorst and Cross, 2001).

The creative event in design then may not be so much a 'creative leap' from problem to solution as the building of a 'bridge' between the problem and the solution by an idea. A creative event occurs as the moment of insight at which a problem–solution pair comes together. This can be such a triumphant feeling that it overshadows all the slow and laborious evolution that went before it. Perhaps that is the origin of the myth of the creative leap.

In the conversational, co-evolution view of design we might be less inclined to make the distinction between problem and solution at all. Indeed, we might see frames and primary generators as ways of negotiating between a problem and solution view of the situation in order to bring about some resolution between what is required and what can be made. But maybe that is going too far: the terms 'problem' and 'solution' are so widely used in common parlance that we cannot ignore them here. And in some design domains the problem may be very clearly stated and success easily measured and thus the process may be more one of moving from a problem to a solution in a fairly linear motion. At the other end of the spectrum of design domains, the formulation of the design problem may only emerge from an extensive exploration of solution possibilities.

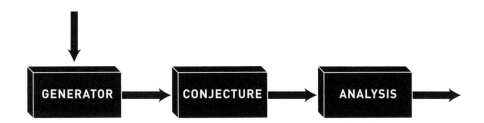

FIG 2.8 Jane Darke's primary generator model of designing

DESIGN AS...
THE CREATION OF SOLUTIONS TO PROBLEMS

Several times in the discussion so far we have seen hints that there is something very special about design problems. In fact, they are so special that we do not really like using the word 'problem' to describe them. This word suggests that they can be solved and therefore by implication that the problem solving view of design is adequate. This is plainly not the case. At times during any design project there may be well-defined problems to solve, perhaps even puzzles with an optimal answer, but overall design is not like this.

In his many perceptive publications Donald Schön claimed that every design problem is unique. Every problem has its own specific situation either in space or time or both. Even tackling the same design problem again is different because it has been changed by our knowledge of the earlier solution. Design problems of the kind we are interested in here are never fully defined. The fact that they are not amenable to the 'classic' problem solving methods has driven the proponents of those methods to call them 'ill-structured' (Simon, 1973) or even 'wicked' (Rittel and Webber, 1973). Perhaps these rather negative descriptions reveal a hint of frustration at the failure of the problem solving methods in tackling design.

More positively, Cross has pointed out that what you need to know about design problems depends upon the approach you are taking to solve them (Cross, 1982). This effectively pulls the rug from under any attempt to describe them in an objective way. What constitutes a problem depends on the abilities of the problem solver so the problem is inherently subjective!

However, we need not despair. It is possible to build some sort of typology of design problems. Lawson used a constraint-based approach to this to create a three-dimensional model showing the generators, domains and functions of constraints (Lawson, 1997). He suggested that design situations differ from each other by the way they are distributed within this model. (This model can be seen with a more detailed discussion in Chapter 4.)

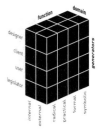

pg.131

Dorst showed that design problems also vary in the extent to which they are determined. He argued that they are neither completely fixed nor completely free (Dorst, 2006). In fact, he suggested three states for this fixity of design problems. Firstly, they can be determined by what he called 'hard and unalterable needs, requirements and intentions'. This would make them more or less amenable to problem solving methods.

Fig 2.9 An artist's studio

BUT, IS IT ART?

Navigating this freedom is the ultimate challenge for
the fine artist; there are no 'requirements' for art. While
design is always to some extent grounded by functionality,
by the obligation to relate to the needs of people and
the requirements of stakeholders, art is not functional;
it does not need to make 'sense'. Artists are more or
less on their own, having to develop a personal and
interesting starting point for the production of works.

But secondly, Dorst argued that a major part of design problems are inevitably under-determined. Perhaps none of the stakeholders have strong constraints, leaving the designer free to make autonomous choices. This is the kind of situation where the work of the designer can touch that of the artist. Such problems need interpretation by the designer. This means that different designers may interpret them differently and that this interpretation is itself part of the creative act of designing. In these aspects of the problem the designer is, to a large extent, free to work according to personal taste, style, interests and abilities. This links nicely with Lawson's model which includes the generation of constraints by designers alongside those created by clients, users and legislators. This designer generation of constraints becomes a vital activity in under-determined design situations.

Finally, some design problems are over-determined according to Dorst. In such situations there are so many constraints that quite simply cannot all be satisfied and there are many irreconcilable conflicts. Paradoxically, there is some freedom of choice in the design process for the designer who has to judge which of the conflicting constraints are going to prevail. This again requires a subjective interpretation step before the design situation can be tackled.

One of the challenges then of design is to be able to spot the kind of situation you are in. It will simply be no good taking a tight problem solving approach to a largely under-determined design problem and vice versa. Expert designers understand this and adjust their approach to the situation. The description by Richard MacCormac of his work at Bristol University in England is a remarkably sensitive evocation of these issues. The project consisted of working with a number of existing houses already used for academic purposes and linking them to create faculty accommodation.

DESIGN AS...
INTEGRATING INTO A COHERENT WHOLE

All of the various demands of the project's stakeholders have to be reconciled within a design. The difficulty here is one of mapping. One cannot design by simply creating individual partial solutions for all the issues that the stakeholders might have and then building together all of these sub-solutions. To arrive at a good solution, the designer needs to create a design in which all the issues and demands of the stakeholders are addressed in an integrated manner. There is no one-on-one mapping from problem to solution. The features of the design are created in such a way that they address many problems at the same time.

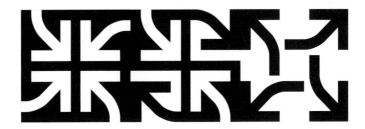

DETERMINED ———————— **UN**DETERMINED

The design that is thus produced must be 'good' as seen from all these different perspectives. These stakeholders all come with viewpoints, knowledge and values from their own world. The designer creates a solution in which all these different worlds must be combined. Attaining a well-integrated design, then, is all about getting the balance right. After concentrating on one stakeholder or perspective on the design, the designer must compensate for the inevitable limitations and bias of that approach by making further moves that balance the first. For instance, if a product has been designed while focusing on form, the designer will have to compensate for this bias by investigating whether the design is technically possible, producible, ergonomically sound, economically feasible and so on. Integration-loops like these are made constantly while designing. To achieve integration, the parts of a design have to be developed more or less in parallel.

Designing sometimes feels like being a Chinese juggler, dashing around frantically keeping a myriad of plates spinning on their poles. Yet from time to time a designer must stop this running around, and create a renewed overview of the design. It is so easy to get much too involved in one pet solution, stakeholder or aspect of the design, and neglect others. Integration is tricky enough to attain in design practice, but the task is severely aggravated by the need simultaneously to reach coherence.

Coherence describes the extent a design is 'unified', free from inner contradictions and can be perceived as a whole; a single entity. The need for coherence effectively limits the amount of compromise a designer can build into a design. Well-integrated and coherent designs are characteristically simple, elegant and give the feeling that everything has been taken into consideration, and is as it should be. There is a glimpse of perfection in an integrated design.

DESIGN AS...
A FUNDAMENTAL HUMAN ACTIVITY

Designers are convinced that 'design' is a special way of thinking, and in their battle for recognition, they spend a lot of time trying to convince the rest of the world of this. But surprisingly seventeen or eighteen-year-old students, new to design school, seem to just start designing. At a simple, basic level of course, but they manage. It does not seem as if they first have to learn an alien, fundamentally different thought process. This tells us that, no matter what designers may claim, apparently there is a certain level of design that can be approached by common sense.

RICHARD MACCORMAC

I know we live in a very un-visual culture and a lot of our problems
come from that, but... the sense I have that architecture is a kind
of analogical or metaphorical way of thinking and I think architects
try and translate the stuff of briefs into some kind of structure as
soon as possible and the most one of the most vivid experiences
of that was in the Bristol University Faculty of Arts scheme,
where one sensed that the scheme could be a kind of model of
a very, of a complex large university department and that's what
it came out really... the real problem is concealed in the way it
is written about as a brief often. And the real problem is some
kind of structural problem, I don't mean in an engineering sense,
I mean in the sense of relationships, in this Bristol case—the
problem which the brief couldn't describe was really the problem
of trying to attach new buildings to listed existing buildings in such
a way that it would be acceptable to the conservation lobby, and
would get planning consent, and yet would give a continuity of
accommodation that would allow a lot of flexibility of re-naming
and different territorial arrangements between existing buildings
and new ones, and so there had to be some kind of a network
and it was in fact a kind of grid if you like, of relationships.

There was another I suppose which could only be hinted at in the
brief which is what physical arrangements tend to produce the
idea of a faculty—and we felt very strongly under these conditions,
apart from this continuity of fabric and social continuity that would
allow the circulation system, which was going to be pretty meagre
in terms of UGC funding, would be amplified if we could string
all the departmental common rooms out along the circulation
system and use them as expansion chambers for lecture theatres,
which otherwise would have caused terrific congestion. Now
those issues don't appear in briefs often, they are the stuff of
the thing which only comes out when you try and solve, when
you try and produce a scheme and therefore the design process
defines objectives in a way in which a brief could never do.

Perhaps this sounds disappointing and we designers would rather be something special, but there it is. But just what is common sense, anyway? This deceptively unassuming name actually stands for an extremely complicated set of thinking strategies that we use to navigate through the world; the things you never explicitly learn, but that you absorb as you grow up. Although expert systems have been built that can, to some extent, deal with large amounts of explicit knowledge, only the most avid artificial intelligence enthusiast would claim that we are ever going to get common sense into a computer. Common sense is just too context-dependent, complex and subtle that we need the human mind to do it. So there is no shame in having a profession that can contain a generous helping of common sense thinking.

The real difficulty in design is not in reaching that very first level of apparent competence; it is in attaining the higher levels. And that is where the design profession sits. Most expert designers certainly employ many more sophisticated cognitive skills, as we shall discover on our journey through this book.

In passing it is worth noting a trend in many other professions, to describe their work as 'designing'. For instance, managers now 'design' company policies, teachers 'design' a curriculum and care models are 'designed' in medical circles. Using this design metaphor appears to suggest the adoption of an open, creative, solution-focused way of working, perhaps unusual in the field, and this may offer new freer ways of working. Some of the tricks and methods that designers use can probably benefit people in many professions. Though it is likely that the way these professions deal with design is probably only just emerging from the 'common sense' level. Designers, with all their experiences of the ins and outs of designing, can play an important role in professionalising design in these disciplines. This is beginning to happen; in fact, designers are spreading throughout society. These days, you encounter people with a design background in all kinds of jobs. These people use their design thinking to create solutions to the problems they face in areas that are far beyond the confines of the 'traditional' design professions.

Many more things can be said about this subject; the second author of this book has published a book that contains 175 mini-essays, all of them stabs at understanding our incredibly complex design profession (Dorst, 2006). But for now, this rough characterisation of design is enough to get a feeling for the field, and provide a basis for some more serious modelling of the design activity in the next sections.

However, we still cannot find a single all-encompassing model of design. Instead we present three models of design or ways of thinking about design,

CONVERSATIONS WITH DRAWINGS
DENISE SCOTT BROWN

Sometimes the hand does something that the eye then re-interprets and gets an idea from and that kind of drawing for yourself and a few other people around the table is Bob's (Venturi) great specialty and those drawings have a nervousness to them and a tension, some of them are just wonderful but they are never done as a piece of art, they are done as a communication with self and with people around the table.

each of which have something useful to say about this most enigmatic and fascinating area of human cognition.

DESIGN MODEL #1:
THE NATURE OF DESIGN ACTIVITIES

In a seminal paper Nigel Cross summarised the scientific knowledge about the activities that make up designing (Cross, 1999). He listed many of the things that designers typically do. According to Cross, designers typically 'produce novel unexpected solutions, tolerate uncertainty, work with incomplete information, apply imagination and constructive forethought to practical problems and use drawings and other modelling media as a means of problem solving'.

Cross then goes on to produce an accompanying list of the abilities designers must have to carry out these activities, and do them well. They need to be able to deal with uncertainty and decision making on the basis of limited information, resolve ill-defined, 'wicked' problems by adopting solution-focusing strategies, employing productive/creative thinking and using graphic or spatial modelling media.

This is an impressive list with a wide range of necessary skills. They do spark immediate recognition in designers, but their very closeness to design practice might also explain an apparent lack of structure in this list. It does not present an overarching model of design, and there does not seem to be one hidden behind it; perhaps there can never be. But in an attempt to impose some sort of order on all this, it may be useful to think of these design skills and group the corresponding design activities under some headings.

The most obvious set of skills employed by all designers are those to do with making design propositions. These are sometimes developed and sometimes abandoned. We might see this whole group of skills as to do with making moves and we shall therefore refer to them as 'moving'. These moves are most often made through some form of representation. They may be described in words or put into computers or, most common of all, visualised through drawings of one kind or another. We shall call these skills 'representing'. Another set of skills are clearly those to do with understanding problems and describing them. We shall refer to these as 'formulating'. The way moves are regulated is most obviously by an evaluation of them against some set of criteria however precisely or vaguely understood. So there is clearly a whole range of skills which we shall refer to as 'evaluating'. In addition to all this there is some group of activities that oversee the whole

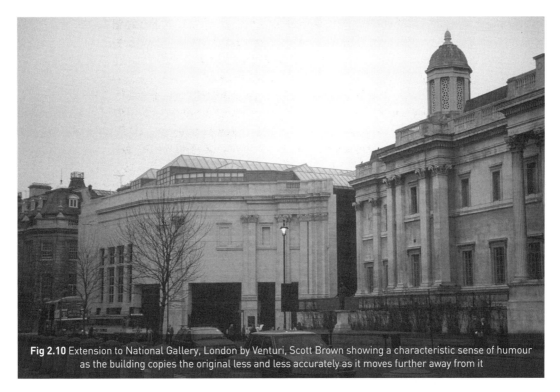

Fig 2.10 Extension to National Gallery, London by Venturi, Scott Brown showing a characteristic sense of humour as the building copies the original less and less accurately as it moves further away from it

ROBERT VENTURI AND DENISE SCOTT BROWN

Robert Venturi studied architecture at Princeton University and the American Academy in Rome. His early architectural career included periods with Louis Kahn and Eero Saarinen. Denise Scott Brown studied at the Architectural Association in London and at the University of Pennsylvania. She has taught at the Universities of Pennsylvania, California at Berkeley, UCLA, Yale and Harvard. They have collaborated since 1950.

Their work includes the decorative arts, furniture, architecture, urban design and planning. They are at least as well known for their writing as for their design. Robert Venturi's book **Complexity and Contradiction in Architecture** is arguably one of the most significant contributions to the debate about the post-modern movement. Robert Venturi and Denise Scott Brown, together with their associate Steven Izenour, followed this with their equally influential treatise on 'Learning from Las Vegas'.

In 1991 Robert Venturi joined a very select band of recipients of the Pritzker Architecture Prize. The jury said 'He has expanded and redefined the limits of the art of architecture in this century, as perhaps no other has, through his theories and built works'.

process and provide support for it. A more or less conscious effort is needed to keep the design activity on course towards its target. We shall refer to these skills as 'managing'.

A model of design skills and activities is beginning to appear. We have groups of activities and skills that are all needed and are commonly found in successful design. They are 'formulating', 'representing', 'moving', 'evaluating' and 'managing'. In the next few pages, each of these activities will be explained briefly, and some first comments will be made that elucidate their application in design practice. If we want to understand the creation of design expertise then we had better have an appreciation of the nature of these constituent skills.

FORMULATING

The design process is a sequence of activities. Logically it would seem that getting a brief and analysing the problem comes before the synthesis of solutions but we have already questioned that assumption. However, there can be no argument that designers must be skilled in finding and stating problems and in understanding and exploring them—maybe not all at the beginning of a project, but as a recurring activity.

IDENTIFYING

In the problem solving view of design these skills include the ability to reformulate and organise ill-structured or wicked problems. In the conversational and learning view of the process designers are said to identify, or as Schön would put it, 'name' elements in the design situation. It is almost as if characters are being introduced in a story and their roles and personalities are being explored in order to understand how they will react to events and behave as the story unfolds. Whether we think of it as the reformulation of problems or the identification of elements, making them explicit and developing their characteristics is not a clear-cut thing but very much part of the design project. This is clearly an important and central design skill.

FRAMING

Perhaps the most important contribution made by Schön and his followers to the debate about design is the idea of 'framing'. This activity involves selectively viewing the design situation in a particular way ('seeing as…') for a period or phase of activity. This selective focus enables the design to handle the massive complexity and the inevitable contradictions in design by giving structure and direction to thinking while simultaneously temporarily suspending some issues. The skill to create and manipulate frames is a central one in determining how the process will unfold. As we will see later in this book, the high-level skill of framing is crucial in the development

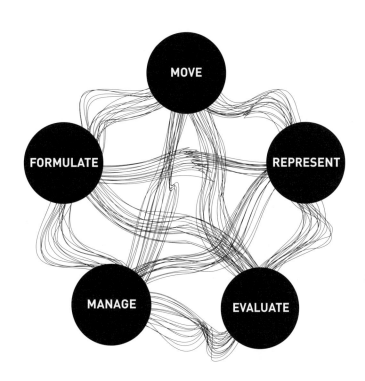

of design expertise, and often the central activity in the working lives of top-designers and architects. The quality of design work produced depends as much on the ability of the designer to frame the problem relevantly and productively, as on the ability to arrive at an interesting solution from this standpoint; maybe even more so.

REPRESENTING

Although it is perfectly possible to imagine design taking place without any externalisation at all, in practice designers almost always externalise their thoughts prolifically. Indeed designers are often characterised by their habitual use of these activities. They draw, write, model, make and compute representations of their inchoate ideas for the design they are working towards. They also shuffle and represent to themselves information about the brief or problem. This extensive use of representation relies on texts, sketches, models and indeed the whole environment as a type of 'external short-term memory'. Design offices are always full of stuff that can spark ideas, feed the intuition or relates more directly to the projects at hand. Designers more or less live within their projects!

CONVERSATIONS WITH REPRESENTATIONS

As Schön has so eloquently put it designers interact with these representations in a conversational way (Schön, 1983). The representations are thus far from being incidental outputs but are rather central inputs to the thought process. Clearly then the ability to execute these representations and manage them is one of the central skills in designing. A designer who cannot sketch is likely not to be able to 'converse' freely with the situation. Drawings are undoubtedly amongst the most central and important of all these forms of representation and those drawings come in several types including most crucially design drawings, diagrams, and visionary drawings. In design practice, some time is spent on managing what can be an avalanche of material around a project, and professional designs can often be seen making periodic overviews of the materials gathered and produced. They see this as a natural and vital part of their professional practice—often to the surprise of design students, who often assume there is some kind of inherent creativity of messiness.

WORKING WITH MULTIPLE REPRESENTATIONS

Most designers do not actually make their designs, but rather they make representations of their designs. They make drawings, computer models, textual descriptions, physical models and so on. In a way the whole point of such a process is that it enables change and experimentation at much lower cost than would be incurred by making the designs themselves. Such a process then is based on the reduction of risk to the designer. Unfortunately,

THE PENCIL AS SPOKESMAN
RICHARD MACCORMAC

Whenever we have a kind of design session or crit review session in the office I cannot say anything until I've got a pencil or pen in my hand and one covers acres, well we have these rolls of paper and you get through them at a fantastic rate. I feel the pencil to be my spokesman as it were, nowadays I suppose most of what I do is freehand...

mostly I'm using drawing as a process of criticism and discovery and tweaking and direction finding.

what we have often seen is that the risk can be transferred to the client who pays for the representations to be made real. The skills of choosing and making representations that minimise this risk and that represent the finished design as accurately as possible to the client and to users may also be ones which are critical in the success of real design processes.

This story does not always hold true for some of the new design disciplines. If you look at web design, for instance, quite a different pattern emerges. In developing a website or an interactive system for a computer, you work on designs that are easy to replicate, and that will be used in the same medium through which they are made. You make things that are going to run on a computer, and you make them on a computer. So you have a realistic 'prototype' at almost any moment during the design process. This allows the designer to do user testing at all times. Designing then changes from a vaguely linear process which leads from small sketches to bigger sketches to presentations to computer models and then on to a prototype, into a process of continuous testing and learning. In these new design professions, design could become a more continuous and evolutionary process; the designer is able to test many generations of the design before delivery (although we would agree with any reader that the above grand opportunities for testing designs have not prevented the proliferation of maddeningly confusing websites).

MOVING

So central to design is the activity of solution generation that the word 'design' is sometimes only used to relate to this group of activities. What we have seen now is that there are several activities under this general heading of making design moves. Firstly and most obviously, a new move may be made which has not been seen before in this process. A feature of the solution is placed, or given some shape or some relation to some other element or given some characteristics. Secondly, a move may alter or develop the existing state of the solution. Where do such ideas come from? We shall develop answers to that question under the section on reflecting.

INTERPRETIVE AND DEVELOPMENTAL MOVES

Not all moves in design are entirely original to the process. Margaret Boden's distinction of 'h' and 'p' creativity is partially helpful here (Boden, 1990). We have four possibilities in a design process. An idea may be entirely novel in all of history (h). Actually such events are relatively rare in our developed and sophisticated world. It might be entirely novel as far as the designer or design team are concerned (p), it might be entirely novel as far as this particular process is concerned, and finally it might derive from another idea that has already appeared in this process.

EVALUATING
OBJECTIVE AND SUBJECTIVE EVALUATIONS

Not only do designers generate alternatives between which choices must be made but also they must know, rather like an artist, when to stop. Clearly then, designers must have evaluative abilities. In some aspects of design this can be considerably aided by technology when numerical criteria can be set, for example the energy consumption of a building. Characteristically though, design involves making judgements between alternatives along many dimensions that cannot be reduced to a common metric. Designers must then have a very particular evaluative skill enabling them to feel comfortable about arriving at such tricky judgements. Designers must be able to perform both objective and subjective evaluations and to be able to make judgements about the relative benefits of alternatives even though they may rely on incompatible methods of measurement. Indeed, designers may develop their own particular tools for evaluating designs against the criteria that are often important to them either because of the kinds of objects they frequently design or because of the guiding principles they have developed.

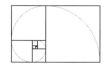

pg.181

THREE QUALITIES

But evaluation in design is much more than just a straight choice between alternatives, on the basis of a more or less clear list of criteria. It is much more of a process of deliberation; because the design discipline implicitly contains many incommensurable viewpoints about what is 'good' and 'bad'. Here we explore three fundamentally different ways of defining quality.

1. Some designers and critics tend to be utilitarian; they would say that a design that people want and buy is, by definition, good.

2. Others would argue that a design can be intrinsically good, regardless of the reaction of the public. They say that quality is deeply engrained in the things we make, and not dependent on the whims of public opinion.

3. Still others argue that designs that are made in correspondence with certain principles which they would hold to be virtues (like simplicity, honesty, care, 'showing the hand of the maker'), and that designs derive their real quality from this.

Discussions about designs often touch upon two or more of these frameworks. Evaluating design then usually involves weighing the relative importance of such incommensurate value systems and building bridges between them.

BEAUTY AND COMFORT

The famous American architect Philip Johnson is reported to have said that: some people find chairs beautiful to look at because they are comfortable to sit in, others find chairs comfortable to sit in because they are beautiful to look at.

SUSPENDING JUDGEMENT

Undoubtedly one of the skills that a designer must have here is to also be able to suspend judgement to allow creative thought to flow and ideas to mature before they are subjected to the harsh light of penetrating criticism. Extremely talented and creative designers are not always very helpful when teaching students as they sometimes fail to appreciate just when and how to do this.

MANAGING
REFLECTION ON ACTION

Since Schön introduced the idea of the 'reflective practitioner' there has been much more recognition of the importance of this concept of reflecting upon actions. In design at least this seems to be capable of two interpretations which we might call 'reflection in action' and 'reflection on action'. The concept of reflection in action is already covered here by combining our formulation, moving and evaluation activities. With such a model the designer is more or less continually reflecting on the current understanding of the problem and the validity of the emerging solution or solutions. As in the example of the idea-sketching activity: the designer fluently moves from making a proposal towards stepping back and reflecting upon it, and deciding on a modification, all in one flow. This can happen on a split-second timescale, as well as in design sessions spanning days or weeks. Reflection on action can be seen as a higher level activity in which the process is monitored rather than the state of the design. Such a concept clearly involves the creation of an overview and a stepping out of the 'flow' of the design activity. It involves a mental 'standing back' and asking if the process is going well or might be steered differently.

BRIEFING IS A CONTINUOUS PROCESS

Contrary to the wishes of many who have tried to establish route maps of the design process, briefing appears to be a continuous process. It is certainly not something that happens exclusively at the beginning but rather represents the problem formulation aspects of designing which are often greatly influenced by the emerging potential solutions. In design, problems do not even necessarily precede solutions in the way normally expected in conventional problem solving. Thinking about solutions and thinking about problems seem inextricably interwoven in the design process. This may well offer us one useful way to distinguish between different design fields. Some design fields have very clearly defined problems that can be quite well described and understood at the beginning of the process or very early in it. Others may characteristically have more open-ended problems that can only be very loosely described and only vaguely understood at the outset.

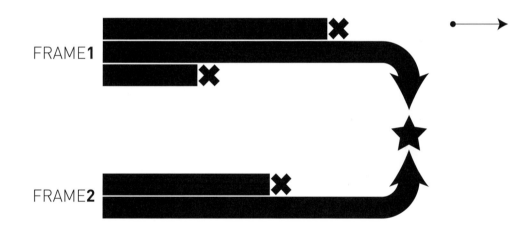

FRAME**1**

FRAME**2**

PARALLEL LINES OF THOUGHT

Designers appear to be able to develop parallel lines of thought about the problem–solution situation. Each line of thought seems to respond to a frame in order to restrict the view of the problem and to rely on a primary generator to develop ideas about the solution. It seems probable that highly creative designers may be able to sustain several of these parallel lines of thought and allow them to be incompatible or even apparently irreconcilable for extended periods during the design project. Judging when to drop some of them or try to resolve the conflicts between them seems to be one of the key skills required for creative design. Indeed, it may even be the case that a creative reframing of the situation allows for a new view in which the various lines of thought can be incorporated into one single higher level set of ideas. The ability to think along parallel lines, deliberately maintain a sense of ambiguity and uncertainty and not to get too concerned to get to a single answer too quickly seems to be essential design skills. This also sheds some light on the decision process that accompanies a design project; clients are often surprised that the design is subject to many changes after the choice of a concept. This is because the choice of a design concept may represent a freezing of a way of describing the problem but not necessarily the solution.

DESIGN MODEL #2:
LEVELS OF DESIGN ACTIVITY

Most readers will recognise many, if not all, of these activities and the accompanying skills from their own work as designers, educators or students of design. This first modelling of design already goes a long way towards capturing design practice. But design is much more complicated than this. We should be aware that 'formulating', 'representing', 'moving', 'evaluating', and 'managing' all take place within design on four distinct levels which we shall call 'project', 'process', 'practice' and 'profession'.

The Malaysian architect Ken Yeang shows an awareness of the 'project', 'process', and 'practice' levels in his comments quoted here and his body of work contributes substantially to the development of our fourth level, the architectural profession itself. Yeang has become known not only for his designs but for consistently pushing forward an agenda about sustainable high rise buildings in the tropics. Through this he has developed an approach to regionalism based not on copying slavishly from the past but on understanding the sound principles behind traditional architecture. He has published these ideas and arguments in many books and clearly sees an interaction between our four levels.

PROFESSION
PRACTICE
PROCESS
PROJECT

1. THE DESIGN PROJECT

Most of the design activities that have been described in our first model drive the design work within a design project (for instance, describing the reflection on the state of the design problem or solution as Reflection *in* Action). Projects are the locus of design work for a client, and they are the main economic element in any design organisation. In a design practice the projects represent income streams, resource needs, timescale and many other features of managing the organisation. Therefore, designers and design researchers alike tend to focus almost exclusively on optimising design performance within the context of the concrete design project.

The training that designers receive is also very much project-oriented; the majority of university design curriculum takes place in 'project work' in 'the studio' (see Chapter 6 for a much more extended coverage of studio-based education). This is almost considered to be 'learning on the job'—and indeed, an important part of design practice is mimicked in the educational environment. Students can even graduate from design school with the impression that being in projects is all that there is. But there is much more to a design existence than project work; many activities in a design practice have to do with the preparation of offers to clients, doing research to support the general development of the office, feeding the inspiration and continuous professional training. There is often a stream of self-initiated design activities that does not fall within the 'classical' project format.

2. THE DESIGN PROCESS

We have already discussed the activities of the design process in detail in our previous mode. We need a brief linguistic intermission here; this is where describing design becomes slippery again. Please note that we use the word 'process' here in a very general sense. By 'process' we mean the methods, ways of working of a designer, and *not* as describing the concrete sequence of steps within a design project. Designers do not just work in (inside) a design project, they also create overviews of the design project to monitor its progress; they have to step back from the hands-on level of working within the project to reflect on what they are doing. This reflection *on* action can lead to devising new 'frames' or 'moves' (or series of moves, patterns of which can be captured in more or less formal 'design methods') to develop the design project.

This process level is an important one; it is here that, through their reflective moments, designers learn from their projects and develop their own approaches to design problems. This is crucial for developing a more

KEN YEANG

Any architect with a mind of his own, whether by design or default will produce an architecture which is identifiable to that architect. Sometimes that's more apparent or evident in the work and sometimes it is more internalised... I had to study ecology, I had to study biology; that was the basis for most of my design work. I'm trying to develop a new form of architecture. We have this climatically responsive tropical skyscraper agenda and each project we try to see whether we can push an idea a little bit further... I give every new member of staff the practice manual to read when they join. They can see not just past designs but study the principles upon which they are based. We work these out over time, over many projects... But in a project I have to be very dependent on my architects and each one of them has their own personal way of doing things, and I try to respect that so they are constantly improving and making things better, there is growth and they get motivated.

I do competitions more as an academic exercise. I treat competitions as research projects... it motivates the office—gets them excited—lets the mind develop new thoughts and themes. I put all the drawings together and publish a book... look in this book, these were our competition drawings for Kuala Lumpur and people said 'how can you spend so much time doing drawings and so on' and I say 'it's research, it develops ideas'.

Fig 2.11 One of Ken Yeang's recent projects illustrating one of his recurring themes—integrating landscape with buildings

KEN YEANG

Ken Yeang was born on the beautiful Malaysian island of Penang in 1948. He studied at the Architectural Association in London and the Department of Landscape Architecture at the University of Pennsylvania. Finally he studied for his doctorate at Cambridge University, which was concerned with the role of ecological considerations in the design of the built environment. He has practiced mainly from Kuala Lumpur and is now also in partnership in London.

In particular Ken Yeang has developed a reputation for designing climatically responsive tall buildings. Dr Yeang himself has also continued to write and lecture on his search for a new form of architectural expression which both has a regional identity and is ecologically sound. He has published many books as well as articles in both Asian and European journals.

Ken Yeang has taught and examined at universities in Malaysia, as well at other schools of architecture in Europe, the United States of America, and Asia. He has been Vice-President of the Commonwealth Association of Architects, and chairman of the Architects Regional Council of Asia (ARCASIA), president of the Malaysian Society of Architects and on the RIBA Council.

strategic view of design, and possibly a distinctive 'style' of designing. This reflection is a vital part of creating design expertise.

3. THE DESIGN PRACTICE

The same basic activities of 'formulating', 'representing', 'moving', 'evaluating' and 'managing' are used again at a level that is a step removed from the concrete project level, that of the development of the professional practice. This can be seen to include the style and assumed role of the designer. This professional stance or personal position is something we shall discuss in detail in later chapters. Suffice it to say here that all designers gradually begin to acquire some attitudes, interests and even principles that govern their work. Along with this comes a set of knowledge and particular experiences which may lead to specialisation. In any case, such awareness must surely change the design process as Theo Groothuizen points out. Experienced designers become familiar with certain kinds of problems or ranges of solutions, technology or groups of users. However, many design practices are not managed by a single individual but may be a partnership employing junior designers. The creation of collective practice design expertise will interest us in a later chapter.

Many recent developments in design have impacted upon this practice level. The increasing complexity of design problems and the growing number of parties involved have led to the development of what is called 'participatory design' or 'co-design'. In these new ways of dealing with design practice, there is a much more active engagement by the designer with the prospective user. In participatory design the user is asked to help evaluate developing design ideas during the design project. In co-design the user is actually part of the design team, actively co-creating the design with the professionals. Each of these new ways of embodying the design profession requires the designer to leave the ivory tower of the studio and to engage with the design situation in a new way. There is as yet no definitive role for the designer in such processes and it is unclear how these trends are going to be developing in the coming years.

The changing nature of business structures in many Western design firms, brought about by the forces of globalisation, is also impacting on design practice. Product design firms, in particular, seem to suffer from a loss of the profitable embodiment (engineering) part of their design projects. That tends to move closer to the countries where the production takes place, leaving the design agencies in the West with a much reduced economic base just consisting of the comparatively few hours of conceptual design; hours that tend to be rather high-risk requiring the more experienced and expensive staff members. But the picture is not all gloomy; other design firms have

THEO GROOTHUIZEN

When you have a lot of knowledge in a field, that is comfortable; but is also limiting. I notice that when I design telephone booths I know so much about telephone booths that designing one becomes more and more difficult. Because if you did a good job on the last one, then that contains many of the optimal solutions, or the optimal choices, or the choices that fit me as a designer... this reminds me of playing chess: it always surprises me how easily a beginner can play. We call that beginner's luck, they are not hampered by too much knowledge. The more you know about chess, it does not become easier or more difficult, but you are able to make many more combinations...

thrived in the same years. Most of them have followed a strategy of self-initiating projects, and selling their design concepts (with intellectual property) to companies. This does require a different, much more entrepreneurial stance from these designers. Perhaps a new business model for design practices is emerging.

Architects too have seen their traditional central role in the project decline. More often than not these days, large developer corporations may initiate projects hiring architects only for design phases and using professional project managers to supervise the process.

4. THE DESIGN PROFESSION

These are just two examples to show that design practice is changing quite rapidly, and that designers might find themselves in the position that they have to re-invent the very core of their professional life. This is the fourth level on which designers work, together defining and redefining the very nature of their profession within what is commonly called in sociology a 'community of practice'. Just as there are collections of individual designers inside a practice then, there are collections of practices that make up the profession. There is then some creation of expertise at this professional level as members come together to develop techniques, publish solutions and exchange ideas. We shall explore this notion of design expertise at the professional level in Chapter 7.

With the introduction of these four levels of activities that are part and parcel of being a designer, we mean to step beyond the overriding focus in design practice, design theory and design education on the design project. Through this fixation on design projects, there are many activities that are an integral part of 'being a designer' that have been neglected by designers, under-funded and unorganised in design agencies and missed by design researchers. They involve vital (but non-project related) activities like the gathering of inspiration, the building up of a stock of useful or admired precedents, and the self-education that is needed to stay abreast of an ever developing field. And most importantly perhaps, they include the critical reflection across projects, through which a designer develops. We need to deal with all of these levels when we want to describe the development of design expertise.

Fig 2.12 Triangular telephone booth—Theo Groothuizen at Landmark. The original model is shown. Colour (an informal bright green) and detailing of the design (with its frameless glass) were developed according to the latest design research insights into what triggers vandalism

THEO GROOTHUIZEN

Theo Groothuizen (1949) started his academic career by studying Architecture, but he was to graduate as an industrial designer from Delft University of Technology in 1978. His major project was the design of a cleverly constructed new triangular telephone booth that was further developed into the new Dutch standard design and also being very influential internationally. This gave him the chance to begin his professional career as a design consultant at PTT, the Dutch telecom company.

After a spell as an independent designer he became the co-founder, with four other experienced designers, of Landmark Design. This firm grew to be one of the biggest and most important product design agencies in the 1980s and early 90s, making a name for itself by creating products for the public domain, with a strong social and ergonomic orientation. Theo has also been very active in national and international designers' associations (BNO, BEDA, ICSID) and has taught at various schools throughout the world.

DESIGN MODEL #3:
TYPES OF THINKING IN DESIGN

This third model of design looks at three types of thinking that can be usefully employed in the process. They represent different approaches that a designer can take to developing the design problem and creating a solution. We can think about effecting a change in the world in a purely rule-based manner, by concentrating the specific problem situation, or by actively creating a new situation through strategic thinking.

1. CONVENTION-BASED DESIGN THINKING

When confronted with a design challenge, one could respond by working according to conventional wisdom, following 'the rules of the game'. This requires some explanation. Firstly, it could be that parts of a design problem can have a very solid knowledge basis that no designer could ignore. When dealing with technical issues, say in the development of a mechanism, anybody will understand that they can only be tackled productively by using the laws of physics and their operationalisation in the fields of statics and mechanics. There are other rules which are much less theoretical in their appearance but nonetheless valuable. Rules-of-thumb, for example, are heuristic ways of getting to a workable solution without employing sophisticated theory. Rule-based thinking allows us to tackle complicated problems with very sophisticated approaches that are often a combination of logic and the experience of many designers before us.

We also find that many of the 'rules' in design are much more tenuous and culturally determined, they are conventions: customs and habits; the set ways of working within a field.

This kind of designing was described by Broadbent as 'canonic' who included planning grids, proportioning systems and other geometrical devices in his canonical rules (Broadbent and Ward, 1969). Perhaps one of the most famous such systems of generating, or at least governing, form was Le Corbusier's Modulor which was based on rules of proportions (Le Corbusier, 1951), but such ideas have a long history in architecture going right back through Alberti to Vitruvius.

These conventions and rules undoubtedly have their uses, and a large part of normal design practice relies on such more or less routine, rule-based behaviour. But an over-reliance on these conventions can lead to standard, run-of-the-mill solutions. Knowing the conventions and successfully applying rule-based thinking is just a first step in becoming literate in the design

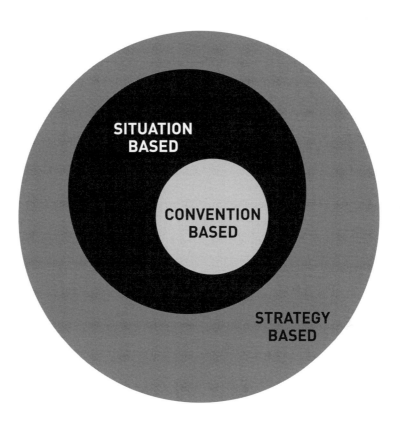

SITUATION BASED

CONVENTION BASED

STRATEGY BASED

profession. There are much more sophisticated and interesting kinds of design thinking to come.

2. SITUATION-BASED DESIGN THINKING

When confronted with a design challenge, we could respond by studying the design situation and trying to create a response that is appropriate in this particular setting. This requires a keen eye for the possibilities within a complex environment and a considerable mental flexibility in formulating a response. Designers often have to improvise to get around the most limiting requirements and use their knowledge and skills in innovative ways to create a fitting design solution. This is where the 'rules of the game' become much less mechanical, acting more as guides. This is where design becomes improvisation, where designers have to use all their wits to scramble out of a problematic design situation towards a satisfactory solution.

Some have argued that the very essence of design is that it is a 'situated' activity (Gero, 1998). Remember that Schön claims, for this reason, that every design situation is unique. Certainly it is often the very special and sometimes unique circumstances of a situation that, in the hands of an expert designer, can help to create very special solutions. The famous opera house in Sydney, for example, was an extraordinary response to a very special site. Frank Lloyd Wright's much-admired house at Falling Water owes a huge amount to his enormous skill but the waterfall it sits over must have triggered much of his thinking. These are rather obvious examples but undoubtedly the skill of recognising not only a special situation, but one that is promising is part of advanced design expertise.

3. STRATEGY-BASED DESIGN THINKING

In strategy-based design, designers formulate a planned response; effectively they consciously design the process itself and create the design situations for themselves. This strategy can be rooted in a general knowledge of the dynamics of a design process and an interpretation of the design situation, but it can also be a personally developed way of working, a 'style' that is imposed upon the problem. The introduction of an original strategy in a design situation of course also introduces the possibility of success or failure of this strategy. This makes the strategy an important object for reflection. Often, the development and use of a strategy are accompanied by a very real sense of personal commitment to the course the design project takes, and to its outcome.

USING THE THREE TYPES OF DESIGN THINKING

The differences between these design approaches can perhaps be clarified by an extended example. In one of the first extensive thinking-aloud protocol

SOME SIMPLE ARCHITECTURAL 'RULES OF THUMB'

A simply spanning concrete beam will need to be about as deep in inches as the span is in feet.

To find the depth of timber floor joists take the span in feet, halve it and add 1 for hardwood and 2 for softwood. This gives the depth in inches for 18 inch spaced joists in a domestic floor.

In a staircase the minimum and maximum pitch allowed can be calculated as follows. Take twice the rise (of each step) plus the going (tread of each step) and the result must be between 550 and 700mm.

A project will take twice as long as you think and cost twice as much.

studies in Industrial Design in the early 1990s, Dorst and Christiaans studied the steps of individual designers working on a design task. The subjects were asked to think aloud, so their thought patterns could be captured and analysed. This study has been extensively reported upon in Dorst (1995), Christiaans and Dorst (1992a, 1992b), Cross et al. (1994), and later led to the Delft Protocols Workshop (Cross et al., 1996). What is interesting from our perspective is that this series of protocol studies was performed with different design students and designers; 12 second year design students, 12 fifth year design students and 12 experienced designers (with a minimum of five years experience, and this dozen included some of the best Industrial Designers in Holland at the time). This gives us a rich source of the three different approaches to design thinking.

A bit of background on these protocol studies is necessary to understand the work of these designers: the design challenge was to develop a new 'litter system' for the passenger carriages of a new Dutch train. All information needed to design a solution (e.g. background to the project, stakeholders involved, dimensions of the train, user research on the existing trains, etc.) was provided. The designers had 2.5 hours to tackle this design challenge, working individually in a lab environment at Delft University of Technology.

Many of the second year students displayed 'convention-based design thinking' in their response to the design challenge. One could say that it is a 'rule' in design that in order to create value you should concentrate on the user, and design from their standpoint. This is exactly what many of these young designers did: they analysed the use situation and developed user criteria from the research they found in the information cards. This naturally led to issues like providing litter bins that are within easy reach of the user (the train passenger), and providing a possibility to store newspapers and magazines for the clean and easy re-use by other passengers. The whole litter system was designed from this standpoint.Other design students and some of the experienced designers clearly followed a 'situation-based design thinking' approach. After some initial thinking about the user, they discovered another party in the life of this litter system that should have an equally strong influence on its form and use; the cleaners of the trains. To see this requires some subtlety of thought since these cleaners were not directly represented in the design situation. Migrating to the standpoint of designing for the cleaners meant stepping away from the 'rule' that the main user comes first. The designs produced by this group of designers were compromises between the passenger-related criteria (that the litter collection points should be easy to reach, and the desire to store newspapers separately) and the

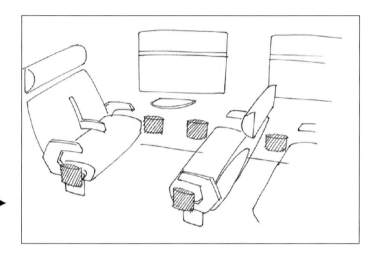

Fig 2.13 Convention-based design thinking in action: the most obvious and immediate stakeholder, the train passenger, is well catered for. The interests of the other important stakeholder, the cleaners, have not been taken into account—in fact, this design creates huge problems for them

criteria of the cleaners (efficient and quick emptying of the bins, no bending, easy cleaning). This clash between different types of users is a common design situation and more experienced designers are likely to be aware of this. For instance, in the design of hospital beds the interests of the nurses (care) and the doctors (the medical process) lead to more stringent and sometimes conflicting criteria for the bed design than the interests of the patient (recovery and quality of life).

Some of the experienced designers took a 'strategy-based design thinking' approach to this problem. In general, they went quickly through most of the information provided to them about the design problem, and they identified what could be called a 'core problem' or 'central paradox' in the problem situation. This paradox was that the requirements of the passengers and the cleaners for the litter system are actually contradictory. We can imagine that an ideal design for the passengers would basically involve a lot of litter collection points spread around the carriage, easily reachable from a sitting position. By contrast the ideal for the cleaners is one central bin that can be emptied quickly and efficiently, without reaching into awkward spaces between seats or bending over. These designers displayed different strategies; some tried to find a way around the paradox by widening the system barrier, looking at the train or the railway carriage as a whole, coming up with original solutions that make use of the possible spread of functions through the different parts of the system (i.e. newspaper racks at the end of the carriage, see Figure 2.15). This is in stark contrast to the designers that followed the 'rule-based' and 'situation-based' approaches, who inadvertently tended to be more focused on the small environment around the user and the seating arrangements within the railway carriage. Other designers followed a strategy in which they made separate designs from the standpoint of the main stakeholders (i.e. a couple of sketches exploring what would be good for the user, and some sketches in which they championed the cleaners), and then they tried to resolve some of these ideas and solutions into an overall design.

Finally, there is the amusing case of an experienced designer who tragically misjudged the design problem, following a rule-based approach and realising too late that he was on the wrong track. This designer, at some point during his analysis, framed the design task very ambitiously. 'Every passenger should be able to throw away his/her litter without rising from the seat, and there should be separate bins for newspapers and other litter'. He went on to develop a concept in which there are one or two bins hanging from every chair (one for newspapers, and one for other litter). He did not consider the problems the cleaners might have until quite late in the 2.5 hours available to him. When he realised that his design made the cleaner's problems a lot

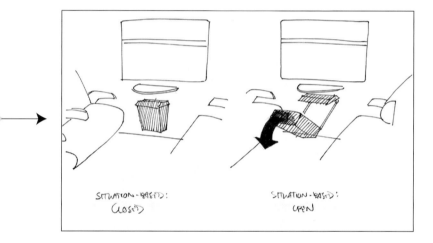

SITUATION-BASED:
(CLOSED)

SITUATION-BASED:
OPEN

Fig 2.14 Situation-based design thinking: the special properties of this specific design challenge are taken into account

worse (more bins, spread throughout the passenger compartment), he panicked. Reconsidering his core idea would have meant starting all over again. He reacted by thinking up and detailing a rather incredible emptying cart for the cleaners (see Figure 2.16) which is much too complicated, and frankly impractical. This is pure designer's panic, expressed in an incredibly complicated Heath Robinson contraption.

It may seem remarkable that this one design brief was able to trigger all these different approaches and indeed so many completely different designs. The range of expertise of the designers involved suggests something significant. It could be that one of the characteristics of creating design expertise is the acquisition of the ability to work in many different ways and to be able to adapt a process to the situation.

We have deliberately chosen this example to help explain the difference between the types of thinking in design by showing them in stark contrast on one project. But the simplicity of this might lead the reader to a limited view of these types of thinking. It does not do justice to the pervasiveness of these ways of thinking, and to the scope of the distinction we want to introduce here. Each of these ways of thinking can be successful, disastrous and somewhere in between; this will depend upon both the situation and the skill of the designer.

For instance, we can revisit the convention-based approach, and realise that 'style' is often a form of convention-based thinking. The established modernist mantra that ornament is wasteful or that 'less is more', which seems to be in the back of the mind of many designers, is just one of those rules. Some designs can be so successful and widely admired that they set a precedent, create a style and dictate the 'rules' for many other designs that are developed in their wake.

An example of such rule-bound stylistic adoption might be the way some superficial characteristics of the Apple iMac were copied. The original design of this colourful, rounded translucent plastic computer was followed by a host of cheap printers and computers suddenly also being released in transparent plastic. It seemed as if the makers of these sorry products must have thought that translucency was the strong point of the iMac, rather than its toy-like and strikingly original appearance. The trend-followers seemed to believe that humanity has an inherent craving for transparent office products. In superficial copying we can see convention-based behaviour at its most mindless.

STRATEGY-BASED: CLOSED

STRATEGY-BASED: OPEN

Fig 2.15 Strategy-based design thinking: the design situation has been changed by proposing a different system border—opening up the possibility of a completely different set of design proposals

CONCLUSION:
TOOLING UP FOR DESCRIBING THE DEVELOPMENT OF DESIGN EXPERTISE

So far in this chapter we have explored the nature of design activity by describing it from a series of different viewpoints. Then we developed three more detailed models of design. The first of these looked at the activities that together make up designing, and the abilities that support these activities. Then we distinguished four levels on which these activities take place and we went on to discuss three types of design thinking.

One could say that these three descriptive frameworks together form a simple categorisation of design activities, some kind of cube with the three 'languages' forming the axes. The 'types of design thinking' outlined involve all of the design activities explored in the first model, and they apply to the four levels of design (project, process, practice and profession).

Such a model could be an interesting avenue to pursue in a more theoretical treatise; one could, for instance, start thinking through the contents of the different cells in this 3D matrix, trying to find examples of each of the design activities. For instance, the example of Ken Yeang used earlier in this chapter clearly reveals an approach to strategy-based design thinking at the practice level. Each project, particularly in the case of competitions, is seen as a form of research to develop the practice strategy. This then in turn is passed on to every member of staff to apply in their own process. We can also see here a careful intention to combine situation-based thinking in each project.

 pg.63

However, for the purposes of this book we will just use the three descriptive frameworks as three 'languages' that can help us think and talk more clearly about aspects of expertise design in the coming chapters. When talking about the development of design expertise, we will continuously do so in terms of the design activities ('formulating', 'representing', 'moving', 'evaluating', and 'managing'), the levels of these activities (project, process, practice and profession) and the mode of thinking that lies behind the problem solving, creativity and decision making that takes place through these design activities (whether that be convention-based, situation-based or strategy-based). Armed with these models, we will now be ready to begin exploring the nature of design expertise.

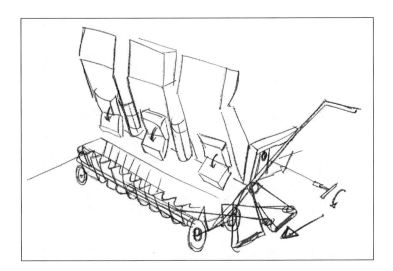

Fig 2.16 The emptying cart, hastily designed to cover the problems created by the design of the litter bins

REFERENCES

Boden, M. (1990). **The Creative Mind: Myths and Mechanisms**. London, Weidenfeld and Nicolson.

Broadbent, G. and Ward, A. eds (1969). **Design Methods in Architecture**. London, Lund Humphries.

Christiaans, H.H.C.M. and Dorst, C.H. (1992a). **Cognitive models in industrial design engineering: A protocol study**. Proceedings of the Fourth International Conference on Design Theory and Methodology. D.L. Taylor and L.A. Stauffer. New York, ASME Press: 131–137.

Christiaans, H.H.C.M. and Dorst, C.H. (1992b). **An empirical study into design thinking**. Research in Design Thinking. N. Cross, C.H. Dorst and N. Roozenburg. Delft, Delft University Press: 119–125.

Cross, N. (1982). **Designerly ways of knowing**. Design Studies 3(4): 221–227.

Cross, N. (1990). **The nature and nurture of the design ability**. Design Studies 11(3): 127–140.

Cross, N., Christiaans, H.H.C.M. and Dorst, K. (1994). **Design expertise amongst student designers**. Journal of Art and Design Education 13: 39–56.

Cross, N., Christiaans, H.H.C.M. and Dorst, K. (1996). **Analysis Design Activity**. Chichester, John Wiley.

Cross, N., ed. (1984). **Developments in Design Methodology**. Chichester, John Wiley.

Darke, J. (1978). **The primary generator and the design process**. New Directions in Environmental Design Research: Proceedings of EDRA 9. W.E. Rogers and W.H. Ittleson. Washington, EDRA: 325–337.

Dorst, C.H. (1995). **Analysing design activity: new directions in protocol analysis**. Design Studies 16(2): 139–142.

Dorst, C.H. (2006). **Understanding Design**. Amsterdam, BIS Publishers.

Dorst, C.H. and Cross, N. (2001). **Creativity in the design process: co-evolution and the problem–solution**. Design Studies 22(5): 425–437.

Gero, J. (1998). **Conceptual designing as a sequence of situated acts**. Artificial Intelligence in Structural Engineering. I. Smith. Berlin, Sprinter-Verlag: 165–177.

Gould, S.J. (1992). **The Panda's Thumb: More reflections on natural history**. New York, W.W. Norton and Co.

Lawson, B.R. (1979). **Cognitive strategies in architectural design**. Ergonomics 22(1): 59–68.

Lawson, B.R. (1997). **How Designers Think**. Oxford, Architectural Press.

Le Corbusier (1951). **The Modulor**. London, Faber and Faber.

Pirsig, R.M. (1991). **Lila**. New York, Bantam.

Rittel, H.W.J. and Webber, M.M. (1973). **Dilemmas in a general theory of planning**. Policy Sciences, 4.

Ryle, G. (1949). **The Concept of Mind**. London, Hutchinson.

Schön, D.A. (1983). **The Reflective Practitioner: How professionals think in action**. London, Temple Smith.

Simon, H.A. (1973). **The structure of ill-formed problems**. Artificial Intelligence 4: 181–201.

Wilson, C.S.J. (1986). **The play of use and use of play**. Architectural Review 180(1073): 15–18.

Wittgenstein, L. (1953). **Philosophical Investigations**. Oxford, Basil Blackwell.

3

EXPERTISE
IN DESIGN

 If one asks an expert for the rules he or she is using, one will, in effect, force the expert to regress to the level of a beginner and state the rules learned in school. Thus, instead of using rules he or she no longer remembers, as the knowledge engineers suppose, the expert is forced to remember rules he or she no longer uses… No amount of rules and facts can capture the knowledge an expert has when he or she has stored experience of the actual outcomes of tens of thousands of situations.
DREYFUS AND DREYFUS 2005

 Art is skill; that is the first meaning of the word.
ERIC GILL

THE NATURE OF EXPERTISE

We are now almost ready to begin exploring the acquisition of expertise in design. First though we must explore this general notion of expertise in a little more detail. Most definitions of expertise are relative rather than absolute. More or less they say that expertise consists of the characteristics, skills and knowledge that distinguish experts from novices in any particular field. This begs the question, as dictionary definitions often have a habit of doing. The Oxford English Dictionary, for example, defines an expert as 'someone having special knowledge or skill in a subject'.

What differentiates experts from novices? One thing that seems common to our understanding of expertise is that it is generally acquired. That is to say that in the great scheme of things experts are not born, they are bred. In the classical psychological battle between nature and nurture, expertise is strongly associated with nurture. In fact, expertise is a wonderful demonstration of the human ability to respond to an environment and adapt behaviour accordingly. We mostly associate experts with many hours of study and practice. At the same time, we also recognise that people probably have a natural predisposition enabling them to develop expertise more easily in some areas than others.

So expertise seems to be a set of learned skills and knowledge probably based on some personal characteristics that facilitate this learning. This then is what distinguishes experts from novices. In this sense expertise is a social construct as well as a cognitive one. It is also the case that expertise exists not just inside individuals but can also be held collectively in teams. We would have no difficulty with the idea that a business or team has a certain level of expertise that distinguishes it in the marketplace. A great deal of designing is done not by individuals alone but in teams of one kind or another. Our exploration of this much more social construct of expertise must wait until rather later in the book.

Are there some general principles that we can identify enabling us to describe the differences between experts and novices independently of the field they might be operating in? Do experts simply know more than other people? Are they just so practised that they are able to work more quickly, be more accurate, or more reliable than the rest of us?

One way of answering this question is to turn back to our dictionary definition where we find the word 'special'. Exactly what then is meant here by 'special'. This can mean 'particularly good or exceptional' but also it can

BECOMING AN EXPERT

The amusing aphorism that an expert is 'an ordinary fellow from another town' suggests that experts are different in the way foreigners are. Getting that way clearly takes a lot of time and effort. A commonly held view is that in most professional fields reaching this status requires something in the region of 10,000 hours of practice. This would amount to 5 years' worth of normal working days. Another common estimate is that it takes about 10 years in total to become recognised as an expert in such fields.

suggest 'peculiar, out of the ordinary and different'. Is it possible then that experts actually operate in different ways to novices?

In general the answer to this last question appears to be 'yes'. In most fields that have been studied extensively experts do appear to operate differently to novices. So becoming expert then is not just a matter of getting faster or more accurate. It is a matter of finding alternative ways of doing things in order to transform the way you operate. One of the key principles behind the development of high levels of skill seems to be the change from a conscious struggle to effortless, even automatic, performance. Novices seem to have to think consciously about many elements of their technique leaving little time to concentrate on the actual target. Those of us who drive a car will remember only too well how, when learning, it seemed difficult to steer and change gear at the same time. Experienced drivers appear to do both entirely effortlessly while holding a conversation with their passengers and listening to the radio.

A common educational or training technique is to give beginners rules to help them perform a new set of skills. So you might teach a novice chess player some simple system of giving each of the pieces a value. The rule then is that any exchange is good when your opponent's piece has a higher value than your own. So far so good and our novice can begin to play and at least make a game of it. Unfortunately, the more expert player might well lure our novice into an exchange of pieces that is attractive under the rules but with a move that also alters the board situation, thus fatally exposing either a much more valuable piece or even the king. The important lesson here is that such rules work in a context-free theoretical world but in any real-world situation they may prove unreliable. Thus, we often have to add a different kind of experiential and contextual knowledge to the theoretical knowledge to become more expert. This is probably the most fundamental way in which so-called 'common-sense' differs from formal learned knowledge.

pg.69

We might thus expect novice designers to rely heavily on the convention-based thinking approaches we outlined in the previous chapter. Such a process can easily produce designs which fail because they are in some ways out of context. Since design is such a situated activity in which theoretically every design problem is unique this sort of failure is more likely in design than in many other areas or professions.

ONE THING AT A TIME...

The great flautist James Galway offers the following
advice for those starting to learn to play the flute:

To start with, the beginner should experiment in making
sounds with the headpiece only, to avoid having to manage the
whole flute and think of half-a-dozen things at once. I believe
in this kind of 'isolation' for working on particular problems,
and indeed for concentrating the mind in daily practice. We all
need to worry as little as possible, so why not identify what
needs improving, isolate it, and get down to making it better?

BREAKING SKILLS DOWN

In his book on the flute, the great flautist James Galway advises the beginner to take the head joint off the main body of the flute before trying to make the first notes (Galway, 1990). He proceeds to teach the novice how to make the stream of air which leaves the lips and is directed across the mouthpiece in such a way that a sound is produced. Only once this sound can be made reliably by the student does Galway recommend attaching the main body of the instrument. Only then does this masterly teacher recommend beginning to think about the many other issues involved in making good notes.

To what extent can such advice apply to learning to design? Much later in this book, in Chapter 6, we shall look at many issues surrounding design education. We saw in the previous chapter that designing is characteristically a process of combining and integrating rather than breaking down and dividing. Perhaps because this is so important and central to design, we tend to assume that we must be integrated all the way through the acquisition of design skills. In Chapter 6 we shall argue that this is not necessarily so. For now let us return to our example of learning the flute for a little longer.

There does not seem to be some finite point in the process when the student can sensibly claim to have 'learned the flute'. Acquiring a sophisticated skill like playing the flute is seen, not only by Galway, but also by musicians in general, as being a life long task. Even the greatest musicians practice scales and still seem to rely heavily on their teachers. They know they must go on learning and practicing their skills. We are used to seeing the coaches of world-class tennis players or golfers accompanying them to the practice court or driving range or watching from the stands ready to give advice at some break in play. In design things seem rather different. The need to learn and practice the skills of design thinking is often hardly addressed at all. While designers may well use the 'crit' or design review to evaluate their output, we hardly ever hear of design master classes in which the very process of designing is developed rather than the end product. Why should this be?

A clue to the answer here is that design is quite different from sport or playing a musical instrument, which are largely physical skills. While designing certainly involves some of these kinds of components, notably drawing, it is much more a matter of cognition. The central tasks in design require us to look and think. Surely thinking is just like breathing, we do it all the time and every day of our lives?

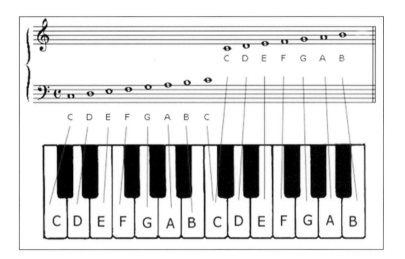

Fig 3.1 The musical scale and keyboard

IS THINKING A SKILL?

In fact cognition may not be as different as some may assume. It was the great philosopher Gilbert Ryle who first suggested that 'thought is very much a matter of drills and skills' (Ryle, 1949). He was later to be supported in this view by the psychologist Frederick Bartlett who told us that 'thinking should be treated as a complex and high level kind of skill' (Bartlett, 1958). Half a century later though we still seem reluctant to consider thinking as something we need to learn and practice. Just as few of us ever like to be told we could improve our driving, so it is with thinking. Most university courses in design hardly touch on this at all, but design demands arguably one of the most challenging and difficult forms of thinking.

And yet many have made a living by writing books telling us just how to improve that skill and become more productive thinkers. There are many such gurus but one of the most well-known is Edward de Bono, who has published simple guides (de Bono, 1991), teaching resources (de Bono, 1976) as well as more theoretical treatises (de Bono, 1969). This book will certainly take the view that design is a special and highly developed form of thinking, that thinking can be considered a skill and that designers can learn to become more expert at what they do.

Since design involves both physical acts and mental processing, acquiring expertise is also likely to be a more complex affair. Indeed, design education is often quite long and few designers seem to reach the peak of their powers until middle age. It is impossible to qualify for membership of the Architects' Register in the UK in less than seven years. A recent book celebrating the work of the best upcoming architects in Singapore defines 'young' architects as those under 45 years of age (URA, 2004). Hugh Pearman claims that 'in architecture, you are young if you are under 50, an infant if you are under 40 and a babe in arms if you are under 30' (Pearman, 2005). We might contrast this with other areas such as mathematics and some of the physical sciences where people are commonly expected to do some of their very best work in their twenties. Professor John Postgate even worries about the poor performance of scientists over the age of 45: 'It would be greatly to the advantage of all concerned if they, like the military, were normally taken on for a career-length term, say 25 years… At age 45 they would, subject to performance, normally be promoted by one grade and retired immediately on half pay' (Postgate, 1991).

But the process of acquiring expertise in design also has parallels in many other spheres of human activity. To illustrate the problem we shall return yet again to our example of learning to play the flute. The advanced

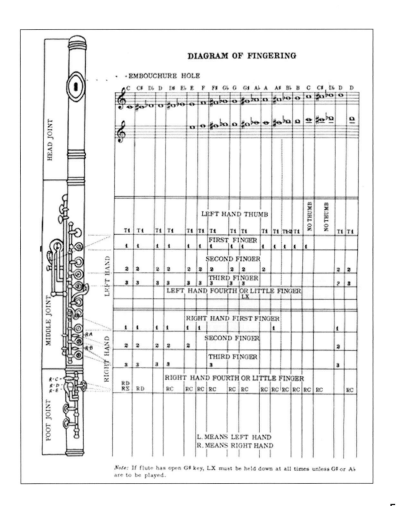

Fig 3.2 The flute fingering chart

flautist, like all instrumental musicians, is expected to perform a series of tasks in order to reach the higher level grades that designate their level of expertise. By grade 8, a flautist must be able to play the major and minor scales based on every note without reading music and without interruption or hesitation. This involves several skills functioning together. First the musician must work out which notes to play in which order, and then they must be physically created with the necessary fingering, breathing and embouchure patterns.

If we take the first part of this task we can see that the flautist shares with many wind instrumentalists a problem not afflicting keyboard and fretted instrument players. On the piano the scale is literally laid out in front of the player. Major and minor scales are always the same sequence of intervals no matter where they begin. The major scale is created by playing the intervals of 2,2,1,2,2,2,1 semi-tones (C major for example is C, D, E, F, G, A, B, C—but there are, of course, no flats or sharps between E and F or between B and C giving the keyboard its characteristic appearance of clusters of two and three black keys). Since, on the keyboard, the keys are arranged in ascending order, it is thus possible to see which keys to press to create the appropriate sequence. The poor flautist cannot 'see' any notes at all. The instrument itself is even out of sight over the right shoulder, but this is not really the major problem. Even worse, the sequence of finger movements to open and close the holes in the instrument are not in a simple logical progression but involve complex patterns of lifting and lowering the fingers of both hands.

The novice flautist then plays a scale in a very halting and deliberate fashion imagining which note must come next and then forming it. One way of speeding this up might be to imagine the notes written on the stave as they appear on a sheet of music. The flautist could 'see' such an arrangement in the mind's eye, as we say. Another technique might be to imagine the piano keyboard laid out in front of you. A third and much more sophisticated way is simply to practice all the scales so frequently that you develop some kind of body memory and stop thinking and imagining altogether but start feeling. These then represent three quite different ways of performing the same task. Of the three by far the most demanding is the third; you simply cannot get there without many hours of practice. This third method requires the least mental effort while playing and can be done semi-automatically. Incidentally, it also incorporates the knowledge about how to breath and form the opening in the lips (embouchure) which is necessarily different for every note.

Now let us give our flautist a slightly higher level of expertise acquired through more hard practice. A great deal of music it turns out uses many

LOUIS ANDRIESSEN SYMFONIE VOOR LOSSE SNAREN

The Dutch composer Louis Andriessen has written a piece, called Melodie that is based on hearing the young neighbour's son learning to play a baroque sonata on a flute, accompanied by his mother. The piece is interesting and excruciating to hear—as a listener, you are willing the performer forward all the time, but it is so slow, so halting, with all beautiful melodic passages and climaxes being missed one way or another. It is also touching and very human to hear. But for the professional musicians that perform this piece this must be very hard to play: they have to force themselves to go back to literal note-reading bypassing all their skills and great abilities.

common phrases. These may be scales or parts of scales or collections of key notes from scales known as 'arpeggios'. Our expert flautist will begin to recognise these even in music that has never been played before. That is to say that each note does not have to be read individually but rather the sequence or pattern of notes is recognised as a single entity. Since the sequences the notes represent have also been well practiced, the playing of these sections is now done with little or no conscious effort. There is a huge gulf then between this performance and that of the novice having to read every note and make the fingering, breathing and embouchure for that note all entirely self-consciously.

Occasionally a composer will write a surprising piece of music that can easily catch out the automated player. In particular, the great composers like to play with our expectations as listeners and this leads to traps for the unwary performer. Above all Mozart was a master of such composition. On these occasions the really skilful flautist may spot the unusual note in a sequence and pay that section of the music just a little more conscious attention. Louis Andriessen has taken this idea one step further!

This is precisely what we find time and time again when we explore expertise. The more sophisticated levels of expertise are not simply the more naïve levels done quicker, more accurately, or more reliably; they involve working in a different way. That different way often releases cognitive effort enabling the performer to pay attention to the situation rather than the process. Whether that situation is a piece of music, a sports opponent or a design problem, the principle seems to hold true. The real expert also knows just when to pay attention to some element in a process that has been honed to a semi-automatic and normally unconscious procedure.

These same principles of recognition can also be seen in the demonstration of how expert readers have come to recognise words rather than read individual letters. This recognition is done from very limited information. Obviously the novice reader who had not yet learned all the common English words would not be able to perform in this way, and we certainly would not recommend this approach to teachers of five-year-old children.

MODELS OF EXPERTISE AND DESIGNING

There are now some fairly well-established models of expertise which we shall examine very soon. In general they imply that expertise is hierarchical and sequential. That is to say we reach one level of expertise and, after some practice, learning some new procedures or acquiring some experience

IT'S ALL SO OVIBUOS

Aoccdrnig to rscheearch at an Elingsh uinervtisy, it deosn't mttaer in waht oerdr the lteers in a word are, the olny iprmoetnt tihng is taht frist and lsat ltteer is at rghit pclae. The rset can be a toatl mses. And you can sitll raed it wouthit porbelm. Tihs is bcuseae we do not raed ervey lteter by istlef, but the wrod as a wlohe

we progress seamlessly to the next level and never look back. The view of design expertise we are going to develop here suggests something rather more sophisticated and interesting.

In designing, the various layers of expertise may offer different potential but they are never exclusive. Reaching another layer of expertise does not strip away the ways of doing things used at previous layers. Just as, for example, a designer who has learned to use computer-aided design, does not stop drawing by hand. Expertise layers thus add new tools to the designer's repertoire of ways of doing things.

This is a similar phenomenon to the idea of shifted paradigms introduced by Kuhn in his theory of scientific revolutions (Kuhn, 1962). He suggested that theoretic advances in science often introduce paradigm shifts. We simply have to start thinking about a situation in a fundamentally different way. A famously accessible example is the manner in which Einstein made us think quite differently about gravity compared with how Newton had described it. This parallel is useful to us here since even all those years after Einstein we still retain Newton's view of gravity. It works well enough for us in everyday life and is easier to operate. Similarly then, we can see that a design student developing a new mode of design thinking does not throw away the old modes but rather has a process enriched by a variety of thinking styles offering more opportunities for tackling design situations.

To understand how this works we shall return yet again to our flute player. When playing the musical scales our novice flautist will probably want to read them from a score. A more experienced flautist may have alternative modes of playing available. Once some basic understanding of the scale patterns has been acquired then a system of imagining the music 'in the mind's eye' or 'seeing' the piano keyboard will both be possible. Once the flautist has become very expert, it may be possible to play from body memory, a much less conscious process. Of course, all the earlier modes of playing remain available even to the most advanced musician. Quite simply the expert can choose on each occasion what mode to use.

However, in design it is probably even more complex than this. Since there are many activities involved in designing, each designer may come to a new layer of expertise with some of those skills already more developed than others. Perhaps our novice flautist has already learned some other instrument to a high level of expertise. In this case the sequence of notes for all the major and minor scales will already be embedded in memory. For example, a pianist learning the flute will already be entirely familiar with the way all

pg.51

the scales are laid out on the piano keyboard. Such a person may well develop their flute scale technique quite differently from a total musical novice.

Students arriving at university to study design come with vastly differing sets of backgrounds and abilities. Some, for example, may have done a great deal of artwork and be very capable in drawing and graphical representation. Others may have studied physics and have a very good sense of structural stability in objects, or come from a craft background and have considerable knowledge of making things. Still others may have studied history and understand something of the sequence of the development of ideas which changed the pattern of design in their field.

There are yet two more intriguing characteristics of expertise we must consider here. Firstly, acquisition of the skill does not necessarily make it easy to describe this process to another. Imagine trying to explain how it is that you stay upright on a bicycle to someone who is learning. Swimming, driving a motorcar and many other everyday skills come into this category. It is often said that trying to teach a spouse to drive is the surest way to end a marriage! Good designers then do not necessarily make good tutors. We shall return to some of these problems in the chapter on education later in the book.

Secondly, we have seen that, once a skill is learned to a level of unconscious effort, then it tends to become transparent and automatic. Quite simply you are no longer aware that you even have the skill. Once you have learned to ride a bicycle you can scoot along happily enjoying the view. Not so when you were struggling to acquire that skill, when all your concentration was focused simply on staying on the bike and hopefully in an upright position. This recurrent theme, that high level skills are often carried out unconsciously, has many ramifications for us in design. One very important advantage for the designer is that what we might call secondary skills can be developed to a level that makes them transparent during the act of designing and therefore no longer demanding of attention by the designer. We shall return to this later in the chapter.

Skills that we have learned generally make our life easier. They enable us to concentrate on other things. Sometimes those very skills can create the obstacle to doing things in a new and possibly more effective way. We all acquire what are sometimes referred to as 'bad habits' in advanced skills. Certainly this is true of driving a car, and many of us will see irritating evidence of this everyday. Moving to another layer of expertise then often involves us in challenging ourselves to a painful period. Perhaps this may be seen to involve 'unlearning' or at least suspending a particularly comfortable skill. When this also involves us in such fundamental matters as seeing and

SHIFTS IN STUDENT EXPERTISE

Most schools seem to implicitly expect their students to develop in a more or less linear way, gradually attaining more expertise. Really letting go of this assumption could have a major impact on design education—more on this in Chapter 6.

If we take seriously the idea that learning to be a designer is not a smooth process at all then we might redesign the course a little. Perhaps first year design courses for example should concentrate on challenging students with the deficiencies in their ways of seeing and thinking about design. Getting a student to realise things could be different is often the first step to progress.

One of the nicest things in design education is to see students take a jump forward in their expertise. You can often recognise that this is about to happen when the student starts producing work that is a lot better or deeper than the student realises. The tutor perhaps needs to spend time explaining what is so good about the student's own idea. These are strange conversations; the tutor is enthusiastic, and the student probably confused and may not really understand what the tutor is talking about. But sometimes it just clicks, and these are defining moments of expertise shifts. Engineering these is what design education should strive for.

thinking, this can be very painful indeed. Each of us is likely to want to progress differently in some ways. Each of us may reach a point of being unwilling to accept any further challenges at different stages.

Design tutors are very much aware that student progression is hardly ever steady and uniform but often reaches a plateau followed by a period of turmoil and sometimes a wonderful leap forward as new approaches are taken on board. This poses all sorts of difficult questions about design education.

Acquiring expertise in design then is influenced by a complex array of factors. Of necessity, this book will present simple and generic descriptions of layers of expertise in a sequential manner. Books tend to be sequential! In reality each designer will develop in their own unique manner based on their own background, personality, motivation and opportunity. Each designer will put together their own way of designing. This book is intended to help designers to reflect upon their own development and position and what might help them progress. It is also intended to be a resource for those trying to help them on their way.

Hubert Dreyfus has proposed a generic model of expertise that we summarise on the opposite page. Dreyfus distinguishes six distinct levels of expertise corresponding with ways of perceiving, interpreting, structuring and solving problems (Dreyfus, 2003). He calls these 'novice', 'advanced beginner', 'competent', 'expert', 'master' and 'visionary'. Dreyfus argues that in each case the nature of the problem is effectively to some extent a function of the level.

TOWARDS A MODEL OF DESIGN EXPERTISE

To explore this step and to see whether the model as it is seems to reflect design reality, we will use some empirical data from design education. The set of data consists of self evaluations from students at the faculty of Industrial Design at Eindhoven University of Technology. In this design curriculum, which is solely project-based, students have to describe their own learning progress in 'self evaluations', which are commented upon by design teachers. These 'self evaluations' are a critical part of the design curriculum in this faculty. No marks are given, but the students are assessed on the basis of the learning progress they report in these self evaluations.

In general terms these student comments do indeed seem to sit comfortably with the generic Dreyfus expertise model. The students do seem to confirm different levels of performance and learning and even to be aware themselves of the transitions between the stages of their development. So this

GENERIC MODELS OF EXPERTISE

1. A **novice** will consider the objective features of a situation, as they are given by the experts, and will follow strict rules to deal with the problem.

2. For an **advanced beginner** the situational aspects are important, there is some sensitivity to exceptions to the 'hard' rules of the novice. Maxims are used for guidance through the problem situation.

3. A **competent** problem solver works in a radically different way. Elements in a situation are selected for special attention because of their relevance. A plan is developed to achieve the goals. This selection and choice can only be made on the basis of a much higher involvement in the problem situation than displayed by a novice or an advanced beginner. Problem solving at this level involves the seeking of opportunities. The process takes on a trial-and-error character, with some learning and reflection. A problem solver that goes on to be proficient immediately sees the most important issues and appropriate plan, and then reasons out what to do.

4. The **expert** responds to a specific situation intuitively, and performs the appropriate action straightaway. There is no problem solving and reasoning that can be distinguished at this level of working. This is a very comfortable level to be functioning on, and a lot of professionals do not progress beyond this point.

5. The **master** sees the standard ways of working that experienced professionals use not as natural but as contingent. A master displays a deeper involvement into the professional field as a whole, dwelling on successes and failures. This attitude requires an acute sense of context, and openness to subtle cues.

6. The **visionary** consciously strives to extend the domain of operation developing new ways of doing things, outcomes, definitions of the issues, opens new worlds and creates new domains. The visionary operates more on the margins of a domain, paying attention to other domains as well, and to anomalies and marginal practices that hold promises for a new vision of the domain.

empirical evidence encourages us to continue developing the argument supported by this model. However, many questions remain. Are these the only levels to be found in design education? Do we find them simply because we are looking for them? How do the transitions between the levels take place? These are all questions that will interest us as we progress through the rest of this book. So most of the generic expertise model levels are intuitively recognisable to anyone involved in design, whether in education (as a student or teacher) or in professional design practice. However, it is not quite as simple as that.

Firstly, these levels of expertise could not be taken as characterisations of a complete designer. These fundamentally different ways of looking at problematic situations can actually co-exist in a design project. Nobody is an expert on all aspects of design; on some problems we might be novices, at others we might be competent, or experts. And these levels can co-exist within a single design project: designers can simultaneously display the rule-based behaviour of the novice in some parts of their work, while displaying the interpretation and reflection that characterise higher levels of expertise in other parts of the design project. The nature of the design problem as seen by the designer depends on the level of expertise of the designer in solving the problem.

We must be careful not to take these levels of skill acquisition as a blanket model for the complete development of a designer. Learning design does not just involve skill acquisition, it also involves the learning of declarative knowledge, and the building up of a set of experiences that can be directly used in new projects. These experiences become a repertoire of earlier solutions that can be applied by the designer. They could be seen as a store of 'frames' in Schön's terminology (Schön, 1983), 'design prototypes' (Gero and Rosenman, 1990; Tham et al., 1990; Vermaas and Dorst, 2007), or as 'design gambits' (Lawson, 2004). We will explore this issue much more thoroughly in Chapter 5.

SYMBOLIC   EPISODIC

pg.127

pg.175

Dreyfus's model of expertise, built over a number of years, was a reaction to other work. The first three steps in the model, from 'novice' through to 'beginner' and 'competent' were particularly targeted at his suspicions about the implied continuity of Artificial Intelligence (Dreyfus, 1992). The AI argument claims that eventually bigger and better computers will be able to replicate all human cognition. So this argument could be extended to suggest that eventually we will be able to get computers to design.

Dreyfus has later argued that this is not necessarily so. Perhaps there are some discontinuities in mental representation that set some cognitive tasks

VISIONARYVISIONA

MASTERMASTERMAS

EXPERTEXPERTEXPERT

COMPETENTCOMPETENT

ADVANCED BEGINNERADVA

BEGINNERBEGINNERBEGINN

NOVICENOVICENOVICENOVICEN

STUDENTS OF DESIGN

Students at the faculty of Industrial Design at Eindhoven University of Technology have to describe their own learning progress in 'self evaluations'. The students are asked to reflect on their development in six basic competencies and four meta-competencies. The basic competencies are:

1. 'ideas and concepts'
2. 'integrating technology'
3. 'user focus'
4. 'social and cultural awareness'
5. 'market orientation'
6. 'form and senses'.

The meta-competencies are:

a. 'multidisciplinary teamwork and communication'
b. 'design and research processes'
c. 'self directed and continuous learning'
d. 'analysing complexity'.

Students in the first three years of study complete about 10 big design projects and 25 assignments. The comments below are from these students at stages we might think of as being comparable with the first three levels of the Dreyfus model and at the transition points between these levels.

aside from others. This work has later been more strongly connected to a fundamental treatise on mental representation, referring to the work of Merleau-Ponty (Dreyfus, 2002). Dreyfus cites the 'situatedness' of problems (a vital component for the 'advanced beginner') as an insurmountable hurdle for artificial intelligence.

The final steps in the Dreyfus expertise model, from 'expert' to 'master' and 'world discloser' (visionary), have been inspired by the existential 'anxieties' as they have been described by Heidegger. More recently, Goel suggested that design cannot be represented using the computational theory of mind (Goel, 1995). That is to say that the knowledge and procedures used by designers cannot be symbolically coded in a manner required by AI.

We largely support this position. Intuitively design feels different from the kinds of tasks so far mastered by artificial forms of intelligence. Some of the characteristics of design discussed in the previous chapter give strong support to this feeling that somehow design is not just a form of very complicated chess but something quite different. It is more like a game in which the board is not defined or even bounded, the moves allowed for each piece are not fixed and even new kinds of pieces might be introduced. If we could imagine such a game then we could not predetermine the range of knowledge that might be useful in order to play it well.

Another problem with applying this Dreyfus model to design is that this activity is not restricted to people who are trained at all, or indeed even realise they are designing. As we shall see in the next chapter, design is an everyday act as well as a professional one. The idea of starting then with a 'novice' level is questionable. Everyday design may be practiced by someone for many years so they are no longer novices new to it, but they may still remain relatively naïve in their approach. Such a category of people cannot be found amongst, for example, chess players or flautists. If you are taking up the flute you realise the minute you pick up the instrument for the first time that you need to do some learning.

But even with these qualifications this model appears useful as a tool for thinking through the development of expertise in a designer. It could offer some insights for both teachers and students in terms of organising and structuring an educational experience. For example, the important step from advanced beginner to competent designer that can be recognised in design education too (Dorst, 2003). This is where involvement and reflection come in to change the problem solving process. This is also where there is a radical shift in the perception and interpretation of the problematic situation: the

STUDENTS OF DESIGN REFLECT ON THEIR DEVELOPMENT

Novice-level:

- I think (it is) an excellent tool in the idea generation process, definitely when you're evolving from a concept to a product.

- What I still miss is some more theoretical background on form (theory of forms). I know there are certain rules in graphical design.

- It strikes me that I never put any effort in learning how to handle requirements while they are a fundamental part of the design process.

Transition from novice to advanced beginner:

- The things I'm learning are changing; at first you really learn project related things. Every project you found out a number of specific things and you wonder how to ever learn all things. But the last periods I'm beginning to see the bigger lines, how all those things relate to each other. You draw connections between things you've seen earlier and new things you see in projects.

Advanced beginner:

- I can hardly believe that for all these different design problems (there is) one process (that) is the most effective.

- Another thing I would like to experiment with is how this method will work on different kinds of projects.

Transition from advanced beginner to competent:

- For me as designer it's important that there are different ways to look at the interface problem so that I can select and follow the appropriate principle for each individual project.

Competent:

- Most of the times when you apply a certain method you will have to adapt it so that it will fit your project.

advanced beginner has to move from a detached view of an 'objective' reality to the involvement and active interpretation of a situation.

EXPERTISE IN SUBORDINATE SKILLS

In Chapter 2 we listed many activities that designers must perform and that we might expect them to become expert at. Clearly at the very heart of design we find the activities that we called 'formulating' or identifying problems and 'moving' or making propositions about solutions. By comparison 'representing' or being able to draw, model and describe design situations, might seem to be more subordinate. However, at least some of the representational skills turn out to be more fundamental than this title might suggest. Donald Schön has famously described a process in which designers have a conversation with the situation through the medium of the drawing. This needs a little expansion here in order to emphasise the significance of this delightful image.

pg.51

Designers are notoriously visually aware and sensitive people. They are usually interested in art, have a heightened sense of dress and fashion, like the iconoclastic and appear different themselves. All these may appear to be superficial characteristics and perhaps they are. However, they are also reflections of a much more fundamental issue about the way designers think. The Artificial Intelligence movement is founded on the basic principle that cognition depends upon the symbolic encoding of knowledge. Two such symbolic systems are well-known to us in everyday life, our spoken and written languages and mathematics. It is assumed that we think when using these methods of representation.

Designers, however, clearly use another form of cognition which is generally described as 'visual thinking'. They think directly by manipulating graphical information which is extremely difficult to encode entirely in conventional symbolic systems as required by AI. This is yet another reason why it seems unlikely that computers can ever be enabled to design in the sense that humans do. The problem that faces the designer is the interface between what we might call perception and imagery. The psychology of perception deals with the way we see and make sense of a world around us. This would include the way we look at drawings. In relying on precedent the designer deals with a second kind of material that is mentally imaged and not physically present. A third even more challenging kind of material is the imagination the designer uses to conjure up designs that have never previously existed. A large part of design thinking then must rely upon relating these three kinds of information.

THINKING IN A LANGUAGE

A normal adult person choosing to live in a foreign country may need to learn a new language. To begin with, this is often done formally through lessons or books and relies upon the learning of vocabulary through translation and the learning of grammar through rules. This skill in the new language is thus acquired in an entirely different way to the experiential learning of a native language around the age of two years. For some time, our emigrating adult will need a dictionary and will think by translating. However, a common question that establishes a certain level of expertise is whether this person thinks directly in the new language, may hear people speak in it during their dreams, and may use it to perform mental arithmetic.

This is largely done through some form of external representation that can bring all three together. This image we have of the designer is of someone sitting at a drawing board using a sketch or drawing to do this. The reality though is that designers also do a great deal of talking, both among themselves and with others. Thinking in design then is characteristically done with these two forms of representation intertwined. This incidentally is one of the reasons why simply studying enforced think-aloud verbal protocols has serious deficiencies as a method of design research (Lloyd et al., 1996).

Since so little design cognition could take place without these external forms of representation they clearly become central to the facilitating of design thinking. A designer not expert in these forms of representation is going to be severely handicapped and unlikely to be able to reach an advanced level of expertise. In subsequent chapters we shall explore some of the aspects of becoming expert in representation. There are, however, two points to consider here of general significance.

Since drawing is likely to be such a fundamental support skill in design thinking, it is likely that it must be developed to a high level of skill in itself in order to leave cognitive effort free to concentrate on the design issues themselves. Designers often talk of the need to spend some of their time thinking in a very rapid and intense way ranging over a very wide range of issues. This is surely because of the integrative nature of design solutions we discussed in Chapter 2. If this is the case then drawing must also be rapid and effortless. Two consequences of this seem important here: the need to develop high-level skills in both drawn and verbal representation.

The great architect/engineer Santiago Calatrava illustrates this point very powerfully in his description here. Calatrava is a particularly good example for us since his process famously depends upon both physical and numerical engineering modelling. However, it is clear that the hand drawing is at the very heart of his creative process. Calatrava is fluent with both a drafting pen and watercolour. Watching him work with these disparate materials shows that he has mastered both to an unconscious level of skill. This enables him to concentrate on the design itself. He uses other types of representations in both physical and computer models but they are more formal in their methods of construction and do not offer the 'dialogue' he clearly finds important.

In the case of drawing, this suggests that a number of sub-skills will be needed. These are all well covered in other sorts of books so here we will restrict ourselves to little more than listing them. Firstly, there is mastery over the technique itself. This implies being able to draw or paint using the

DRAWING SANTIAGO CALATRAVA

Drawing is very important to me; it is a beautiful process. You see the thing in your mind and it doesn't exist on the paper but then you start making simple sketches and organising things and then it comes more and more and then you start doing this layer and this layer and this and then you look at the drawings and they are very different one from the other and you see there is a kind of revolution but it is very much a dialogue. This is why I like to draw quite small, but even a thing like that (he points to a drawing of a cathedral project) you know because it's very large, you see I could also take a big piece of paper and then draw the whole thing but I like much more to concentrate. (He draws on A3, A4 and sometimes A5 paper.) I don't draw perspectives I prefer to imagine... because the reality is always better than any perspective... three dimensional representation is only to let someone else see, you do that for someone else and not for yourself. I am talking here about drawings that are a dialogue with yourself.

The model is important in a certain period of the design process after that we don't look very much at the model. I don't use them too much for relating reality. You see because the model that we use it is black and white, and the reason is also very simple because I want to have an abstraction, I don't want to have a hyper-realistic model but it is really blank and so it is abstract... I have learned also to appreciate the models as autonomous things. A model is beautiful because a model can be beautiful. It is a certain guarantee that building will be also... will have a certain beauty but only a small guarantee...

I like very much the unbelievable precision with which you can work (on the computer), you know sometimes especially in engineering works it is very important this precision. If you want an arc going between two points and you want to see immediately and you cannot achieve it by your hand you see what I mean. It is too imprecise by your hand, you can maybe say to the computer I want to do an arc then the computer is very helpful.

Fig 3.3 Railway Station at Lyon Airport by Santiago Calatrava—a typical example of his expressive dynamic structures

SANTIAGO CALATRAVA

Santiago Calatrava is one of an extremely rare breed of architect-engineers. He grew up in the Spanish region of Valencia going to evening classes in Arts and Crafts as early as the age of eight. He studied architecture at the Escuela Tecnica Superior de Arquitectura de Valencia, and then moved to Switzerland to study civil engineering in Zurich receiving a doctorate studying foldable frameworks. His practice has offices in Zurich and Paris.

Santiago Calatrava has designed jewellery, created sculptures, street furniture, bridges, railway stations and opera houses among many other buildings. His approach defies categorisation in that his engineering is highly sculptural and his architecture exploits the power of innovative but logical structural form. Underlying all his work is a consistent attempt to make structural form expressive and appropriate. The influence of his early life in Valencia and more recent years in Switzerland can perhaps be seen in a totally new approach to form that appears to combine and develop the traditions of Gaudi and Maillart. He has won many prizes in design competitions. He has been awarded the Gold Medals of both the Royal Institute of British Architects and the Institute of Civil and Structural Engineers.

media with facility. This would include being able to draw thick and thin lines, straight and curved lines and put flat and graded layers of colour in precise areas and so on. However, drawing from life also requires the skills of articulating proportion, colour, distance and many other normally implicit features of the three-dimensional world and making them explicit in order to choose appropriate forms to graphically represent them. Learning to do this repeatedly through sketching would thus seem important. If design students take pictures with digital cameras and make presentations of their designs with computers they are unlikely to be practicing freehand sketching and developing skills that are central in supporting their very fundamental design thinking. Of course new representational skills in digital media will also bring other benefits but overall this may distort design expertise in ways we are yet to understand.

In the case of verbal language we shall see in due course that the acquisition of concepts and ideas that can be expressed in words is another central support skill for a designer. Design conversations simply cannot take place unless meaningful languages can be developed. There are many implications of this process but one illustration may be useful here. Lawson has argued that architects have developed a language for the description of complex roof forms that is simple and yet extremely powerful (Lawson, 2002). In particular, a very few words enable us to describe features and parts of such roof forms. The words 'ridge', 'eaves', 'hip', 'valley' and 'verge' cover every possible edge or fold in traditional roof forms. Once we add the simple concepts of 'pitch' and words to describe flatness and curvature it is possible to describe very complex three-dimensional form.

This example also helps us to understand how different design domains do indeed require some different supporting skills. Some design research implicitly assumes that design is a generic skill and indeed many of the central design skills may well be generic. It is more likely that the support skills vary. Architects may frequently manipulate space and geometric form and may need to be highly skilled at line drawing. Fashion designers may work with more organic forms and make more use of colour and texture, suggesting they may need to be more skilled at painting. Design researcher Michael Tovey has described the fascinating and intricate language of car stylists. They too have their own highly developed language of design form through which they discuss solutions and problems (Tovey, 1992).

So far, of course, we have assumed that the design fields we are studying here all produce physical objects. Other design fields such as system design do not and their designers may only need fairly crude diagram drawing capabilities. Of course, software designers need a whole raft of skills to do with

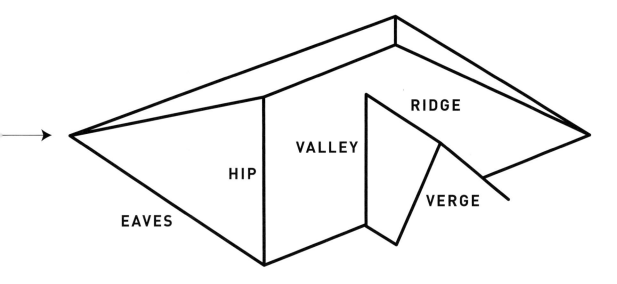

Fig 3.4 A language for describing roof forms

symbolical representation in software. Interestingly the new field of web-design creates virtual physical objects. That is to say it creates objects we look at which are nonetheless implemented through formal symbolic computer languages. Within this field, the behaviour of the 'objects' within interaction scenarios is the defining quality. Thus, web-designers design behaviour, design interaction scenarios and the software 'objects' that will make them happen. The language needed to support the critical design thinking in this domain is still developing.

AUTOMOBILE STYLISTS DESIGN LANGUAGE

Michael Tovey describes how the highly specialised designers working on the immensely complex shape of a car have borrowed many words from our common language about human bodies, and redefined them to describe the car bodies they are creating. They talk about the 'eyes' (lights), 'forehead' (rim of the hood or bonnet) and 'shoulders' (overall wheel-well breadth) of a car. The drawings they make also contain a certain code, in that they have developed a very subtle way of drawing the reflections on a car's surface, that (for them) precisely define the shape of the car. The mouth-watering drawings they produce may look like glossy presentation-drawings, but they are not. The accomplished car stylist can look at these drawings and read the three-dimensional shape of the car in much more detail than a layman could.

REFERENCES

Bartlett, F.C. (1958). **Thinking**. London, George Allen and Unwin.

de Bono, E. (1969). **The Mechanism of Mind**. London, Jonathan Cape.

de Bono, E. (1976). **Teaching Thinking**. London, Temple Smith.

de Bono, E. (1991). **Six Action Shoes**. London, Fontana.

Dorst, C.H. (2003). **Understanding Design**. Amsterdam, BIS Publishers.

Dreyfus, H.L. (1992). **What Computers Still Can't Do: A critique of artificial reason**. Cambridge, MA, MIT Press.

Dreyfus, H.L. (2002). **Intelligence without representation: Merleau-Ponty's critique of mental representation**. Phenomenology and the Cognitive Sciences 1: 367–383.

Dreyfus, H.L. (2003). **The Spinoza Lectures**, University of Amsterdam.

Dreyfus, H.L. and Dreyfus, S. (2005). **Expertise in real world contexts**. Organization Studies 26(5): 779–792.

Galway, J. (1990). **Flute**. London, Kahn and Averill.

Gero, J.S. and Rosenman, M.A. (1990). **A conceptual framework for knowledge-based design research at Sydney University**. Artificial Intelligence in Engineering 5(2): 65–77.

Goel, V. (1995). **Sketches of Thought**. Cambridge, Mass, MIT Press.

Kuhn, T.S. (1962). **The Structure of Scientific Revolutions**. Chicago, University of Chicago Press.

Lawson, B.R. (2002). **CAD and creativity: does the computer really help?** Leonardo 35(3): 327–331.

Lawson, B.R. (2004). **Schemata, gambits and precedent: some factors in design expertise**. Design Studies 25(5): 443–457.

Lloyd, P., Lawson, B. and Scott, P. (1996). **Can concurrent verbalisation reveal design cognition?** Analysing Design Activity. N. Cross, H. Christiaans and K. Dorst. Chichester, Wiley: 437–463.

Pearman, H. (2005). **A river of talent?** The Sunday Times. London. 9434: 24–25.

Postgate, J. (1991). **Bring in the Long-service commission—Science should follow the army's example**. New Scientist 1753(26 January): forum.

Ryle, G. (1949). **The Concept of Mind**. London, Hutchinson.

Schön, D.A. (1983). **The Reflective Practitioner: How professionals think in action**. London, Temple Smith.

Tham, K.W., Lee, H.S. and Gero, J.S. (1990). **Building envelope design using design prototypes**. ASHRAE Trans 96: 508–520.

Tovey, M. (1992). **Automotive stylists' design thinking.** Research in Design Thinking. N. Cross, K. Dorst and N. Roozenburg. Delft, Delft University Press: 87–98.

URA (2004). **20 Under 45**. Singapore, Urban Redevelopment Authority.

Vermaas, P.E. and Dorst, C. H. (2007). **On the conceptual framework of John Gero's FBS model of designing and the prescriptive aims of design methodology**. Design Studies 28(22): 133–157.

4 STARTING OUT AS A DESIGNER

I am enough of an artist to draw freely upon my imagination. Imagination is more important than knowledge. Knowledge is limited. Imagination encircles the world.

ALBERT EINSTEIN

I have yet to see any problem, however complicated, which, when you looked at it in the right way did not become still more complicated.

PAUL ANDERSON

A designer can mull over complicated designs for months. Then suddenly the simple, elegant, beautiful solution occurs to him. When it happens to you, it feels as if God is talking! And maybe He is.

LEO A. FRANKOWSKI (THE CROSS-TIME ENGINEER)

EVERYDAY DESIGN

Today it is possible to study degree courses in many different kinds of design. Most design professions are defined by the kinds of solutions their members create. So architects design buildings and industrial designers create everyday objects, though, as we saw in Chapter 2, the reality is often not quite so simple and straightforward. A whole range of specialised designers now exist to create interiors, urban settings, landscapes, furniture, fashion, websites and graphics. Many of these designers are highly professionalised within their societies and some, like architects, even protect their title with national and even regional legislation.

And yet in spite of all this professionalism, design also remains an activity carried out by all of us more or less unconsciously. We make everyday decisions that look remarkably like designing. We contrive our appearance, lay out letters and documents on our computers and arrange our homes and workplaces. Buying clothes and combining them into an outfit looks like a simple form of design. We might take on more ambitious projects such as landscaping our gardens and refurbishing the interiors of our homes. We might even say that everyday consumer choice turns us into designers. On special occasions we might entertain some friends. Looking through recipes, putting a menu together, going out and buying the food required, preparing the food and finally arranging and serving it, all looks like a process of designing.

However, we need to be very careful here. Many activities may look like design but in reality they turn out to be little more than a series of choices or perhaps simple problem solving; and design is more than that.

Hatchuel's nice example of finding a movie to watch and planning a party explains some important differences here (Hatchuel, 2002). To complicate matters further, the everyday tasks that Hatchuel would not regard as design can often be found inside design processes. Designers do many things. At some stage in a project they may well select from a limited range of predetermined choices. At other times they may well solve highly constrained and even clearly defined problems. So these everyday design look-alikes are worthy of our attention as long as we recognise them for what they are. They also enable us to illustrate a range of complexity in the sorts of situations that designers must learn to work with.

Large complex and expensive purchases require choices to be made that often combine normally irreconcilable factors. Consider buying a car for example. The choice will vary between individuals but might involve decisions about

DESIGNING A PARTY HATCHUEL

Hatchuel imagines a group of friends coming together on a Saturday evening and looking for a good movie in town. This might look like a very simple form of design but Hatchuel argues that they are really just making a choice from a set of alternatives already provided for them. They are really just problem solving.

Hatchuel then imagines these same friends setting out to have a party. In this situation they are, in Hatchuel's view, involved not in problem solving but in design. Now the situation becomes a project rather than a simple problem. There are no instantly available solutions to choose from but rather the friends must imagine various possibilities.

In fact Hatchuel argues that there are four key differences here that distinguish design from simple problem solving. Firstly, there is a creative step in actually defining what you mean by a party, whereas this cannot be said about watching a movie. Secondly, there is a lack of pre-packaged solutions for parties. Thirdly, in design, there is a need to use what we might call 'learning devices' in order to get a solution. These might include experiments or imagined or simulated solutions. And, finally, the whole process itself needs to be created. In other words, our group of friends need to develop and agree ways of reaching solutions and how to decide which one they will choose.

such factors as purchase price, running costs, appearance, performance, comfort, convenience, reliability, safety, perceived status and many others. We saw in Chapter 2 how one of the common characteristics of design is the inescapable need to combine such different factors together into single integrated decisions. But there are no rules or theories about how to do this. We went through a period in the mid-twentieth century when some argued that cost-benefit analysis could provide a procedure for dealing with such situations by reducing all factors to a monetary value. However, we soon realised that all this did was to move the subjective aspects of the decision making to a dangerously invisible part of the process.

So there are no common metrics or measurements that connect the cost, appearance and reliability of, for example, cars. How much will a car driver pay for styling? How much performance might a car owner sacrifice for safety? Which is more important, appearance or reliability? These are exactly the sort of questions that form characteristic ingredients in design problems. Just as the designer of an automobile has to deal with these impossible conundrums, so does the purchaser. How then do we come to these everyday tricky design-like conclusions?

Everyday 'designers' generally rely on little or no experience and knowledge. People working in this way are often assisted in this decision making process by consumer support material.

For example, the Which Magazine in the UK (http://www.which.co.uk/) or Consumentengids in Holland (http://www.consumentenbond.nl/) will test a whole series of items such as lawn-mowers, refrigerators, washing machines and of course cars. Their published reports show how well the items were judged along a whole series of dimensions. Some of these may involve physical measurement, such as size or weight. Others will involve tests for which there are quantitative results, such as petrol consumption. Still others such as convenience may require subjective judgements. For the everyday consumer such support is helpful then in two ways. Firstly, it identifies the key characteristics of the designed item under investigation and thus educates and prepares the consumer to be more discerning. Secondly, it presents some hard and soft data comparing actual designs with each other.

Often such publications arrive at an overall score and declare one or more winners or 'best-buys'. While they may declare their weighting system in the small print, such publications hardly ever address the really difficult and important question of the relative values of all the criteria. As we go through our model of design expertise then it will quickly become apparent that

CHOOSING A VACUUM CLEANER

	A	B*	C
weight (kgs)	8	6	7
cord length (m)	9	7	8
FEATURES			
telescopic tubes	Y	Y	N
variable suction	Y	N	N
bag full indicator	N	Y	Y
reusable paper bag	Y	Y	N
PERFORMANCE (1–5)			
dust pickup	3	4	4
fibre pickup	4	5	5
cleaning edges	1	2	2
suction power	1	3	3
noise	2	4	3
ease of use	3	5	3
TOTAL SCORE (1-10)	**4**	**8**	**6**

*Best buy!

dealing with such tricky decision making in a rather more sophisticated manner is just one of the skills needed by professional designers.

These examples of design-like activity are in reality simply a matter of making a series of choices between prepared alternatives. At the next level of sophistication everyday designers also deal with issues of combining such choices into some overall solution and, in doing so may need to take account of some special local conditions.

An example of this might be redesigning a kitchen or perhaps a bathroom. Here a series of items have to be selected and combined together, such as storage cupboards, work surfaces, cookers, washers and refrigerators and so on. But the consumer's kitchen will already have a predetermined size and probably have fixed doors and windows. Support for this more complex task may be provided in the form of help with measuring up and drawing out, selecting and representing alternative designs. Most retailers will now offer a computer-aided design package to support all these activities. Essentially this de-skills the process as much as possible and thus provides the consumer with a range of solutions to choose from as if buying a complete single entity.

Inevitably design often involves some decision making that may look rather like this. Although what happens in a kitchen showroom may look to the uninitiated very much like what an architect or interior designer would do, it is in fact far from it. The professional designer is almost certainly considering whether the doors and windows should be moved and the dimensions of the kitchen altered. Using different ranges of fittings and even designing some new ones may come into the equation. Perhaps there is even some consideration of whether we are using the right space to be a kitchen. Of course, when designing a complete dwelling from scratch, all these things are up in the air at once as it were.

At this much more skilled level then there can be no reducing everything to a series of simple choices. The problem solution situation becomes far more fluid. This suggests that we are no longer talking about everyday 'design' but rather are in the realms of some higher levels of expertise. This is surely what the great architect/engineer Santiago Calatrava was telling us about using a process that involves drawing by hand rather than allowing ourselves to select pre-packed solutions from catalogues.

The kind of simple computer-aided design system offered in a kitchen showroom is no longer likely to be helpful in supporting this process. Sadly, many creators of computer-aided design tools seem to have failed to arrive at this

" DRAWING BY HAND
SANTIAGO CALATRAVA

It is necessary to get spontaneity; you see a product has
a freshness and a spontaneity that you probably can only
achieve when you are working by hand. Whether it is a lamp
or a handrail or maybe the way in which you touch a wall
or whatever. You have to draw by hand, you see, because
this spontaneity is not something that you pull out of a
catalogue. Even if things are a little bit similar there is also
the possibility of this spontaneity... Sometimes the degree
of freedom is not very large, you see, it is like moving in
a very narrow band. You cannot do like this, you cannot
do that, you have to work very strictly according to the
millimetres that they give you. So sometimes on the one
hand it needs a lot of constancy or perseverance but you
see on the other hand I think it needs a lot of spontaneity.
Drawing by hand is a very beautiful process. I wish to
draw. I do many drawings. I wish not to repeat myself... "

simple conclusion and have provided tools far too crude for more expert designers to find useful.

The recent proliferation of 'makeover' programmes on television show just how much everyday design depends upon support. These programmes show how to change your bedroom, bathroom, kitchen, living room or garden to make it appear to have been professionally designed. The adjective 'designer' encourages consumers to believe that objects are somehow superior and desirable because they carry famous designer labels. Of course, the design process behind them may indeed have been a more thorough, comprehensive, creative and imaginative one, but the label itself is no guarantee of this.

Everyday design, then, often depends on copying solutions or fragments of solutions without any real understanding of the principles involved. This process may consist of emulating a relatively superficial set of attributes of existing designs. In terms of our three types of design thinking this is very much rule-based design. The rule here is that a particular design was admired; therefore, all of its attributes are worth copying. The results may appear to be very direct and often inappropriate forms of visual quotation and the re-use of ideas out of their original context can, to the more expert eye, seem inappropriate and even absurd. The situation-based design approach then would question if such a doggedly convention-based copy was relevant to the new context or situation.

pg.69

Clients, therefore, can come with many different levels of expertise in design. Increasingly, major manufacturers or organisations who procure buildings frequently may have very sophisticated professional clients who are them-selves educated as designers. Other clients may have little or no experience of designing and briefing. Clients are inevitably consumers themselves and thus also operate as 'everyday' designers. Designers must learn to deal with all these levels of client expertise.

This inevitably means that one of the designer's tasks may be offering some form of design education to explain their more sophisticated process to cli-ents. The Czech architect Eva Jiricna has obviously worked with a number of such clients and she shows very clearly how this happens.

STARTING TO STUDY DESIGN

In many subjects the main degree curriculum can be found between the cov-ers of one, or perhaps just a few, textbooks. Students of design are not going to find life so simple. There is no overall general basic undergraduate design textbook. This is not because design tutors are too busy to write such books.

DESIGNING FOR A 'KNOWING CLIENT'

Experience shows that one of the most difficult challenges to the patience of an interior designer can be working on private houses, when one of the owners of the house has done a course in 'interior design' or was an avid reader of some popular Interior magazines. This often means that these people are full of preferences and opinions, which they can clearly express—but they might still lack any idea of what a 'design process' is like, and may have no basis for discussing their preferences, criteria or the design ideas put forward. It is very hard to negotiate a design space when working with people who overestimate their abilities to contribute to it, and feel they can be judgemental at any moment in the design process.

To quote Aristotle:
"Real thinking starts when judgement is suspended."

It just is not that kind of a subject. There may be many who write books that appear to theorise about design but more often than not these are statements of personal value systems. Such authors are usually telling you what they enjoy and value and what seems to them to be good design.

Indeed, life has tended to get more difficult for design students in recent years. Design styles have proliferated in the writings of design critics. Since the breakdown late in the twentieth century of the monopoly that the 'modern movement' had over design, there no longer even seems to be a consensus about what defines contemporary style. Many designers will say that style does not interest them and that they do not think in stylistic terms. In earlier days a designer had at least some certainties provided by the historical styles of design. A Greek temple, a Palladian building, or a Queen Anne chair were all objects that lay firmly inside the rules of styles that could be clearly articulated and which were studied and understood by the students of the time. The rules and conventions of a single dominant design style is no longer a nice easy starting point for the novice student of design.

The examples of everyday design we have looked at above show largely convention-based thinking. We might expect that early student work would rely more on this relatively primitive thinking strategy than that of more expert designers. In terms of the generic model of expertise we examined in Chapter 3, this is really at the 'novice' level. Design education often uses early projects that are deliberately designed to shake students out of their unquestioned conventional assumptions. Characteristically novice students are likely to do relatively little reframing of problem situations.

pg.69

Early student work is largely at the project level rather than the process, practice or professional levels that we introduced in Chapter 2. Not surprisingly, to begin with the average student has little opportunity to develop a practice context for their work. In searching for this, students may well begin to pick this up from their tutors and if this is done unconsciously it can create significant problems later on. Perhaps one of the weaknesses of the so-called 'unit' systems of studio teaching is that it appears to offer a model of the professional practice. But there are considerable deficiencies in this studio model; there is little continuity, the authority of the tutor and motivation of the students is very different, the relationships with clients and users is often remote and timescales are likely to be very short. Inevitably also, to begin with students are most likely to focus on the project and may pay relatively little attention to building a process or their overall practice. After all, it is the project that brings marks to the student just as it brings fees to the professional designer.

pg.61

EDUCATING CLIENTS
(WORDS AND PICTURES)
EVA JIRICNA

What I try to do is to express in words what they (clients) want, and in the same way—in words, I try to twist it into a different statement and make them accept a verbal statement and then draw it. Because if they have a verbal explanation for what we are doing, well that is something which happens all the time. For example, we have got a client who wanted, who has bought himself an 1822 building and he wanted to convert it into what he thought would be an interior very similar to the original one. It finished up with a glass staircase, he finished up with some suspended ceilings, he finished up with stainless steel picture rails, Japanese blinds at the windows, diagonal bracing, just completely different. He has bought now some furniture which is period furniture but as far as the shell of the building is concerned there is not one single classical detail. We started talking about which cornice, which skirting; he had books of different types of classical staircases and so on and I just had to explain to him that on a basis of analysis what the skirting, the cornices and the ceilings used to do in that period of time, we can replace it with a similar articulated design which is not based on classical detail. Basically cornices were to cope with the junction of the horizontal plane with the vertical plane and it was a junction which was always very messy, so what we did we let the junction go through and then we suspended a floating ceiling underneath so instead of having cornices this way we just had a floating ceiling underneath, which made it possible for us to hide all the mess of wires and cables and lighting. Explaining like this is the only way because he doesn't know he has never seen anything in his life apart from cornices.

FIG 4.1 Joe's Café in Sloane Street, London by Eva Jiricna showing her elegant use of high-tech materials

EVA JIRICNA

Eva Jiricna was born in the Czechoslovakian town of Zlin where her father, Josef Jiricny, was an architect for the Bata organisation. In spite of her father's discouragement she went to university in Prague to study architecture. She never joined the Communist Party and, after attending a UIA conference in Paris, Eva Jiricna resolved to cross the then 'iron curtain' more permanently. She initially joined Jack Whittle who helped her at GLC Architects' Department before moving to Louis de Soissons to work on the Brighton Marina where she was to learn a great deal about materials. She left in 1978 to start a series of practices co-operating with others including Jan Kaplicky of Future Systems, and with Richard Rogers on the interior of the Lloyd's building. In the early 1980s she established her long running close association with Joseph Ettedgui for whom she has designed a well-known series of high quality interiors. The 'Joseph' shops and the associated cafe were followed by fashion stores for other clients, night-clubs, and domestic interiors.

Students beginning design degrees have a long road ahead of them. It will likely be difficult and frustrating, but also potentially hugely rewarding. Design remains one of the most tantalisingly tricky and intractable of all human skills to teach and learn. There are a number of reasons for this.

LOOKING FOR THEORIES

Just as design students will search in vain for textbooks, they may also wonder where the theory is. Laura Willenbrock's puzzlement seems to come at least in part from her transfer from a degree with a more orthodox approach to knowledge than architecture (Willenbrock, 1991). Design of the kind we are discussing in this book, does not have some overarching theory in the way many other subjects do. There is no theory of relativity or quantum theory in design and not even the equivalents of the laws of gravity, friction, force, mass and so on that enable engineers to calculate the sizes of structural components. Designers do not then have a set of systematic rules that enable them to move from a problem to a solution. As we saw in Chapter 2, design problems and solutions are simply not connected in logical, predictable or even describable patterns.

Nigel Cross refers to the 'Method in their madness', nicely adapting a quotation from Shakespeare here in the title of one of his many publications on the nature of designing. 'Though this be madness, yet there is method in't' whispers Polonius as he struggles to fathom Hamlet's actions. In using this title, Cross nicely summarises the feelings of those of us who try to understand not only the actions but also the thoughts of designers (Cross, 1996). They often seem to behave in illogical and curious but nevertheless effective ways. This is quite simply because design situations are not amenable to pure logic but require the application of imagination. They are seldom progressed step by step inexorably from problem to solution but often by the introduction of ideas from outside the situation originating in quite unpredictable sources. Thus, design proceeds more often by the introduction of knowledge about things that might work rather than by theories about how to get from problems to solutions.

Scientific theories are very attractive in that they structure knowledge and suggest courses of action. They give rise to models which in turn allow us to predict and to understand behaviour. Bannister amusingly portrays the way this works in psychology (Bannister, 1966). Such theories allow people operating in those fields to describe why one situation is different from another and to predict what might happen under certain circumstances. This book advances a model of design expertise based on some other theories about the

BEYOND CONVENTION-BASED DESIGN

A colleague used to set students of architecture and engineering an apparently abstract project. The brief was remarkably simple. It demanded that a series of identical loads were to be suspended in space. The point of suspension of these loads all had to be a minimum height above ground. The loads must have a minimum distance between them. The task was to produce the simplest and most efficient structure to perform all this. The students would work away on this for a day or so coming up with proposals that were presented only in outline sketch form or a simple model.

In fact, the brief was that for an electricity pylon. The loads were the various power cables and the distances were all required for safety reasons. The discussion at the end of the project was always not so much about the detail design but whether any designs had really come up with anything original. The whole point being that it would have been even more difficult to break away from the traditional pylon design, if the students had known that was what they were designing.

A PUZZLED STUDENT
LAURA WILLENBROCK

I transferred into architecture in my sophomore year. I had enrolled initially in Miami University's nationally known International Studies program… I remember feeling very anxious about my early days in the undergraduate architecture program at Miami University. I was unsure about the way we were being directed toward knowledge, although I was willing to trust that there was a particular design in the minds of our professors. Whether I was patient, optimistic, or fighting cynicism I am not sure.

nature of design problems and design activity. In part this model also draws on generic models of the acquisition of cognitive expertise, but it cannot invent or discover a theory of design. Such a thing simply is not there.

Of course, students of design may well study many of the theories and structures of knowledge we have discussed above. They are very likely to learn some stylistic history. They will need mathematics, certainly geometry, and they may find value in the kinds of calculative theory that engineers use. But they will not be able to develop design expertise by studying theory. Nor will they be able to rely on the design pattern books and stylistic rules of earlier generations. So just what kind of knowledge do designers have to study in order to become experts?

EPISODIC KNOWLEDGE IN DESIGN

It turns out that design knowledge tends to be of a nature known as 'episodic' rather more than 'semantic'. This argument has been made extensively elsewhere (Lawson, 2004a; Visser, 1995) and we shall only cover it briefly here. However, the distinction is an important one since work on long-term memory suggests that these two kinds of knowledge are held separately and differently in the brain. Simple illustrations of these differences are abundant in everyday life. The sad way in which older people with memory loss begin to forget recent events while retaining their ability to construct grammatical sentences is perhaps one of the most poignant. Lawson has illustrated this distinction in design terms by recalling an event as a student when he sat with several fellow students to draw up rules to enable them to reconstruct plans of historical buildings in examinations. While he could clearly recall this event he could not recall the rules themselves (Lawson, 2004a).

Ismail Samsuddin studied the way students taking a dual degree in structural engineering and architecture made use of knowledge. They described their experience in architecture as either 'very' or 'quite dependent' on episodic knowledge. By comparison, the same students described their use of knowledge in structural engineering as either 'very' or 'quite dependent' on semantic knowledge (Samsuddin, 2008). We shall return to this in Chapter 6 when we explore the implications of these issues for the education of designers.

The attraction of episodic memory can be seen in its use to transfer knowledge in many societies. Examples of the telling of stories that communicate socially approved behaviour and values, and even theories of existence and deity belief systems, are to be found all over the world. The Aboriginal

THEORIES AND MODELS
BANNISTER

All psychological theories seem to imply some sort of model man, some notion of what man essentially is. Thus psycho-analytic theories suggest that man is essentially a battlefield. He is a dark cellar in which a maiden aunt and a sex-crazed monkey are locked in mortal combat, the affair being refereed by a rather nervous bank clerk. Alternatively, learning theory and stimulus-response psychology generally seem to suggest that man is essentially a ping-pong ball with a memory.

TYPES OF KNOWLEDGE

SYMBOLIC   **EPISODIC**

'dreamtime' stories are perhaps one of the most famous and elaborate systems of such knowledge.

There is another distinction between episodic and semantic memories that is of importance to us in the context of this book. Episodic memories include, most obviously, events and occasions in our lives; things we have seen and done, places we have been to and so on. Semantic memories include the rules and structures that guide us in speaking a language or performing simple arithmetic. Episodic memories are generally case specific and experiential. That is to say, they are lodged in a structure related to events, occasions and existing typologies. Symbolic memories, by contrast, are lodged in a structure that encourages their use in a generic way using rules and relationships. The illustration above of students trying to 'cram' semantic knowledge into their heads for an examination reminds us of a characteristic we are only too well aware of from our own experiences. Trying to remember semantic knowledge for examinations is unpleasant, feels unnatural and requires effort. By contrast, we remember events episodically often with no conscious effort whatsoever. Many theories of learning have taken this as a point of departure in order to develop effective methods of acquiring knowledge.

A very well developed example of this can be seen in the Harvard Business School that uses the case-based approach. Several thousand case studies are documented relating to every aspect of business, management and marketing. Students thus learn by working on these cases enabling them to simulate common situations which they may be expected to encounter in their later professional careers. So far, design has no published equivalent, at least on that scale. Most design cases are presented in a structure more related to their final outcome than the processes which led to them let alone the practices responsible. Published design studies of this kind also usually reside inside the professional boundaries separating the design fields. So architects are unlikely to read case studies for industrial designers and vice versa even though in process terms there may be much common ground.

DESIGN PRECEDENT

So why is it that designers seem relatively dependent on episodic knowledge rather than theoretical knowledge? At least one important reason is the complex relationship between problems and solutions discussed in Chapter 2. In the kinds of design fields we are discussing here there is no simple mapping between parts of problems and parts of solutions. It is generally not possible to list the design problem comprehensively but, even when a range of important issues are listed, they are likely to represent quite different kinds of

KNOWLEDGE CONTAINED
IN NARRATIVE
THE THREE SISTERS

Long ago in the Blue Mountains there lived three little Aboriginal sisters. They were Meenhi, Wimlah and Gunnedoo, whose Witch Doctor father was called Tyawan. They feared the Bunyip* who lived in a deep hole. When Tyawan had to pass the hole, he would leave his daughters safely on the cliff behind a rocky wall. One day he waved goodbye to his daughters and descended the cliff steps. On top of the cliff a big centipede suddenly appeared and frightened Meenhi, who threw a stone at it.

The stone rolled over the cliff and crashed into the valley. All the creatures stopped as the rocks behind the three sisters split open, leaving them on a thin ledge. The angry Bunyip emerged to see the terrified sisters in the valley. Tyawan saw the Bunyip close to his daughters so he pointed his magic bone at the girls and turned them to stone to keep them safe.

But the Bunyip chased Tyawan who found himself trapped, so he changed himself into a Lyre Bird. Everyone was safe, but Tyawan had dropped his magic bone. After the Bunyip had gone, Tyawan searched and searched for his bone. He is still searching as The Three Sisters stand silently watching him from their ledge.

* A Bunyip is an evil spirit said to live in swamps
  or billabongs in Aboriginal folklore.

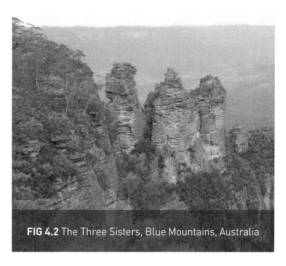

FIG 4.2 The Three Sisters, Blue Mountains, Australia

THE ABORIGINAL DREAMTIME

The Aboriginal 'dreamtime' is a collection of stories that contain knowledge passed on through the generations. What is effectively the oldest of human cultures is still kept alive this way today. It is the story of how the culture believes the universe came to be. A series of stories tell how the Rainbow Serpent created the landscape features by crawling through space. Other stories tell how animals and human beings were created and how the Aboriginals believe the creator intended humans to function within the cosmos. Interestingly for us here, Aboriginals believe that every event leaves behind some traces in the place it happened. For this reason certain rituals must be performed in approved places. In fact, the movement through space guided by the stories almost replaces the calendar that enables most western societies to move through time. This memory of beliefs, rules and societal structures is then encoded into events and places making it accessible to episodic memory. This example of how the famous rock formation known as The Three Sisters in the Blue Mountains came to be formed also explains other parts of the local geography, why the area is an important location for women's rituals and the bower-building behaviour of the Lyre Bird found in the Jamieson Valley.

aspects. Lawson has proposed a model of design problem constraints by categorising them along three dimensions. The first dimension considers who generates the constraints ranging from designers themselves through clients and users to legislators. The second dimension considers whether they are entirely internal to the object being designed or whether they involve contextual issues. The third dimension considers whether they are concerned with functional, practical/technical, compositional or symbolic material.

Two things are particularly interesting about this model for our purposes here. The first is the huge range of kinds of constraints that designers must learn to deal with. The second is the way solution features can combine disparate kinds of problem issues. A well-known example of this phenomenon is the use of dished forms for farmyard cartwheels documented by George Sturt. This ingenious solution form was found to have many advantages over a flat wheel (Sturt, 1923). These advantages ranged from issues of assembly through strength, manoeuvrability, and even load capacity; thus many different kinds of problems were solved by the one solution idea of dishing the cartwheel. In analysing building forms, Lawson has shown that a single idea such as that governing the sectional form of a building can often simultaneously solve problems as different as environmental control, view and circulation (Lawson, 2006).

So it is sensible to see a design solution as an integrated response to a range of problem issues. Rules for generating solutions from problems are often thus of little real value. Indeed, generic rules are even less likely to be of value due to the highly situated nature of design. This means that design problems are often significantly composed of what Lawson's model would call 'external constraints'. These constraints in some way link some aspects or features of the designed object to a context over which the designer has little or no control. Obvious examples of this in architecture would certainly include the site and climate. Such factors are sufficiently common in design to make situation-based thinking strategies an essential constituent of design expertise.

Schön and his followers have tended to see all design situations as unique and special. While technically this may be correct, it is nonetheless somewhat misleading. It is possible to look for precedents that share reasonably common characteristics with some design situation though, of course, they cannot be successfully copied in their entirety. We shall see the modes of design thought available to more expert designers that enable them to see wider ranges of parallelism and to copy in more adaptive ways.

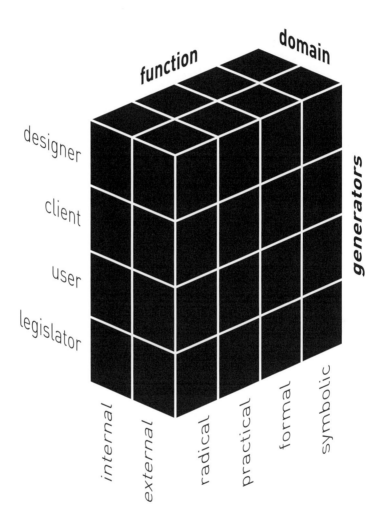

Fig 4.3 Bryan Lawson's model of design constraints

Designers then acquire knowledge not so much of theoretical structures but of solutions or ways of doing things. Of course we do not necessarily use complete solutions to the complex problem at hand. In most design this is highly unlikely. What is far more common is to find some aspect, quality or subcomponent that has sufficient similarity to one in a situation already experienced—this then becomes useful. For example, in urban design it might be a way of opening up a vista down a street; in architecture it might be a way of arriving and entering a building; in a product it might be a way of creating visual balance in a design.

One advantage of being a designer is that you are literally surrounded by examples of design, good and bad. Designers then accumulate experience of designed objects both from their own field of design and others. Many designers habitually carry small sketchbooks in order to draw things they see. Some do this in a very casual manner while others, like the architect John Outram, appear to use more formal analytical techniques.

In fact, designers frequently claim to have gained inspiration from examples of work well beyond their own field. The great industrial designer Raymond Loewy cited 'Shakespeare, Seurat, Monet, Conan Doyle, Picasso, Nureyev, Chanel, Archipenko, Maugham, Saki, Cortaza, Diaghilev, Escoffier' as coming to mind first (Loewy, 2000). We might recognise designers such as Chanel among this list and not be too surprised by painters such as Seurat, Monet and Picasso. The ballet as represented by Diaghilev and Nureyev seem more remote. But it is perhaps the presence of a chef (Escoffier) and writers (Shakespeare and Conan Doyle) that might surprise us most. However, such claims are not extraordinary in the writings of designers so we must take them seriously.

This great array of experiences seems to offer clues or hints for designers about some aspects of how things might be. It is not the job of design to describe the world, but rather to suggest how it could or even should be. The designer draws inspiration from seeing many ways of putting objects, buildings and place together. But designers are not restricted to only looking at other designs. They may equally well turn to art and sculpture for their ideas. They are not even restricted to looking at things created by other humans and often draw ideas from nature. The creation of these analogies with nature is even used within a creativity technique called 'Synectics' (Gordon, 1961).

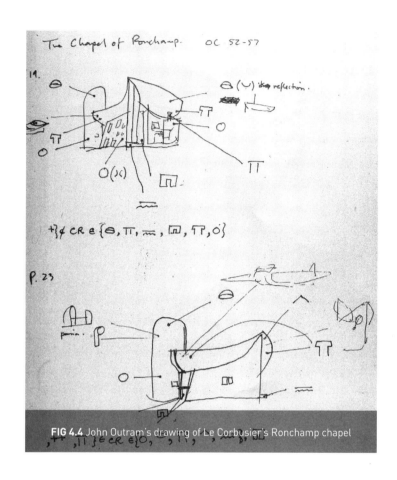

FIG 4.4 John Outram's drawing of Le Corbusier's Ronchamp chapel

INSPIRATION FROM NATURE

Inspiration can be found in nature for creating solutions to many mechanical problems in the field of product design. Evolution has often provided us with optimal solutions. Leonardo da Vinci was aware of this in his time, but even now we can turn to nature to learn a good lesson. The landing gear of some US marine fighter planes that needs to absorb enormous shocks when they land on aircraft carriers has famously been modelled on the legs of grasshoppers. The awesome ingenuity and efficiency of some of nature's 'designs' often inspires, but there are some fundamental restrictions in these analogies. For example, in nature no living thing can turn around an axle. If this had been the case, nature would probably have been full of wheels.

DEVELOPING CONCEPTS AND CONSTRUCTS

Let us imagine that a novice design student stumbles across a Le Corbusier chaise longue. What is he or she to make of this interesting object? It might be recorded in some way, by sketching or by photographing, or these days perhaps by collecting an image from an Internet website. But how is this information filed in the mind of our developing designer? What is important here is that all of this information will be in the form of a personal construct system. It is what this particular designer makes of this object that matters rather than some intrinsic features of the object itself; though of course it would be a most unusual designer who had a construct system entirely disconnected from objective form. It is very much a matter of perception as to how the knowledge of the object is likely to be stored and later used in design by our student.

Firstly, let us ask some questions about recognition. If the novice design student is not yet aware of Le Corbusier and his work in furniture design, then this object is not a Le Corbusier chaise longue at all but simply a chaise longue. If the notion of the chaise longue does not yet exist in the mind of the student it may simply be a couch, perhaps a rather curvy one that tests our student's notion of what defines a couch. Perhaps a very naïve student may not even have developed the concepts that enable the distinction to be made between various types of sitting objects. In which case, this thing is simply a chair, perhaps a slightly odd one, but still a chair at that. The important point here is that what this object represents to the student of design depends upon what concepts he or she has developed for discriminating between such objects. As we have already hinted, however, this is a two-way process. The odder the object in terms of the existing acquired concepts, the more the student may question the boundaries of the concept itself and be inclined to sub-divide it or to develop an entirely new concept. This is the very essence of such learning.

However, it is much more complex than our simple example has illustrated so far. Perhaps our student might think about this newly discovered object along some other dimensions. Is this object modern or old, for example? Well a good student probably knows that Le Corbusier lived in the twentieth century and may even know that the chaise longue dates from around 1928 so it is normally classified as modern.

For a moment though let us imagine a rather odd creature; a student of design who is really very experienced and operating on fairly sophisticated layers of our expertise model, but who has never ever seen a Le Corbusier chaise longue before and indeed has no knowledge that Le Corbusier ever designed

DESIGN CASE STUDIES

The various design fields have never built up such a strong repository of cases. Many of the case descriptions of projects in architecture and design reside in the professional journals, where they tend to be rather superficial, and often uncritically described 'success stories' of design projects. Within these case stories it is often unclear where reality ends, post-rationalisation starts and where that moves into all-out fabrication.

This lack of good case studies has really limited design researchers in their attempts to understand design in practice, and it has hampered the thoughtful design professional who would really like to learn from the work of others. Consequently, there has been very little 'flow' of knowledge and experiences from design practice into design science, and vice-versa. A new design journal is now being proposed that will try to fulfil this need for in-depth, systematically gathered data on design processes. The substantial and varied set of design cases that is being gathered will support our thinking about design, from a professional and from a design science perspective.

such a thing. Would this student therefore have no knowledge about the likely date of the chair? Almost certainly the object would be recognised as twentieth century even in the absence of the knowledge of its designer. There would here be a reliance on some ideas embedded in the concept of modernism, and probably some knowledge about the history of technology. Quite simply the proportions, lines, forms, lack of detailed decoration, use of materials and many other features would suggest that this object was modern to any reasonably well-educated designer.

We are not specifically interested in either modernism or chairs in this book. The questions here are 'how do concepts of these kinds get developed in the minds of designers' and 'how are they used in design?'. To answer such questions we could turn to the classic works on concept formation exemplified by the work of Jerome Bruner (Bruner et al, 1956). Bruner explored how we, particularly as children, acquire concepts in just the sort of way suggested by our example of the design student and the chaise longue. The work of Bruner and his followers tells us how children usually begin with very large indiscriminate concepts such as 'cow' to represent all four legged animals. As time goes on they discover that not all four-legged animals give milk and say 'moo' so they might sub-divide the concept recognising that those that bark are more sensibly called 'dogs'.

While this appears useful to us in fact it does not help us very much for several reasons. The classical concept formation work sees concepts of this kind as largely based on objective physical features such as number of legs and barking sounds. It also sees concepts as largely discrete entities and hardly deals at all with the relationship between concepts. Modern cognitive science has developed similar ideas with schemata seen as a series of slots, which can hold values to represent specific cases or instances of the schema (Minsky, 1975). In this model, when we receive new information through our senses, our memory will try to match it with these mental templates, enabling us to recall the whole schema from any appropriate value of any slot. This helps explain the metonymic nature of memory. The mere mentioning of 'birthday' brings forth memories of birthday parties, friends and diverse emotions (Schank, 1982).

Others have gone on to argue that our understanding of concepts is fundamentally linked to our physical relationship with the world around us, and that bodily experiences are our most natural and powerful forms of memory (Lakoff and Johnson, 1980). It is worth remembering here how we discussed the importance of body memory when learning to perform sophisticated skills such as playing the flute (see Chapter 3). Such a view goes on to argue that more sophisticated, deeper and more abstract concepts, which cannot

Fig 4.5 Chaise Longue by Le Corbusier

be held as pure bodily memory, are referenced back through metaphor. This suggests that metaphor is not just some neat literary device but a very fundamental cognitive mechanism. These ideas point to the dynamic interplay between low-level episodic experiences and high-level symbolic semantics in human memory, with metaphorical thought depending heavily on this dynamic interplay. Certainly, the use of metaphor is often heavily encouraged in design education and appears to be a common and very powerful tool in creative thought and the processes of expert designers. We shall return to this issue in later chapters.

The work on personal construct theory began most famously by Kelly enables us to see in more detail what is happening with our design student (Kelly, 1955). Kelly's constructs are more atomistic in themselves than the traditional view of a concept. Yet they build up together into a complex hierarchical and networked personal construct system. We need to consider this system in its entirety to help us to understand design thinking. For Kelly and his followers a construct is most easily understood as a dimension along which objects can be placed. At its most simple we can see a construct as represented by a scale between two adjectives having opposite meanings. The construct 'new-old' for example has already been used in our overworked chaise longue scenario. It is worth remembering that the adjectival scale is not the construct itself, which may be unconscious and non-verbal, but simply a convenient way of externalising it. We shall return to this important argument again as we deal with even higher levels of design expertise.

Words and images both have roles to play in design processes and design thinking. It may be the case that design has become associated much more with the graphical image in our minds. This may in part be due to the often interesting and attractive nature of many design drawings which can often be confused with art. Such images are strong, powerful and have longevity. The words used by designers while developing their designs and discussing them with other stakeholders are much more likely to go unrecorded. They are nonetheless important for that.

One of the advantages of words over images is their very ambiguity. In an elaborately constructed sophisticated language such as English, words can take on a variety of meanings and often shade from one to another without clear boundaries. During early design process phases this may offer positive advantages, allowing thought to be appropriately vague. We know that designers like to use different kinds of tools for sketching depending upon their degree of certainty and confidence. Richard MacCormac discusses this very clearly.

WHAT IS IN A WORD? QUITE A LOT IT SEEMS

In the example of the design project to create a new litter system for the Dutch trains, introduced in Chapter 2, we can clearly see the tricky relationship between the designers and the words they use to describe their creation. In the course of his design work, one of the designers had split up the existing litter bin into its constituent functions, through a simple functional decomposition. He then started redistributing these basic functions (in its simplest form 'input', 'storage', 'output') throughout the railway carriage, creating a central litter storage area under the belly of the train (that could be emptied directly from the outside). Yet while he had effectively created a 'chute-system' he still kept talking about the passenger throwing things in an imaginary 'bin'. The good part of the story of course is that he apparently did not let himself be limited by the use of the word 'bin'. Other designers seemed to immediately limit the design challenge, which was carefully worded in terms of a 'litter system', to the design of a litter bin.

This must make it really hard to design something for which there is no word yet. Words are important 'thinking tools'—having no word for something must limit our possibilities to think about it, and to develop it.

It seems likely that they like to use words too in a rather rough and ready sort of way. Perhaps Eva Jiricna can be seen to be consciously exploiting this characteristic of words in her conversations with clients. She can argue through, and reach agreement on, a set of ideas that can then be followed through with images that earlier on in the process may have seemed too definite and strange to a client (see Chapter 3).

For now it seems important to recognise that the novice student must begin the long process of acquiring knowledge of design solutions and other related sources of potential design inspiration. There is much evidence that designers operating at the more advanced layers of our expertise model make use of this material during their design process. Commonly such material is referred to by designers as 'precedent'. This turns out to be a rather confusing name but since it is in common usage we shall stick with it here. We need to explore some characteristics of design precedent in order to clarify the special meaning of the word in this context.

The word 'precedent' is also used in law to refer to the practice of establishing a parallel case which was judged in the direction you would like to see found this time around. Here the lawyers may argue as to whether the precedent is a sufficiently accurate replication of the situation, but in design we are much less bothered by this. Design precedent may be useful simply if it reproduces a few of the characteristics of the current situation, as Goldschmidt has pointed out (Goldschmidt, 1998). In design several precedents may be used and combined. To a designer it does not matter whether a precedent precisely replicates the situation; what matters is that in some way it helps in the progressing of the design process. In any case, as we have already argued, design situations are hardly ever really likely to be accurately replicated. Indeed, as Gero has convincingly argued, the very situatedness of design problems represents one of their most representative characteristics (Gero, 1998). Goldschmidt has therefore argued that the term 'precedent' is misleading and should be replaced by the term 'reference'. This would be a perfectly sensible argument were it not for the fact that 'precedent' is common parlance among designers.

FROM FRESHER TO GRADUATE

Any experienced tutor in a design school will tell you that the gulf between their freshmen and graduate students is colossal. In the generic model of expertise such graduates are probably at least Advanced Beginners. They are still at a relatively early stage in a lifetime project of learning to become designers. As we shall see, there are many stages of development ahead of

VISIONARY VISIONA
MASTER MASTERMAS
EXPERT EXPERTEXPERT
COMPETENT COMPETENT
ADVANCED BEGINNER ADVA
BEGINNER BEGINNERBEGINN
NOVICE NOVICENOVICENOVICEN

pg.101

ROUGH AND PRECISE REPRESENTATIONS
RICHARD MACCORMAC

There's that very fast ideas/creative period which throws out this proposition and you use perhaps felt tips or soft pencils or whatever, you get it down very quickly. Then there's a period of testing which involves using a quite different frame of mind, moving to quite a different frame of mind and then the first person who taught me this when I worked with him was David Lee who is a contemporary of mine and he would inspect things very carefully, he'd get into one to a hundred drawings, he'd use a 2H pencil, he would get dimensions and everything right and it's very difficult to do that because you very quickly see what's wrong with your proposition but you have to be very cool and careful to investigate it. And then there's a critical process where you say well actually it doesn't work, then you work out why it doesn't work, then you feel very depressed then you go back into that crazy phase again and come up with something else to test and criticise and eventually you get there, so there are these different frames of mind which involve different instruments actually for producing/representing what you are doing.

them and a huge amount of learning, practising and gathering of experience to do. Somewhere along the way during a degree design course, most students manage to transform themselves into useful and creative designers capable of working with experienced and expert professionals. So just what has happened?

Students need to gain experience not just of design precedents that might be useful but also of the process itself. Throughout design, judgements must be made more or less continuously about the way the process is going. This reflective process becomes increasingly unconscious as designers develop more expertise. In the early years, however, students need guidance not just on appropriate content for their designs but on how to manage the process itself.

We can see this happening in the example shown here of a student design tutorial (managing the process). The more experienced tutor is trying to suggest gently to the student that the process needs to be more adaptive. One of the most common experiences in design education is to find students who are stuck or unable to make progress through their unwillingness to challenge their own rigidity of process. Sometimes such things seem blindingly obvious to the expert and not to the novice. Previously, students may have been advised of the need to work in a certain way, perhaps to have a clear programme or concept for their design. This revelation can be so striking that for a while it takes over and dominates the process in an unquestioned manner. Students often need help turning convention-based thinking into situation-based or even strategy-based thinking.

LEARNING FORMS OF REPRESENTATION

We can also see that students need guidance on how to bring their secondary or support skills to bear on the design and good tutors appear to be entirely familiar with that. The example shown here is of a more experienced practicing architect tutoring a second year architecture student. In this excerpt we have stripped out most of the discussion about the design itself from what was originally nearly half an hour of conversation. The remaining exchanges here then about choosing appropriate forms of representation to develop the design thinking. This is yet another example of a general move from convention-based thinking to situation-based thinking. The tutor appears to feel that the particular situation here is that the student prefers a particular kind of representation (painting) that is not enabling him to see the issues in the design situation that now need exploring.

pg.69

MANAGING THE PROCESS
A DESIGN STUDENT TUTORIAL

TUTOR

It strikes me that you've got an idea which you are trying to force to work at one level, right. And I think what you need to do is to be flexible a little bit more to accepting the principles of what you're doing as a kind of a programme that identifies different issues. So I think the courtyard that you're creating is really a fundamental space.

STUDENT

Yeah, right. Right now I'm thinking that by having two buildings soaring up like that, I don't think you really need to do anything with that courtyard space because at night time, with the lights that will project the lights on to this building here, and into that courtyard... it will all be coloured just by the lighting.

TUTOR

I think again the principle is fine. But to me that's the space you enter. Is that your point of entrance?

STUDENT

You can enter anywhere. There's no main entrance.

TUTOR

Well how... I mean, don't you have a main entrance to your house?

STUDENT

That was the concept as well. I wanted people to feel lost.

TUTOR

Yeah, but the concept is only a way... a concept has to be questioned as to the value it serves or what the purpose of that is going to be. Now, if you say there isn't an entrance, how do people arrive to this national gallery, peace museum, you know. How do they go into this? There's a kind of a logical process that we move through buildings you know. You arrive at the university here, everybody knows where the main entrance is, through a hierarchical organisation of spaces. So it's good to have a concept but you have to keep questioning it.

DESIGN STUDENT TUTORIALS

These are all excerpts from protocols that were all collected by Khairul Khaidzir at Sheffield University. They were normal tutorials between students and their tutors, which were recorded. The students were second year architects and the tutors were all experienced practicing architects who also acted as studio tutors.

Menezes studied the way first and final year architecture students described sketches to see if there was some development in the way these possible precedents were being analysed and conceptualised (Menezes and Lawson, 2006). The experiment involved some sixty students, half from the first year and half from the sixth and final year of a normal architecture course. In each session a student was asked to describe two sketches to another student from their own level of expertise. The other student, who could not see the original sketch and could not ask questions, was required to produce a drawing from the description. Both sketches were of a kind that design students might quite normally be expected to look at during their studies. However, one was specifically a design sketch from their domain, a drawing by Mies van der Rohe when he was working on his Hubble House project of 1935. The second image was a sketch called Double Island done by the artist Paul Klee in 1939. The first two images shown here are of the Paul Klee sketch; the first version a novice student pairing and the second, much more accurate, version is a graduate student pairing.

This design of experiment allowed Menezes to ascertain if there were any differences between the ways more experienced and sophisticated students thought about a sketch both from their own domain and elsewhere. Firstly, both groups of students spent longer on average describing the architectural design sketch than the non-architectural, and this difference was greater for the more experienced students. More importantly the same effects, but showing an even more marked difference, were found in terms of the number of different ways used to describe the drawings. In other words, both first and final year groups found more things to say about the architectural sketch and this difference was much larger for the final year students.

Taking these results together then, the final year group produced richer descriptions of the architectural sketch compared with the non-architectural one. This effect was much less noticeable for the first year students. Thus, all of these results suggest that the architectural sketch was capable of yielding more interpretations and that more ideas emerged from looking at it when the subjects were more expert in the domain.

In terms of our concerns here, Menezes did something even more interesting with his data. He asked a small group of tutors, operating at an even more expert level, to assess all the drawings produced from the descriptions. They were asked to rank them in terms of the extent to which they were accurate reproductions of the originals. He then compared the descriptions which had given rise to the most accurate and least accurate drawings. Not surprisingly, he found that the most accurate drawings came from longer and richer descriptions. He also found an important and significant difference in the

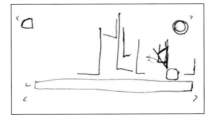

Fig 4.6 Novice student drawing from description of Klee original

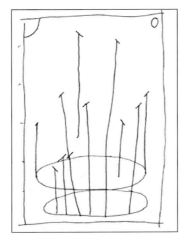

Fig 4.7 Advanced student drawing from description of Klee original

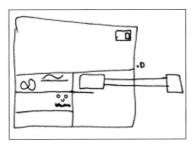

Fig 4.8 Novice student drawing from description of Mies original

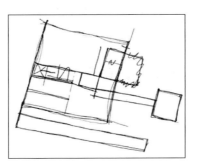

Fig 4.9 Advanced student drawing from description of Mies original

kinds of descriptions used; the more successful descriptions relied far more heavily on what Menezes calls symbolic rather than formal ways of conveying information. In essence symbolic methods rely on conceptual structures whereas formal ways rely upon geometrical abstractions.

Formal descriptions then rely upon using references to such characteristics as proportion, 'this one is about twice the size as the other', or simple shapes, 'an oval', or degrees of repetition, 'there is a whole line of these'. By contrast, symbolic descriptions rely upon references to ideas not physically embedded in the drawing such as 'it looks like a sun' or 'there is a sausage here' and 'it's like a flag'. The drawing with the quotes alongside it was created by a student listening to a description with exactly these phrases in it (Figure 4.10).

Now what Menezes showed here was that the drawings appeared to be more accurately reproduced when more symbolic or conceptual ideas were used in the descriptions. His data also showed that the more expert students increased their use of symbolic descriptions to a far greater extent for the architectural sketch. This seems to us to be a very real demonstration of the extent to which one of the characteristics of expertise is the acquisition of concepts about the domain that allows for richer discussions about instances from that domain. Two sketches shown before (Figures 4.8 and 4.9) are of the Mies van der Rohe sketch with the first being from the novice pairing and the second from the graduate pairing.

Bearing in mind all this then we are not surprised to see novice design students being taken on field trips, to museums and art galleries and being encouraged to keep sketchbooks with them at all times. Such educational devices serve to establish both a set of values about the importance of acquiring precedent and the skills to record and retain the information. However, associated with all this is the need to encourage students to develop conceptual structures that enable discussion and debate. In fact, unless students learn which precedents are generally regarded as part of the canon they will increasingly find debate difficult.

THE DEVELOPMENT OF PERSONAL DESIGN SCHEMATA

So we are beginning to see a clear pattern develop here about an essential characteristic of design expertise. Because all design is theoretically unique to some extent the context of a particular design problem becomes a significant issue. This is a way in which design is really much more sophisticated and complex than games like chess. Chess, with all its frustrating

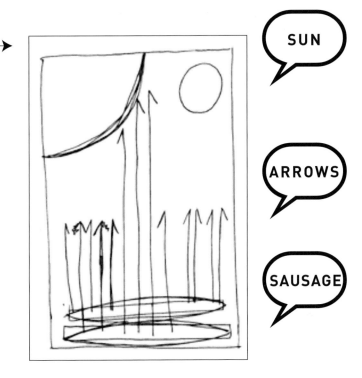

Fig 4.10 Student realisation of Paul Klee image in response to descriptions from another student

and intriguing complexities, still remains a bounded universe of possibilities. The only things of relevance in a chess situation are within the boundary of the chess board. There are no external influences.

Design students then must not only learn to recognise situations but they must also be able to draw parallels with situations from other contexts. This is a subtle and sophisticated process that lies right at the very core of creative thought in design. Students will stand very little chance of carrying off this cognitive trick unless they develop their own mental structures for storing potentially useful knowledge. A major task for the design student then must be the creation of some organising structure within which sense can be made of the design precedent gathered. Precedents are not simply stamps stuck into some mental philatelic album country by country; they are complex phenomena that need evaluation along many dimensions. As the design student develops the number and organisational complexity of these dimensions will surely increase.

When introducing the idea of recognition of precedent we relied on the personal construct theory of George Kelly. In fact Kelly's ideas are not so much a theory of cognition as a complete approach to the psychology of the human condition (Kelly, 1963). Kelly sees us not as passive creatures but as active, predictive ones. He argues that our very identity is defined by the way we construe our personal world. In this view of human psychology we are all seen as scientists in the sense that we use our constructs to predict the world around us. Effectively we try things out or experiment to see what works and what does not. The more adventurous of us will constantly rebuild our construct system when it appears inadequate to predict accurately. For Kelly then our personal construct system is effectively our own personal scientific (in a phenomenological sense) theory about the world. We use it to predict the world and reconfigure it when it proves inadequate. In these terms then, learning is this very process of making more sophisticated personal construct systems.

A further and important point for us here in our discussion of design precedent is that the notion of a construct is not specifically a cognitive one. Constructs can be as much about emotions and feelings as they are about logic. For designers this is vital. Design is certainly about emotion as well as logic. Designers need constructs that help them to evaluate and store ideas about how design possibilities feel and work.

An important tool in construct theory is the repertory grid with its junior partner the semantic differential. The repertory grid is a simple but powerful way of making explicit a personal construct system. Typically it

FORMS OF REPRESENTATION
A DESIGN STUDENT TUTORIAL

STUDENT

I came up with this idea for my theatre of memory, which is a ramp. The ramp shows the journey and continuity for a (number) of bridges, show the connection between different memories. And then, these little separate rooms coming up with like temporary exhibition in. So, this ramp will show like the journeys of different people like migrating. So it starts from the past and then coming up to the future at the top. But then, anyway this is my ramp in my model. And I looked at it whether it will be a kind of light structure with a very heavy sort of like box surrounding or whether it will be a really heavy enclosed structure within a lighter... So I'm going to do it like really heavy within light. And then these are my plans that I did. This was for my review. But I think these need to be bigger because 1:200 seems a bit small.

TUTOR

I would have a look at blowing those up to 1:100 and start working on them. You've set up a very strong diagram here, haven't you?

STUDENT

Yeah, but I don't want it to be very... I just don't really like straight lines. I don't think... it's just not right. I don't want it to be like grids and... I quite like it to be free like messy, not messy but...

TUTOR

I wonder whether, you know... because you like drawing and painting... Whether you... I would set about working this up to a larger scale. To keep working on the plans and see how the circulation and everything works. But I'd also do a painting of that view showing this thing, sort of coming out, nosing out and the glass and the lightweight-ness of this skin that's surrounding the rest of the building and see whether you like it... a painting showing the glass and how this thing could contrast... you'll be able to see through and maybe get clues as to what you've been talking about, gaps and slots in this thing. Maybe you can read them through this glass elevation as well to get an idea of how this thing's inhabited. You need to see how it all works in section.

consists of a rectangular grid along one side of which the subject places a list of people or objects. Triads of these are examined in turn to find ways in which one of them is seen as different form the other two. Each of these becomes a construct placed along the other side of the grid. Of course, the system as a whole consists not just of the constructs themselves but the ways in which they overlap or correlate with each other.

The semantic differential tool, which has been much used for evaluating design, is simply a prepared grid in which the constructs are predetermined rather than created by individuals. This, of course, has the advantage of enabling us to compare the way different designs are perceived by groups of people or alternatively the way different groups of people perceive the same design. While this is very convenient for the researcher it does rather lose the fundamental underlying phenomenological principle of constructs being personal. Here we are more interested in the personal development of design expertise. The central theme of personal construct theory sees us as anticipatory creatures with new possibilities opening up as we re-construe the world around us. Such a notion fits beautifully with our image of the creative designer always looking to reinterpret and generate new forms of design.

One job of design education then must surely be to facilitate this development. It needs to challenge conventional, traditional or commonly held constructs and patterns of constructs in order to enable designers to see familiar situations in new ways, or as Schön would put it, reframe them. A very limited example of this might be the way the novice architecture student makes sense of brick walls. How do different instances of brick walls get differentiated in his or her personal construct system? The likelihood is that initially this will be through rather superficial and very generic constructs to do with size and colour. Later the student will learn about the whole range of different patterns of arranging the brick in the wall known as 'bonding'—perhaps English, Flemish, garden wall bond and so on. The student will also discover a series of ways of finishing the mortar joint, perhaps flush, bucket handle, recessed, etc. Before long, the more sophisticated student will know a little about the manufacture of bricks and see them as self-coloured, sand-finished and as having a range of strengths and be resistant to frost. We could go on, but this will surely suffice to illustrate our point here. To the everyday designer a brick wall is a brick wall but to a student who has developed all of these constructs it is a very complex object indeed and it is increasingly unlikely that any two examples will ever be seen as identical.

A design student has a further complication to deal with here. Normal everyday consumers need not concern themselves further with a design they do not like. However, the design student must learn to appreciate design ideas

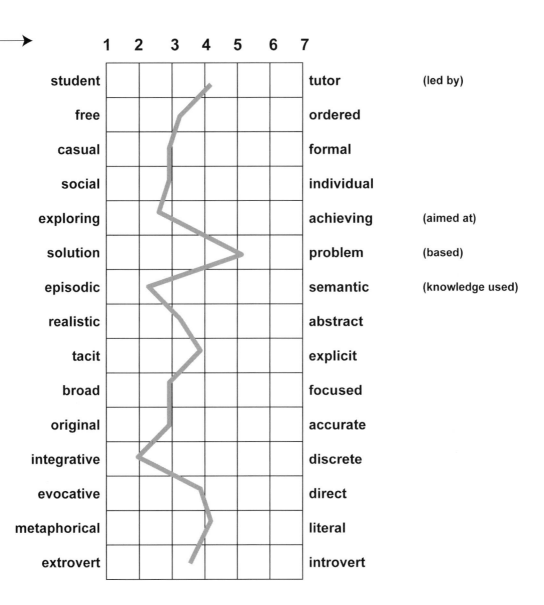

	1	2	3	4	5	6	7		
student								tutor	(led by)
free								ordered	
casual								formal	
social								individual	
exploring								achieving	(aimed at)
solution								problem	(based)
episodic								semantic	(knowledge used)
realistic								abstract	
tacit								explicit	
broad								focused	
original								accurate	
integrative								discrete	
evocative								direct	
metaphorical								literal	
extrovert								introvert	

Fig 4.11 A semantic differential grid showing students of architecture describing their education

in terms of how well they realise their objectives rather than being overly concerned with personal preferences. As a design student you need to be able to perform a sort of Aristotelian suspension of judgement. The object you are looking at may not be to your taste but it may still be of value to you. So you need to learn to study a painting that you would not want to hang on your wall and a piece of music you would not keep on your iPod. You need to engage with the way the object is put together and be prepared to learn lessons from it that might be transferable to other situations.

In its earliest professional stages, design education needs to help the student to form constructs that will be genuinely useful in making sense of the precedent being gathered. Often this is done through a limited amount of formal tuition accompanied by large doses of exemplars. How, for example, does a novice student of design develop a construct of 'modern' in the context of design? Such a construct is likely to be quite high in the hierarchy of any designer's system. It will probably rely on many lower level constructs to do with simplicity of form, lack of decoration, use of materials and so on. However, it is also important here to appreciate that constructs have ranges.

One of Kelly's original theoretical postulates was that 'a construct is convenient for the anticipation of a finite range of events'. It is perfectly possible to use the notion of modernity differently in different aspects of the world. For example, the idea of modernity when applied to say comedy or literature could be substantially different. Of course, this may ultimately lead to some uncomfortable lack of consistency at even higher levels in a personal construct system. But that is often how people are; we can be paradoxical creatures as well as logical ones. Indeed sometimes the very ambiguity of our constructs can often become a source of inspiration in design. The process of taking an idea from a current design problem, putting it into a totally different context where it may have quite different meanings, and then bringing those ideas back into the design, is a relatively well-established trick of creative thinking.

Although constructs and, in particular, their relationships are entirely personal, nevertheless the likelihood is that many are extensively shared with others. Perhaps one of the problems with the design community is that it tends to develop commonly shared constructs that seem obscure or unfamiliar to its clients and users. However, we might expect that the early years of design education involve a considerable amount of communication attempting to develop shared constructs. Some of these will be very low level constructs while others will be higher level and more evaluative constructs. Examples of the former might be simple descriptors of design form such as

FRESHNESS

Some students start their design projects not with an in-depth study of the design problem but by generating design concepts. Perhaps they expect their 'freshness' to deliver brilliant ideas. Primary generators can be useful but unless accompanied by rigorous analysis this strategy can lead to naïve, uninteresting, standard solutions.

A common misunderstanding is that the more you know about the design area, the more set you will be in your use of design constructs and the harder it will be to come up with original solutions. This is a legitimate fear; 'design fixation' can happen all too easily. But remaining uneducated is not the answer; you need to conquer design fixation by knowing conventional constructs well enough to challenge them. For this, you need to engage with them, not run away.

symmetrical, or axial. However, some involve the development of what we might more appropriately call schemata.

These are complex concepts such as the notion of 'scale'. This concept involves a more sophisticated combination of simpler ideas. A building can be said to have a 'large scale' even though it might be quite small in size. This may be achieved through the use of a whole range of design devices such as over-sized windows and doors, high ceilings, a podium, and so on. Architects will commonly converse using such schemata and developing them further into, for example, the idea of 'domestic scale'. Taken together this system of shared constructs and schemata form a common basis of communication through which design ideas can be discussed, explored and debated by students and their tutors. One day interviewing the members of a design practice, Bryan Lawson heard the word 'belvedere' used several times by different people (Lawson, 2004b). This clearly suggested that the practice as a whole was making use of the complex set of architectural ideas that can so easily be summarised by this one word. As we shall see in the next chapter, the higher layers of professional design expertise appear to require shared schemata and constructs within design practices in order for them to perform effectively and efficiently.

The sharing of schemata and values may be seen as one of the inevitable outcomes of the highly social process of design education so commonly found around the world known as 'the studio'. Here groups of students work on the same or similar projects under a single tutor or common group of tutors. Thus, team teaching is very common as is group working among the students.

Margaret Wilson showed exactly this process of shared construct systems developing among students from two different schools of architecture (Wilson, 1996). Students were shown 26 colour images of contemporary architecture selected to represent a wide range of architectural styles from among the most notable architects. The students were asked to classify them in terms of their preferences on a 12-point scale. They were also then asked to explain why they liked the buildings in their most preferred group. Wilson used groups of students from each of the years of the architecture course which is seen to be 6 years long including one year in professional practice. Her data is quite remarkable in showing how the first year student groups from the two schools of architecture had fairly similar sets of preferences. However, as the students progress through their course the sets of preferences move further apart until, in the final year, the students from the two schools of architecture had quite distinctly recognisable sets of preferences about architectural style.

BELVEDERE
A SOPHISTICATED ARCHITECTURAL SCHEMA

The Encarta World English Dictionary defines a belvedere as: a building or part of a building positioned to offer a fine view of the surrounding area. The word is derived from the Italian meaning 'fair view'. There was quite a fashion for such buildings in sixteenth century Italy not least stimulated by one on a hillside above the Vatican Palace. The concept is sophisticated in the sense that it can take many architectural forms; most obviously turrets, towers and cupolas, but galleries or loggias and many other forms can be regarded as belvederes.

Reinterpreting this result in terms of construct theory suggests that the constructs seen as having preferable architectural qualities are learned by students in a socially facilitated way during their education. Disturbingly, what this also shows is that, even in the late twentieth century, British university schools of architecture appear to be teaching stylistic preferences. This is almost certainly something they would deny doing consciously or even aspiring to do.

The concern here must surely be that novice and perhaps graduate student designers are not able to use precedent in the way more expert designers can. Denise Scott-Brown expresses exactly this worry.

There is a commonly expressed view in design education circles that if students are given examples of what is thought to be good design during projects, they will simply copy those examples. This would certainly be supported by the generic work on expertise that suggests novices tend to see examples in different ways from experts and that experts are more able to extract generic value from examples by detected deep underlying structures. We shall return to that argument in later chapters. The experiment by Heylighen and Verstijnen seems to demonstrate this effect in the architectural studio. By contrast, we shall see in later chapters that more experienced and expert designers frequently use examples very remote from the problem in hand.

We have begun to discuss some issues that impinge on the way design is taught formally at university. We shall return to the whole question of design education again in Chapter 6. For now, we must move on to the levels of expertise we find in practicing professional designers.

DENISE SCOTT-BROWN

It's very interesting that a young person learns by copying their master, by copying the forms of their master and quite often in a retrospective exhibition of an artist you will find that the early paintings look like the artist's master and then this thing of 'who am I' begins to grow as you get technical proficiency, you don't need this crutch any more when you look into yourself, but the early stages of copying someone I don't think is a bad idea and I don't think Bob (Venturi) does either, it's so funny because it sounds like a contrast of what you say. We were taught not to and yet we copy ideologies.

GENERIC LEARNING FROM CASES?

Heylighen and Verstijnen made a series of example case studies available in a computer tool to students working on two design projects (Heylighen and Verstijnen, 2003). One project required a library while the other a school. Of the nine cases inserted into the case-based computer tool, eight illustrated libraries and only one a school.

The student designs were assessed for quality by independent judges. These design qualities were then correlated with the extent to which the students had made reference to case studies. Only students working on the library showed significant positive correlations. This strongly suggests the students were not extracting generic knowledge from the case-based examples or precedents and were only able to make use of material from examples very closely associated with their problem.

REFERENCES

Bannister, D. (1966). **A new theory of personality**. New Horizons in Psychology. B.M. Foss. Harmondsworth, Penguin: 361–380.

Bruner, J.S., Goodnow, J.J. and Austin, A. (1956). **A Study of Thinking**. New York, Wiley.

Cross, N. (1996). **The Method in Their Madness: Understanding how designers think**. Delft, Delft University Press.

Gero, J. (1998). **Conceptual designing as a sequence of situated acts**. Artificial Intelligence in Structural Engineering. I. Smith. Berlin, Springer-Verlag: 165–177.

Goldschmidt, G. (1998). **Creative architectural design: reference versus precedence**. Journal of Architectural and Planning Research 15(3): 258–270.

Gordon, W.J.J. (1961). **Synectics: The development of creative capacity**. New York, Harper and Row.

Hatchuel, A. (2002). **Towards design theory and expandable rationality: the unfinished program of Herbert Simon**. Journal of Management and Governance 5(3): 260–273.

Heylighen, A. and Verstijnen, I.M. (2003). **Close encounters of the architectural kind**. Design Studies 24(4): 313–326.

Kelly, G.A. (1955). **The Psychology of Personal Constructs**. New York, Norton.

Kelly, G.A. (1963). **A Theory of Personality**. New York, W.W. Norton and Co.

Lakoff, G. and Johnson, M. (1980). **Metaphors We Live By**. Chicago, University of Chicago Press.

Lawson, B. R. (2004a). **What Designers Know**. Oxford, Elsevier-Architectural Press.

Lawson, B.R. (2004b). **Schemata, gambits and precedent: some factors in design expertise**. Design Studies 25(5): 443–457.

Lawson, B.R. (2006). **How Designers Think** (4th Edition). Oxford, Architectural Press (an imprint of Elsevier).

Loewy, R. (2000). **Industrial Design**. London, Laurence King Publishing.

Menezes, A. and Lawson, B.R. (2006). **How designers perceive sketches**. Design Studies 27(5): 571–585.

Minsky, M. (1975). **A framework for representing knowledge**. The Psychology of Computer Vision. P.H. Winston. New York, McGraw Hill.

Samsuddin, I.B. (2008). **Architectural Education: Peer culture in design studio and its relationship with designing interest**. Architecture. Sheffield, University of Sheffield. PhD.

Schank, R.C. (1982). **Dynamic Memory**. Cambridge, Cambridge University Press.

Sturt, G. (1923). **The Wheelwright's Shop**. Cambridge, Cambridge University Press.

Visser, W. (1995). **Use of episodic knowledge and information in design problem solving**. Design Studies 16(2): 171–187.

Willenbrock, L.L. (1991). **An undergraduate voice in architectural education**. Voices in Architectural Education. T.A. Dutton. New York, Bergin and Garvey: 97–119.

Wilson, M.A. (1996). **The socialization of architectural preference**. Journal of Environmental Psychology 16: 33–44.

5

BEING
PROFESSIONAL

Creativity is allowing yourself to make mistakes.
Art is knowing which ones to keep.
SCOTT ADAMS (AMERICAN CARTOONIST)

Although I think my work has changed a lot over the
years, I do not think that others see much difference.
There is a consistency; a certain simplicity, logic, that
stays… I have not changed the feeling that is the basis
for my design work. I just believe that I have come
to know more and more about that feeling, and that
the feeling has become more conscious, leading to a
different way of designing… My designs have deepened.
JOKE BRAKMAN

MOVING INTO PRACTICE

The graduating student has begun to acquire a considerable knowledge of precedent, has a general understanding of all the major concepts and ideas and probably appreciates the wide range of design situations that commonly occur. However, because of the timescales involved in design, it is unlikely that a freshly qualified graduate will have first-hand knowledge of bringing many design solutions into being. In many design fields students are still given considerable periods of practical experience. The normal qualification period for architecture students to become full members of their professional institute is 7 years, only 5 of these being in full-time education. Skill-based activities usually cannot be learned to an advanced level of expertise without practical experience. Airline pilots cannot learn their job theoretically but need a number of 'flying hours' to acquire the first-hand bodily experience of doing the job.

In design this is likely to be reached only after some years of gaining first-hand experience. Only then is a designer normally able to handle and understand all the common kinds of situations which occur within the design domain being practiced. Such a designer will have seen many situations in the field and worked through the whole process of designing a number of times.

In essence the professional designer is one who can do the job. Such a designer is obviously capable and can offer the client at least a competent service. The question that interests us here is just what happens to designers as they graduate, become professional and gain practical experience. One possibility is that this experience is used to reinforce the application of more or less standard solutions in an increasingly routine manner. We might see this as the development of proficiency. In some professions such proficiency may indeed be desirable, but in the case of design there is also a downside to this. Creative and innovative design is based on the ability to see new possibilities and the questioning of traditional or established solutions. Jan Lucassen makes it very clear that in order to progress, like sportspeople, designers need to push the boundaries.

While, theoretically, all design solutions are unique, there are likely to be only relatively small differences when competent designers who have become proficient tackle common problems; for this reason, they may not have their work extensively studied by their peers. It often seems to be the case that designers who are more admired are those who have developed greater differences, probably having a degree of specialisation to the point of having some reputation for a certain kind of work. This emphasis on peer approval rather than client or user approval could easily be seen as a failing of

PUSHING THE BOUNDARIES
JAN LUCASSEN

You have to keep developing. It is like in sports. If a sportsman does not put his goals higher than he can achieve, he will never progress. You have to keep pushing the boundaries. Many designers don't do this. They put the bar at a height they can jump, and keep jumping to that same height. And as a result, they will fail to achieve that height after a while.

JAN LUCASSEN
Jan Lucassen was trained as a designer at the Design Academy in Eindhoven. He co-founded Tel Design, one of the biggest design firms in Holland and headed that firm for 15 years before returning to the Design Academy as the chairman of the board. He was leader of this important design school for 16 years.

designers. Many clients may well be extremely pleased with traditional and reliable solutions, preferring them to risky innovative ones; who is to say they are wrong? It might also be thought that the cult of originality is to some extent a phenomenon of twentieth century western culture. It has not always been so 'necessary' for designers to be different. The proficient designer is almost certainly taking fewer risks and is more likely to produce a design without unpredicted failings. Perhaps a weakness of contemporary design in general—and certainly architecture—is a willingness on the part of designers to take risks on their client's behalf for the sake of originality which they may not always properly inform the clients about.

Perhaps the most obvious characteristic of proficiency comes from having done the job enough times to know that you can do it. Such confidence is perhaps even more important in design than in many other fields. It is well known that sports performance is remarkably dependent on confidence. This is quite understandable since, almost by definition, in competitive sports there is a fine and yet very obvious line between winning and losing; between success and failure. Such a distinction is hardly relevant to design, but here we have the huge uncertainty that it is inevitably part of the territory when one is expected to be creative. Richard MacCormac surely told us this right at the beginning of the very first chapter of this book when he described design as an 'insane' way of earning a living.

There is no theoretical or even pragmatic way of calculating the resource required to complete a design. Even more disturbingly for the inexperienced, there is no guarantee that you can produce something to satisfy the client let alone all the other stakeholders involved. So in that sense the confidence that comes from having 'found' the idea many times before makes a huge difference to the way the proficient designer can approach the task. Many of the 'crutches' that student designers so often lean upon can, as a consequence, be discarded.

One example of this often seems to reveal itself in a more relaxed attitude to the information given at the start of the project. Clients often think that their designers will require extremely detailed information in the form of an extensive brief. Student designers often pester their tutors for more certainty and detail in the way their projects are set. By comparison, it is common to find that professional designers express a wish to be involved as early as possible in projects long before the brief has even evolved. Michael Wilford articulates this very clearly.

Fig 5.1 The Lowry Centre in Manchester by Stirling and Wilford showing the interactions between routes and use of bright colours and original forms that characterised this period of their work

GETTING EARLY INVOLVEMENT
MICHAEL WILFORD

What is an ideal brief for an architect or a design person? We have found over the years that the ideal brief is probably one or two pages even for the most complex project. And that basic mission statement is really what they're after and then that's supported by a room list and then more detail can be added to that and as the process continues in discussion other possibilities arise that we hadn't even thought of so the architect can actually contribute to the brief writing and things like numbers of light switches and socket outlets and gas taps in laboratories are of no interest. Many clients think they've got to pro- duce something which is two inches thick before an architect can even put pen to paper. We pre- fer it the other way round, we prefer the thinnest possible information so that we can get a grasp on the whole thing and then gradually embellish with the detail later as it's required, so working with a fairly minimal brief we will generate.

MICHAEL WILFORD

Michael Wilford studied architecture at North London Polytechnic and the Regent Street Polytechnic Planning School. Even before completing his studies he was working for James Stirling and James Gowan. That partnership broke up in 1963 and Michael Wilford became an Associate Partner with James Stirling in 1965. The practice of James Stirling Michael Wilford and Associates was formed in 1971, and the association between James Stirling and Michael Wilford thus represents one of the longest running periods of sustained co-operation at this level of design. Sadly this was terminated by the untimely death of James Stirling in 1992. The work of Stirling and Wilford is well known around the world. They are particularly admired for their work in universities, museums and art galleries where they have frequently been able to contribute to the public domain.

Michael Wilford has also been heavily involved in education himself and has lectured and examined widely. He has taught at schools of architecture in the USA, Canada, Britain and Australia, and held visiting professorships both in the USA and UK.

DESIGN SCHEMATA

By this stage, professional designers are able to recognise very common patterns of problems and solutions. Because design is highly situated, generic solutions usually provide poor outcomes. The creative designer needs to be able to appreciate not only generic solutions but also their exceptions. Designers thus depend upon the ability not only to recognise parallels with well-known situations but also to detect subtle variations. They also need to see beyond the superficial aspects of a situation to find parallels from apparently remote circumstances. Ways in which one solution may differ slightly from another and why, are both key parts of the knowledge held by the more expert designer.

pg.155

Tovey, writing about automobile stylists, argued that they 'use a shared but exclusive language, which involves tacit knowing, a subliminal appreciation of what is appropriate in the creation and development of the automotive form' (Tovey, 1992). It is clear that these designers have evolved a language uniquely suited to describing the kinds of form they most frequently use (see also Chapter 3).

Eckert and Stacey also showed that the conversations between professional designers are often couched in the form of references to previous solutions, combining them in new ways, and the exceptions or variations to these. They studied fields as different as fashion design and helicopter engineering and found remarkably similar characteristics to their conversations. They suggest that a very common form of communication between designers about new designs is in terms of variations to previous well-understood designs (Eckert and Stacey, 2000).

Fashion design presents us with some interesting and rather special characteristics which are almost certainly present in most other design fields but much less explicitly so. We use the very word 'fashion' and the French version 'mode' to refer to a set of design ideas that are temporarily defined as being desirable. The whole point of fashion is that it changes and what is in fashion one year will not be the next. Of course this set of ideas can be applied to design styles in any field. However, in other fields such as architecture the time cycles involved are much longer and many styles may co-exist for years if not decades.

Fashion designers then are characteristically faced simultaneously with three problems. Firstly, they must detect the current fashion, recognise and identify it and understand it as a set of generic concepts. Secondly, they must learn to design objects that lie somewhere inside the boundaries of

CONVERSATIONS ABOUT FORM
MICHAEL TOVEY

Michael Tovey suggests that, what he calls 'automotive stylists' often work in small groups and thus need to converse about the development of a design. He demonstrates how they use a 'typically idiosyncratic form of language'. On the one hand this enables them to exchange ideas very easily and effectively about the kinds of forms commonly found in automobiles, but on the other hand this excludes others from their conversations. The language is clearly suited to the highly curved and irregular shapes that make up 'that bowed, soft or hard, shaped surface' used in the body of the modern vehicle. This language also concentrates on how complex three-dimensional curved surfaces can be thought to comprise simpler more geometrical shapes such as cones, spherical sections and so on.

'Terms might be used such as slippery, exciting, fluid, soap bar, bath tub, tailored, shear, razor look, blitz line, whip lash, sweep spear, tiffany, and wind split'.

the complex schemata that define this currently acceptable style. However, they also probably want to identify themselves as special or different within the style. This last requirement is perhaps the most challenging of all since it requires them to understand precisely not the very centre of the solution space defined by the style but its periphery. Only then will they be able to attempt designs that are acceptable within the current fashion but that also push the boundaries. Thus, by studying the working conversations of fashion designers, we might reasonably expect to hear evidence of the struggle to identify and communicate design characteristics.

The concept that design ideas, particularly in stylistic terms, have current boundaries is perhaps better understood in some design fields than in others. In fashion and industrial design products will sell only if they sit inside these boundaries. At the same time manufacturers and suppliers are looking for distinctiveness. In such cases both designers and their clients are trying to identify these otherwise undefined and elusive boundaries.

The famous industrial designer Raymond Loewy is particularly associated with the use of the invented word MAYA to describe exactly this quality. MAYA means Most Advanced, Yet Acceptable. Loewy, who worked on such futuristic environments as the Skylab for NASA also successfully designed more everyday objects including refrigerators, cars, and even buildings. He pointed out that many otherwise interesting pieces of design failed initially because their designers went beyond these limits (Loewy, 2000).

Others have suggested that quality in design should not always be associated with originality for its own sake. The Pritzker Prize-winning Australian architect Glenn Murcutt is fond of a quotation from Thoreau that his father taught him. 'Since most of us spend our lives doing ordinary tasks, the most important thing is to carry them out extraordinarily well'. In a similar vein the English architect Bob Maguire talks of striving for 'a high standard of ordinariness' (Maguire, 1971). This suggests that highly professional design may often be a matter of refining a set of ideas rather than inventing entirely new ones. As Mies van der Rohe put it: 'certainly it is neither necessary nor possible to invent a new kind of architecture every Monday morning'.

It should not surprise us, therefore, to find Eckert and Stacey also went on to show that conversations between helicopter engineers revealed remarkably similar characteristics to those of their fashion counterparts. They interviewed senior designers from GKN Westland, well known for highly customised helicopter design. Helicopters are obviously far more complex objects than anything a fashion designer may have to deal with. Indeed, they are so complex that a series of highly specialised designers is needed to put

DESCRIBING DESIGN SITUATIONS
ECKERT AND STACEY

These researchers studied the communication in fashion design including conversations and graphical and textual information in the form of mood boards or style sheets. These characteristically consist of collections of design examples that all comply with the rules of the style that is being defined. In one example they show four images of women's clothes under the banner 'understatement' and accompanied by the text 'the triumph of essential styles under the profile of understatement and influenced by New Age philosophy. Clear geometric, minimalist lines are emphasised by straight skirts, monochrome suits in neutral or grey colours'.

Conversations, however, could short-circuit lengthy descriptions and complex collections of graphics simply by references to past designs that might also be recombined and subtly changed. 'A cardigan like the one in Vogue, but in pink mohair,' or 'a jumper like the one last year but a bit longer and with a V-neck'. What is meant by 'a bit longer' or even by the simple word 'blue' is also known by these designers to be interpreted within the currently understood style boundaries.

the whole thing together. In fact, the members of these design teams are so specialised that they would struggle to explain the totality of their responsibilities to each other. So, but perhaps for different reasons, we see the same pattern emerging in their conversations. These were based on past modifications and combinations of modifications that were well understood within each design specialisation.

Much of the design that we are interested in here probably lies somewhere between these extremes of fashion and helicopter engineering. In fields such as architecture and industrial design there are quite likely to be issues both of fashion and style as well as issues of specialised teams. We may expect to hear conversations between designers that are substantially reliant on this reference to past solutions, modifications and re-combinations. Indeed, unless able to conduct such conversations, designers are unlikely to be considered as 'competent' by their peers.

In this sense existing well-understood designs have become complex schemata in their own right. That is to say a complex set of ideas can be communicated simply by naming the design solution. The competent designer may also work within a design practice that shares a common understanding of the relative importance (as the members of the practice see it) of various known design schemata. In this sense a design schemata consists of a coherent set of design elements interrelated in ways that relate consistently to sets of guiding principles, which we shall introduce later in this chapter.

pg.181

One problem that inevitably arises from such a method of thinking and communicating is that lay people standing outside the design domain itself are unlikely to be able to make much sense of the conversations. In a study done at Sheffield University of architects' websites we found the most common feature was a display of previously created designs. The least most common characteristic of these sites was any form of description of process. Thus, the novice client approaching such a site would find it very hard to obtain the kind of information that would assist in choosing an architect. Other architects, however, would quickly be able to appreciate the kind of architect who owned the website. One wonders to whom these websites were really addressed.

CHALLENGING EXISTING SCHEMATA

Being a proficient designer may well offer a comfortable rather than challenging existence. Staying in this professional mode over a prolonged period may not show any great sign of development. Some designers may feel quite

FINDING PARALLEL PATTERNS
A DESIGN STUDENT TUTORIAL

TUTOR

Do you know Stirling's Staatsgalerie... In Stuttgart? The central space. He kind of put in a ramp and went around this and down the other side (sketch outline of central ramp of Staatsgalerie).

STUDENT

It was nicer in a way. It looked like a really sort of, almost quite an ordinary sort of shape and then inside everything was so fluid. It's the kind that I want to...

TUTOR

It might be a bit of an overkill on the scheme of this size, somehow, I don't know. You would need to modify it to be more intimate...

TUTOR

One I saw in New York where one off one of the big squares, for some reason (sketches) a building has been removed or collapsed from an organised façade. And somebody's taken that space which would be no more than the width of this room. And it's about sort of that height (continues sketch), probably three stories high, and they've just put a little kiosk in there. And the wall itself is just a granulated concrete. So water trickles into the top and runs down the face of that.

STUDENT

I suppose that would give you the dynamic effect?

TUTOR

I suppose you could put some sort of that kind of climbing plants or something which is less dynamic. But I think it's got to be a landscape effect. That seems too physical, really...

STUDENT

Whereas after going to Cheetham's in Manchester, I thought a really sort of rich library like that is really a nice place to work.

TUTOR

I've seen something like that, maybe it was Hertzberger... I would just perhaps be a bit more subtle somehow, so you keep the enclosure of the space in the darkness and sombre light and just see (sketch).

happy with the relatively low levels of risk that their work entails. As we shall see, challenging this comfort zone may produce more original and creative results, but it may well as a consequence also increase the level of risk that designer and client are taking. The design critic Stuart Brand has claimed that 'all designs are predictions; all predictions are wrong' (Brand, 1995). While he may exaggerate for effect, the point is well made. Design by its very nature is a risky business. A key question is how that risk is assessed, controlled and shared. Perhaps it was during the second half of the twentieth century that we really began to appreciate this. The increasingly rapid rates of technological, economic and social change led designers into ever higher levels of novelty and of risk. Eliminating risk from design is likely to lead to a conservative sterility and is thus neither desirable nor even really possible. However, sharing knowledge with clients and users about the levels of risks, and where in the solution they are being taken, seems to be yet another of the skills that a professional designer needs to acquire. It is a tricky business to get right.

In process terms a competent designer is likely to be able to create the design situation itself through strategic thinking. This means that by now, in addition to the representational skills being acquired earlier, such designers must be able to develop a brief with clients and understand the needs of their users. In addition, they must have a certain amount of technical knowledge about the making and maintaining of the objects they design. They also need to be able to analyse those objects and evaluate them in terms of performance. However, as we know these skills and the knowledge they depend on cannot be entirely separated from the process of designing. Contemporary design research would suggest that designers must be able to develop a problem–solution situation and engage with it.

pg.69

Perhaps the introduction of more sophisticated situation-based designing is one of the features that might mark out the more interesting design from the mundane. If every design problem is unique, then perhaps it is those unusual aspects of the problem situation that give the more courageous designer a hook upon which to hang a more adventurous design. Designers who can raise their game to the expert level are probably responding to an inner need to find variety and originality as much as anything else here. This is surely what the great architect/engineer Santiago Calatrava is telling us.

EXPERTISE AGAIN

In order to explore the higher levels of expertise in design, we first need to return to our more general exploration of expertise itself. In the general

SITUATION-BASED DESIGNING
SANTIAGO CALATRAVA

Sometimes, especially when I started, you see I used to do design for itself, for example I started to design pillars, you see, a pillar in a bridge, or a bridge as an arch. But I can no longer design for example, a simple beam or a pillar or an arch. You need a problem, a very precise problem; this in my opinion is very important. You need a place; I think the relation with a place is very important as it can conditionally affect a pillar or an arch. This means having an argument. This is the way to mature as a designer. I mean a house like the Falling Water by Frank Lloyd Wright is so much related to this place. You see it is almost the place and you see it is so beautiful. This is very mature design. You need a problem, otherwise you have just empty talk, and in my opinion landscape is the argument.

literature about very high levels of expertise of this kind, there are a number of indications that this layer may be characterised by an ability to reduce dependence on analysis in favour of more or less automatic recognition of situations. While the rest of us work hard at analysing situations, experts appear to work intuitively and rapidly. Somehow the expert appears to be able to use the information available in a more efficient or effective manner. Experts can recognise very much more complex patterns than their novice counterparts.

Of course we develop expertise about all sorts of things and in many tasks even from early childhood. Studies of how young boys could recognise and describe dinosaurs have provided an interesting insight into changes that take place in the knowledge structures used (Chi and Koeske, 1983). It seems that we organise our knowledge differently in domains where we have expertise to the way we do in domains we are novices in. Chi and Koeske showed that boys who knew a lot about a particular group of dinosaurs had more integrated and cohesive knowledge structures to represent this than they did for a set of less familiar dinosaurs. It seems this allowed them to reason and develop arguments about either a single instance or when comparing instances. In Kelly's terms they had richer construct systems.

Importantly, there seems to come a point in the development of this knowledge structure when it becomes so efficient that we can use it in significantly different ways. Those of us who struggled with problems in mathematics or physics will perhaps remember that the most difficult part of the process was seldom the actual application of formulae but decoding the problem type. It seems that good college students can easily categorise mathematical problems into types, and can do this very quickly, sometimes after reading only a few words (Hinsley et al., 1978). These categories are associated with formulae and procedures which can then be applied routinely. Others have shown similar results when studying the way students solve problems in physics (Chi et al., 1981). Quite simply, the internal knowledge structure held by such experts enables them to recognise problem situation types rather than have to extensively analyse them. It is as if they had done the hard thinking before the problem was presented, and in a way they have by building up their knowledge structure through experience.

This categorisation into types also has another important effect on our mental performance. We are able to 'chunk' a great deal of information together under the heading of a category; and then recall the detail by reconstructing it from what our knowledge structure tells us should be there, rather than actually recalling it from memory. This important technique can be illustrated by simple short-term memory experiments. It has long been

VISIONARY VISION/
MASTER MASTERMAS
EXPERT EXPERTEXPERT
COMPETENT COMPETENT
ADVANCED BEGINNER ADVA
BEGINNER BEGINNERBEGINN
NOVICE NOVICENOVICENOVICEN

pg. 101

REMEMBERING

SEQUENCES

These sequences of 9 apparently random letters are difficult to remember

ITTRHACCE

CAHIETCRT

But these sequences are much easier by relying on 3 syllables

TIC CAT HER

CIC RAT THE

CAR HIT TEC

This single word makes the 9 letters very easy to remember

ARCHITECT

MNEMONICS IN MUSIC

The notes represented by the lines on the treble clef, bottom to top.

Every Good Boy Does Fine (EGBDF)

The notes represented by the spaces on the bass clef, bottom to top.

All Cows Eat Grass (ACEG)

MNEMONICS IN CHEMISTRY

International Classification of Hazardous Substances

1. Explosives
2. Gases
3. Liquids
4. Oxidising
5. Toxic (and poisonous)
6. Radioactive
7. Corrosive
8. Miscellaneous.

Extra Good Layers On These Really Cold Mornings

recognised that our short-term memory has a very limited capacity, normally thought to be around 7 items (Miller, 1956). Simple experiments ask subjects to remember and then recall sequences of digits or letters. With sequences up to around 7 items long performance is quite accurate, but it normally tails off dramatically with increasingly long sequences. However, we can rearrange these same letters into recognisable syllables or words and then easily remember 7 of these. If they are arranged in some meaningful way into a sentence, then the whole sentence can be remembered and used to reconstruct other details. This is the principle behind mnemonic devices used to help students recall the sequences of Kings and Queens of England, chemical compounds, the number of days in each month and other such apparently meaningless lists.

This effect of 'chunking' groups of items into single representations has long been understood and many examples of it have now been found in a whole series of domains. In this sense, a chunk becomes a single entity rather than an aggregation of smaller objects. Thus to someone learning a language a word is a collection of letters. To an expert in that language the letters can be recreated from the word. The direction of thought has thus virtually reversed. For example, Adelson showed that expert computer programmers could remember and recall much longer sections of program code in this way (Adelson, 1981). Chase and Simon famously showed that expert chess players divide the board up into areas of attack and defence and remember the locations of the relevant pieces (Chase and Simon, 1973).

In fact, chess turns out to offer us an interesting set of examples of how problem recognition may work in design. De Groot and his followers studied how expert chess players 'see' the board differently from average ones (De Groot, 1965). It seems the chess master does not *analyse* the chess board but rather *recognises* it. Effectively, the situation on the board to a player of this layer of expertise is known as a Gestalt. The whole situation is recognised and can be given a name. It is thus categorised in the manner we have seen in the simpler examples above. In the case of chess players, this no doubt comes about, not only through playing but through gaining what we call here accelerated experience, by studying the recorded and documented games of great players. This studying of previously documented games that contain seminal moves or gambits provides the chess master with the equivalent of studying design precedent.

The idea of a gambit seems an important one in understanding how design knowledge might develop. In chess a gambit is generally seen as an opening move. In fact, the word comes from the Italian phrase 'Dare il gambetta'; literally 'stick out a leg'. This, in turn, is a term taken from wrestling and

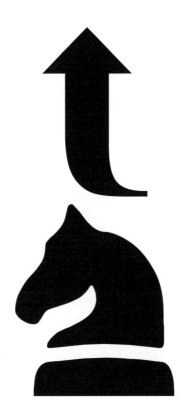

represents how the bout is moved forward from simple jostling for position to actual wrestling.

Perhaps in design we should not see a gambit as necessarily a beginning of the whole process, but rather a way of starting a line of thought about how some aspects or features of the design might be developed. Designers clearly develop an understanding of many of these features in quite generic terms from studying precedent. For example, in architecture the organisation of the plan around an entrance is a well-understood way of progressing a design. There are many varieties of this including, for example, a central doorway on an axis of symmetry, a doorway in a recessive corner to draw people in, and so on. Such ideas can be used to begin an investigation of how the design might be.

EXPERTISE IN DESIGN

We have a great deal of anecdotal, and some empirical, evidence that designers operate in this way; Schön and Wiggins' work suggest something very similar (Schön and Wiggins, 1992). Also recent recordings of staff tutorials with architectural design students gathered at Sheffield by Khairul Khaidzir give further indications that this is happening (Khaidzir, 2007). Conversational elements were categorised as being 'moves', 'formulations' or 'evaluations' (as defined in Chapter 2). Tutors talked about possible moves seven times longer than students did. Tutors also spent about a third of their time trying to make moves, whereas students only spent about a tenth. In this time tutors were found to be engaged in what Khairul identifies as 'content-based' move actions. This means that they were effectively drawing on their practical experiences. Students, with much less experience, could only manage less than a quarter of this output.

pg.51

During these sessions, tutors would often make remarks such as 'this is a situation where you could do…'. Interestingly, such remarks often already indicate an intention to generate solutions rather than explicitly to recognise problems. Indeed, sometimes remarks suggest a reconstruction of the problem by the student in order to take advantage of a particular design move. 'You could bend this a little and then you would be able to do…'. The student tutorial shown here offers an example where a more experienced design practitioner first tries to understand the design situation created by the student, then recognises a pattern and suggests two alternative gambits. These are expressed as if they were generically recognised strategies. Then the expert tutor can immediately put forward practical ways of realising these two gambits in the context of this particular design. This strongly

RECOGNISING THE SITUATION
A DESIGN STUDENT TUTORIAL

TUTOR

What's that 'kink' in the plan here?

STUDENT

It's been really annoying me... I don't like it so I'm going to kind of scrap it! It kind of helps with the shape but it...

TUTOR

You can make some decisions about this. You can say, okay, this is about two cubes and there's a coming together of the two cubes which may introduce something else (kink). You know, if there's a meeting of things, there is a possibility for something to occur. Or you can say well this isn't about two cubes which was just the starting point for me to get going and it's about having this block which has this circulation dropping down through the middle of it. So I think if the former is the case and this is clearly about articulating two cubes, then that (kink element) becomes quite key and I wouldn't ignore it. I would think about how it's treated and how it could be expressed as the point which they come together. Or you can sort of say I don't really want that and I'm just going to follow the building line which is entirely legitimate.

STUDENT

Yes... it's just a small idea in my mind. I can't decide do I really like it or really not like it? I can probably justify both quite well, but...

TUTOR

Yeah, well that can often end in a kind of 'greyness', you know. So I think you have to decide what do. I really want to go with this. Is it worth fighting for?

STUDENT

I do want it because... I'll show you in my other drawings.

TUTOR

OK, right. Well that means that this becomes important, doesn't it? This line that you're showing here starts to mean something... maybe that's something expressed in structure. It might be something that lights into this space. It might be a slot that runs through...

suggests that gambits are learned from particular situations, such as buildings, and then generalised. In application, the process is almost reversed as the generic idea is tailored to the situation. An important skill to build then, in the creation of design expertise, must be the ability to recognise the deep underlying structure of these situations.

There is other evidence that expert designers appear to 'think ahead' in the process more than novices. A study of aerospace engineering designers showed that, where novices tended to implement ideas immediately and then evaluated them, more experienced designers evaluate them before implementation (Ahmed et al., 2003). In general, this ability to think forwards rather than backwards seems to be a common characteristic of expertise in many areas. The expert thus assesses the extent to which an idea might be worth developing before expending the effort in doing so. Similar cost-benefit strategies have been observed in other fields. The expert appears to be able to weigh up the potential benefits of a course of action and set them against the potential effort required. The novice, perhaps carried away by the excitement of the idea, rushes into development—only later to evaluate and be disappointed not only by the idea but also by the amount of time and effort expended. This seems to be a very powerful characteristic of expertise potentially saving vast amounts of time in the process. Some of Khairul's tutors' comments to their students seem to be encouraging them to adopt the more forward thinking approach. Evidence from studies in other areas suggests that experts may be able to do this forward evaluation so quickly that they may not even be aware of it as a conscious strategy. This further suggests that experts are able to recognise situations and perform almost instant forward evaluations of them as a result. These findings also suggest that evaluative skills may be a more important component of creative expertise than is normally assumed.

GUIDING PRINCIPLES

We have studied a range of cognitive activities here in order to understand something of the ways in which expertise might be established. However, design is different from most of these other situations in at least one very important way. We saw in Chapter 2 that design problems are open-ended and poorly specified compared with many other more conventional problems. The knowledge needed to solve a design problem very much depends upon the approach the designer is taking to it. Chess is sometimes seen as almost as open-ended as design, since the total number of possible board situations is so vast as to be effectively infinite. Nevertheless, chess is highly constrained compared with design. The board is predefined as 8 by 8 squares

" GUIDING PRINCIPLES (MATERIALS)
EVA JIRICNA

We always try to limit the amount of materials on each scheme... I believe that each material has got its own language and every time you use it, you just learn one more word, one more expression, a little bit of grammar. If you use too many materials they just don't go together, so in the beginning we just try to establish very carefully what we are going to use and what we are trying to achieve in terms of materials that are related to the concept. So if, for example, it's a public building, so what is durable? What materials will survive in a specific environment? Of course the cost aspect comes into it from the beginning and then we say, okay, let's try to do it in say stone and timber and stainless steel.

So the material is a very early decision. I think that in a way material dictates the concept... you can only interpret certain concepts with certain materials because materials are not inter-changeable. In terms of space it depends on whether you clad with say aluminium panels, or fibrous plaster or just paint the walls. The material really is the starting point of the story and use of the material somehow helps to put together a concept. You will probably find this a completely heretical view because most of the people I have ever worked with start by making little sketches and trying to put together some ideas. We usually start with full size details because once we have some ideas of how to create different junctions, then we can create a layout which would be good... materials only join with certain way comfortably... for example a point where you have a joint of the ceiling, walls, vertical or something coming from the staircase or balustrade... because you can have the most brilliant concept but if you cannot handle the detailing the concept falls apart. It doesn't mean that we ignore the spatial concept because we look at the plan and re-do, go through an investigation/analysis of what you see, what the proportions are, what the scale is, sitting down, standing up, looking at different distances, it goes on in parallel, but you know we just don't go from concept which will be based on say creating little boxes and so on and then leave the details to the end.

and the pieces all exist and have their numbers and allowed moves specified. A design-like version of chess would remove all of these constraints allowing for the continuous redesign of the pieces, their moves and the board. So while it is possible for a chess master to study a limited array of knowledge, this is not possible for a designer. Chess masters need only learn all of the important previously played games and the key gambits associated with board situations. Of course, this is potentially a huge task but nevertheless it is at least defined. The designer has no such guidelines in terms of deciding where to look for precedent that might be helpful. So just how do designers learn to direct their attention?

DETERMINED ——— UNDETERMINED

pg.43

One clue to this seems to lie with the idea of 'guiding principles' first suggested by Lawson (2006). These are collections of overarching interests and values that expert designers appear to acquire over time. There seems to be an almost limitless set of possibilities for the domain of guiding principles. For some they may be about form, shape or proportion; for others they may be about an approach to technology or sustainability. For yet others they may be about the process rather than the product, perhaps a way of working collaboratively with users. The Czech architect Eva Jiricna obviously has a set of guiding principles about the importance of understanding and using materials and has built a design process around those ideas.

The process of developing guiding principles almost certainly starts quite early on in design careers and may well even begin during the student phase. For the expert they have become so well-established that they may be clearly articulated in public. Clients may even appreciate and understand them and indeed may select designers partly on the basis of their guiding principles. When this happens the designer may have already completed a body of work that exemplifies these ideas and thus there is a spiralling process of reinforcement. Here each design project is informed by the designer's guiding principles but, in turn, becomes yet another research vehicle for further developing those ideas.

The most illustrious designers can effectively choose their clients and projects and thus maintain the integrity of their approach. If Michael Wilford is typical of this select band then this clearly becomes a most important issue. However, what this illustrates is the extent to which design at this level is almost invariably a matter of a collective rather than an individual. It is perhaps paradoxical that the most successful designers are the most likely to employ larger numbers of designers in their studios, and yet these are the very people who become known as signature designers. This perhaps leads us, it must be said via a great deal of current design criticism, to the erroneous conclusion that all the work of the practice is done by the titular head.

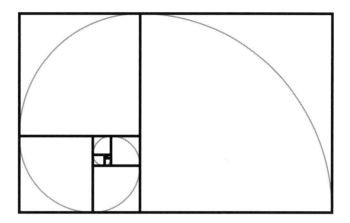

CHOOSING A DESIGNER
MICHAEL WILFORD

We find it very difficult to operate in situations where we're having to sell our-selves to the client, where you're in the market place in a competitive situation, where the client says well it's an office building. I mean I don't mind, there are a dozen architects who can do it. If you want to do it fine, 'what's your lowest fee'? You know we're not in that sort of syndrome though we've often got involved, we've got sucked into situations, particularly in America, where friends of ours will say "look there's this huge project going downtown somewhere, are you interested in going in with us?" And we say ok fine, then you find that you are one of fifty people who are submitting and then the client will choose maybe that firm but is indifferent to us and it's very difficult I think to operate in that climate, for us anyway. Our experience is that the best buildings are produced is when the client comes to us and says you know, I've seen A+U*, and I've seen AD* and I quite like the variety of things that you do and I'd like you to do a building for us.

*Architecture + Urbanism and Architectural Design are international architectural journals

The English architect John Outram is quite explicit about the problems this poses for his own staff. Clearly, working in a practice that has strong sets of guiding principles involves buying in to those principles and, as it were, signing up to the agenda and agreeing to work with it.

These guiding principles then form a vitally important part of what, in Chapter 2, we referred to as 'practice' issues. They develop in and through designing but they transcend any individual projects.

It is worth noting here that authorship in design is very often different from authorship in art. Although some art is quite significantly the work of a team, this is almost always so in design. Michael Wilford portrays this through his analogy with the process of editing a newspaper.

The most admired designers seem to be ones who produce work that sets the agenda and changes the design domain. Their work is likely to be published and studied as part of the precedent pool by both students and professional designers. It is highly likely that such work is normally done by designers with very well developed sets of guiding principles. Their work shows a new way forward not previously imagined by other designers in some way.

PROFESSION
PRACTICE
PROCESS
PROJECT
pg.61

RECOGNISING SITUATIONS

Research described earlier on chess experts shows that they recognise board situations and know the kinds of gambits that can be successfully used in those situations. In fact, such players often play demonstration matches against ordinary club players, perhaps taking on more than one opponent at the same time, moving swiftly from one board to the next.

This apparently extraordinary feat is only possible because of two conditions. Firstly, the expert has the ability to recognise a situation, which means they don't waste time analysing. Secondly, the expert has the knowledge that standard gambits are likely to be sufficient to defeat opponents. The masters of chess, though, create new gambits. It is their moves that are studied and added to the pool of knowledge studied by others. In truth, of course, a chess master is unlikely to beat another master playing at the same level with any of the well-known and studied gambits. Of course, design is not a competitive game, nor is it conducted in a restricted and defined environment such as the chess board. But the master designer is just as interested in moving the field on and has studied sufficiently well to know how to create fairly standard responses. Totally new ideas are rare and precious indeed.

pg.175

THINKING ABOUT
THE PRACTICE
JOHN OUTRAM

I think probably it's necessary if you're going to be a practising designer to be able to handle the language of pure design and I think it's like a process of analysis and synthesis you know, you break down the language and then you have a sort of ability to be original, to understand the security that you obtain. That anything you compose will be beautiful even if it doesn't mean anything, and then the search for meaning is something separate.

Architecture is a collaborative process, which isn't to say that I am not ultimately in control because I am, but I respect ideas from wherever they come. Obviously they come from structural engineers, mechanical engineers, the clients themselves; they all act. In the early stage you know, I've always felt that you must sort of attract as much energy as you can out of people. I've evolved what I suppose is a design vocabulary like a design language, which you see can cope with all this diverse input because in the end it all gets translated into the Outram architecture. The longer they (his staff) stay the more adept they get, if they refuse to speak it at all then there is a mutual parting as it were. But, the staff that get on best are the ones who regard it like another aspect of the game that they are required to play you know. There is the district surveyor, there's the quantity surveyor, there's the structural engineer and there's John Outram. And the ones who are adept at negotiating with these are those who, as it were, sincerely believe and want to practise the system and there are those who regard it in a more detached professional way and just learn the system. And of course those people I like working with, you see I like people who can contribute but who don't destroy.

Fig 5.2 The interior of the Judge Institute in Cambridge by John Outram showing his characteristic flair for symbolic decoration, colour and texture and classically inspired forms

JOHN OUTRAM

John Outram was born into a British military family and spent his early years in the India of the British Empire. A boyhood fascination with aircraft and flight led him to train as a pilot with the Royal Air Force, whilst his architectural education was gained at Regent Street Polytechnic and the AA.

John Outram developed a more recent interest in the semiology of architecture and urban form. He has argued for a rejection of the Modern Movement and the vision of buildings as machines as exemplified by 'Hi-tech' architects. He also rejects the superficiality of much 'post-modern' architecture and has argued that buildings should be both poetic and symbolic. He has also developed a highly practical approach to the construction of buildings inventing a kind of exposed crushed brick aggregate concrete which he calls 'Blitzcrete'. He has called his approach to design 'popular classicism' which is a suitably contradictory phrase with which to encapsulate this unique combination of influences.

A delightful example of this can be found in Richard MacCormac's description of the development of his design for a headquarters and training centre for Cable and Wireless. The scheme has a series of partially overlapping wavelike roofs that sail over the main spaces. Note how MacCormac not only makes reference to the great Finnish architect Pietilä and the masterly Jørn Utzon but also how he relates their work and draws out the beginnings of generic idea from them which he reuses in his own work.

SETTING THE AGENDA

Design work done at this level thus effectively changes the world. Designs of this kind can have an influence well beyond their own life. An example of this might be the revolutionary work of Alec Issigonis in creating the famous Mini automobile design. Issigonis had already designed the Morris Minor which itself was pretty revolutionary since it brought family motoring to the British masses on a previously unimagined scale. But it was the design of the Mini that really changed motoring forever. Today it is hard to believe that so many innovations now in common use were introduced in this one car. It is also remarkable in that the design was completed in an unusually short timescale.

The Mini had a transversely mounted engine with gearbox below and front-wheel drive. It used a rubber cone suspension system invented by Moulton, another master designer. The driver sat inside a stripped down interior. But the compact exterior was perhaps more remarkable in that it dispensed with the traditional rear luggage box. The Mini was also a response to the first major fuel crisis following on from the Suez dispute which alerted consumers to the need for fuel economy.

Issigonis always described himself as an engineer and was unhappy at later descriptions of his work in stylistic terms. Even so, the shape and distinctive curves of the Mini added to the engineering innovations to make it a style icon of its age. Although there had previously been 'bubble cars' it was surely the innovations of the Mini that paved the way for a whole succession of small cars that continue today. Indeed, the newer BMW version of the Mini still pays very considerable homage to the original design.

We talk of 'classic' pieces of design which seem to us to be timeless. The idea of the design classic is difficult to pin down and describe but easier to recognise. Such pieces of design might include the Anglepoise lamp, curiously in terms of our story here, designed by an automobile engineer George Cawardine in 1932. This was the first desk lamp that you could position to direct

DESIGN PRINCIPALS AS EDITORS
MICHAEL WILFORD

It is certainly my experience that the greater the body of work, the more you do tend to delegate work to others and become more and more a decision maker. But in terms of the process I think one does tend to leave that to others more and you tend to guide it. The analogy that I often use when asked... I think it's like a newspaper editorial office.

Basically we assign a project architect... it's often an associate... he will have a couple of assistants... he will sign the brief at that particular building and he will be responsible for generating ideas about how that brief can be satisfied. We will have ideas from talking to the client, experiencing (the site) environment, about the way the building should be organised and so on. We will have discussions about that, and these people will generate ideas/sketches, which we will then work over and modify and add to or subtract and that kind of thing. So largely the initiative comes from those staff who have been here several years and know how we worked and.... because in a way, they kind of felt, they'd generate ideas and then we'd (James Stirling and Michael Wilford) work with them where needed and come back next day and say I think these two approaches are very appropriate, this one is hopeless—forget about it, don't waste anymore time on it, let's push in this direction. So, that's the way it develops from a very small nucleus and then it gradually expands and so then the team will build up as the building firms up, in other words for us it's a systematic process and almost a boring, methodical, sequential process. Let me just go back ... so if you can imagine about twelve people doing that kind of activity backed up by others drawings, the process of editing is as I say just like a newspaper editor who will take copy and say well I think the slant of this is kind of wrong, I think that you have not covered this aspect of it, let's focus here, let's balance this, re-do it, I don't like this. So it's very much this kind of process and in the end the design has that personal kind of touch, that slant if you like of the editor in its final form. But the generation of the idea is not entirely the editor's, it's the result of the complete kind of labyrinth of ideas that somehow come together and get sort of ordered, sifted, prioritised.

light at a task from any angle, without needing any fixing, and yet remain permanently stable. The Anglepoise itself went through a number of minor stylistic developments but it triggered a whole slew of imitations.

It is said that Cawardine invented the lamp by accident when looking for uses for his new springs. It is generally recognised that James Dyson's revolutionary vacuum cleaner was the result of him first solving another problem and then looking for alternative applications of his cyclone. Perhaps then one way of developing what we might call a 'design classic' is to transfer an idea from one context to another in such a way that it then seems obvious and easy. Quite how the human mind does this is what tantalises those who research design processes.

Some design classics are the result of the designer exploring a new material, or transferring a material into a novel context. The amazing work of Charles and Ray Eames using bent plywood for medical splints and chairs would be obvious examples of such a process. Charles Eames was once asked if his famous lounger chair design came in a flash, and he replied 'yes a thirty year flash'. Eames' point, which he developed in a design timeline was that design of this kind cannot sensibly be pinned down to a moment. Some sudden reframing of a situation may well appear to be the key moment in a process but in reality it depends on many years of thought, development and creation of all the precedents that have influenced the designer. Perhaps then Eames was right in trying to dissuade us from the rather populist notion of design being a sudden idea. The recent tendency to see the 'lightbulb' moment as the only source of creativity is not helpful to those learning the skills of design. This is an important theme that recurs in this book. If we want to understand design it simply will not do only to study individual projects. It is the way designers build up their knowledge and expertise over a series of projects and other experiences that deserves our attention. This is what we have referred to here as their 'practice'.

PROFESSION
PRACTICE
PROCESS
PROJECT
pg.61

Relatively little research has been conducted on the working methods and capabilities of our best designers. That work which has been done suggests some common themes. One of the strongest of these themes centres on the ability and willingness of such designers to accommodate uncertainty. Making a design turns out to be a very different process from making a physical object. When we make an object—a piece of furniture, a model, a house—we see evidence of our work progressively growing in front of our eyes. However, when we make a design, often this is not the case. It is certainly not the case that a design must grow progressively. There may be little sign of it until quite late in the process; it is often the case that you may need to be engaged with an idea for quite a while before you see the relevance of it.

FINDING DESIGN GAMBITS
RICHARD MACCORMAC

It was a series of static events so that the overlap was about a sort of sense of flow. I suppose what tweaked me with that was suddenly seeing Pietilä's Finnish Embassy in India in World Architecture with his kind of crinkly amazing sort of roofs, almost like sort of, fragile—like egg shells, and that sort of started a line of thought...

...a sort of base, but with substance, with very delicate steel elements supporting the wave so that it's hovering over this datum really, so that was incredibly difficult to sort out. It was so important that the lid, that the beams on the frame were level, at one stage they were high under the high part of the wave and low under the low part, but eventually they were absolutely at datum to the site with the wave taking off. I think that for me has quite a lot to do with what Utzon used to write about the Sydney Opera House, that sense of establishing a base and letting something fly on top of it.

THE MYTH OF A SINGLE MIND

Design on a substantial scale is essentially a collaborative effort. This is where design historians, often educated as art historians, sometimes find themselves in trouble in their research. They tend implicitly and automatically to look for the elusive single author of a design or design idea, in an effort to describe the history of design as a series of geniuses that single-handedly change the world. However, the ideas in a design firm often emerge from a collaborative creative process, rather than from a single contribution. Some young designers work under the same misconception. When they start working in a design agency or architectural firm, they are afraid that their ideas will be 'stolen', or claim that they did all the work in a successful project.

For many people such a state of affairs may be quite disturbing. If you are one of those people who like to stand back and see what they have done at the end of every day, then design may feel rather unrewarding. If you are one of those people who like to measure their progress against some pre-ordained target then design may feel rather dangerous. If you are one of those people who like to show others how you are getting on then design may feel rather frustrating. If you like to know how much work you have left to do then design may feel unsettling. You will never hear a designer, when asked how they are doing, reply 'well I have done about half of it'.

PERSONAL CHARACTERISTICS

All this suggests that good designers are likely to be comfortable with such a situation and therefore may show unusual personality characteristics. A variety of evidence tends to confirm this. In a famous series of studies completed at what was then known as the Institute of Personality Assessment and Research at Berkeley, its founder Donald MacKinnon studied the personality of successful American architects (MacKinnon, 1962). These and other similar studies showed strong tendencies in this group to be tolerant of ambiguity and be open to new experiences. Studies with a different set of personality measures have also shown similar characteristics. This work used the more recent Myers–Briggs measures of personality (Durling et al., 1996). This system uses four bipolar scales one of which is the judgemental-perceptual scale. The study showed designers to be characteristically and unusually at the perceptual end of this scale, whereas the general population tend to be at the judgemental end of the scale. In simple terms, this means that designers are more likely to be open-ended, flexible and spontaneous in their approach.

All this suggests that some personalities may be more comfortable using convention-based design thinking. Such thinking tends, by definition, to be more formulaic in its approach and to be more likely to lead to the removal of doubt and uncertainty. Perhaps then the willingness to use the more sophisticated situation-based and strategy-based thinking may come more naturally to those with personalities more heavily represented among the design professions as revealed by this research.

pg.69

However, we think the situation is rather more complex than such a simple and direct analysis would suggest. Studies of the thinking styles of school-children have revealed a coherent set of results from which inappropriate conclusions can easily be drawn. Hudson studied schoolboys who scored highly on creativity tests and compared them with those who scored highly

TIMELESSNESS

The brilliant Japanese product designer Naoto Fukasawa describes his design philosophy in a couple of very clear statements. He wants to create objects of use that look natural, in the sense that everybody can relate to them. They look like they have always existed, almost self-evident. Yet this line of thinking could easily lead to superficial cliché products—that is why Naoto Fukasawa takes the utmost care in detailing his products, making them attain a subtlety and a sensitivity to human needs that he hopes will make people enjoy them at a much deeper level. They should have an enduring quality that goes beyond their instantaneous attractiveness.

on traditional intelligence tests (Hudson, 1966). He called these groups 'convergers' and 'divergers'. This is a reference to the way intelligence tests reward a kind of thinking that focuses down onto one correct answer; converging. By comparison, creativity tests demand the production of many answers; diverging. Hudson showed that the high-convergent ability schoolboys tended to favour the sciences, while their high-divergent ability counterparts tended to favour the arts.

Lawson has argued that this alignment of creativity with divergent thinking is somewhat misleading, at least as far as design is concerned (Lawson, 2001). We are struck by the comments of the great Dutch architect Herman Hertzberger here talking about what he calls 'real' and 'fake' creativity. He calls into question the notion, perhaps rather popular in design schools in recent years, that originality and creativity are one and the same thing. Students in design schools may feel rewarded and approved of by their tutors when they have novel or original ideas. Of course, it is very important in design education to encourage students to move away from purely convention-based thinking, and perhaps this is what lies behind this. Unfortunately, the inference often drawn by students is that all they have to do is to be original. One might contrast this notion with the famous saying of Edison that 'genius is 1% inspiration and 99% perspiration'.

Clearly, the idea that design involves only divergent thought and that science requires only convergent thought is far too simple. Studies of the famous discovery by Crick and Watson of the structure of DNA suggest that they beat their close competitors by using divergent thinking methods. That is to say, rather than thinking through the logic of what the data was telling them, they looked for possible spatial structures that might be useful. Design then surely must involve both kinds of thought. Perhaps it might be more useful to think of masterly designers as having the capability to turn either on or off in response to the situation.

Further support for this notion comes from more of the results of the personality studies of designers. Prior to Hudson's work, Getzels and Jackson had also compared children who scored highly on creativity tests with those who scored highly on traditional intelligence tests (Getzels and Jackson, 1962). They found that the more 'intelligent' children were often seen by their teachers as more conforming and compliant. The more 'creative' children were seen as more independent, setting their own standards and caring less about approval. In general they were less well-liked by their teachers. MacKinnon's work suggested that his successful architects had a disregard for social conventions, together with a lack of concern of other's opinions of

'REAL' AND 'FAKE' CREATIVITY
HERMAN HERTZBERGER

Design is not looking out of the window and looking at the blue sky and asking God to help you, it is just this taking into consideration all the things you know. But there is a difference between analysis of the problem and solving the problem. Most people want to do it at once. I mean you have football players who get the ball and sometimes you are in the situation where the ball comes and you have to direct it in one touch, but most of the time when you are not under this stress so you first stop the ball and then go with it you know, so what you must do is first have the problem analysed on the table. What is at stake, what is involved, and from that try to find a solution... Just take an example, stairs for the entrance of a school, you have to realise what is the problem. The problem is you have certain moments that many children that have to go through, the problem is also that sometimes you have a small number of people waiting, the problem is that sometimes it rains and then it is not very nice to sit there, the problem is ... And then you get this whole list of things that in fact in altogether represent the problem, and then you can say well listen, given all these things, the stairs should not be too small, should not be too large, it should be covered over, should be... and so on. Always there are these contradictions. This is for me creativity you know, that you find the solution for all these things that are working contrary and the wrong type of creativity which is not real creativity is only fake creativity is that you just forget about the fact that it sometimes rains, you forget that sometimes it is for many people and you just make the beautiful stairs from that one idea you have in your head.

them. The work of Durling et al. (1996) also suggested that designers were internally driven, single-minded and self-centred.

DESIGN AS A SEPARATE INTELLIGENCE?

Designers and design researchers alike tend to want to identify what distinguishes design from other disciplines. Some have done this by claiming that design is a special kind of reasoning in addition to deduction, induction, and abduction. In the end, logical analysis of design does not seem to bear this out but rather suggests that design involves all of these kinds of thinking.

In discussing the nature and nurture of design abilities, Nigel Cross suggested that there might be eight key design knowledge attributes and skills, together defining 'the design ability' (Cross, 1990). He argued that designers must have the ability to: (1) produce novel, unexpected solutions by (2) applying imagination and constructive forethought to practical problems, (3) using drawings and other modelling media as means of problem solving. In doing this, they need to (4) deal with uncertainty and decision making on the basis of limited information, (5) resolve ill-defined, 'wicked' problems. They do this by (6) adopting solution-focused strategies, (7) employing productive/creative thinking, and (8) using graphic or spatial modelling media.

This impressive list of requirements has considerable resonance with the model of design activities that we developed in Chapter 2, and indeed we discussed Nigel's paper when arriving at our model. Our concern here is slightly different; we are trying to answer a very difficult question: does design require a special and distinct form of intelligence? There does not seem to be an underlying coherence, a single core 'essential design ability' or guiding principle behind the list Cross has drawn up. Indeed, some of these abilities are not particularly special and might commonly be found among other professions. Some can be learned or taught in a fairly straightforward way. However, others are less common and very difficult to teach, such as resolving wicked problems. Some are probably rather dependent on personality traits such as dealing with uncertainty.

pg.51

This discussion also brings us close to the idea of six intelligences advanced by Howard Gardner (Gardner, 1983). He suggests that there are several, relatively autonomous human intellectual faculties. He discerns the following six forms of intelligence: linguistic, logical/mathematical, spatial, musical, bodily/kinaesthetic and personal.

Design does not seem to fit easily in any of these distinct intelligences, or to be especially related to any of them. What then, could be the 'core' of design?

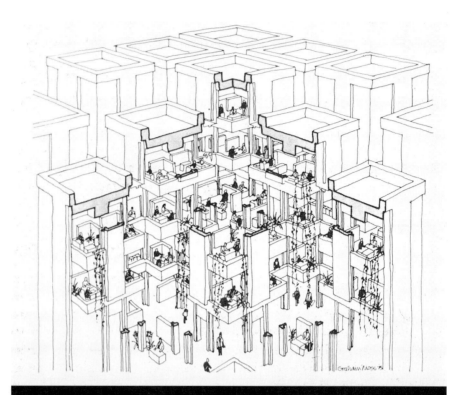

Fig 5.3 The seminal design of an office building for Centraal Beheer by Herman Hertzberger—an interior that changed the way architects thought about how work environments could be humanised

HERMAN HERTZBERGER

Herman Hertzberger was born in Amsterdam and educated at the Technical University of Delft. His practice has designed seminal buildings including schools, old people's housing, and the Vredenburg Music Centre in Utrecht. His office building for Centraal Beheer completed in 1972, most succinctly expresses his concern about the users of architecture.

Herman Hertzberger began the highly influential Dutch architectural magazine Forum which he edited with several others including Jaap Bakema and Aldo van Eyck. He has argued that function should be seen as much a response to form as opposed to the other way round. He developed the 'structuralist' idea that architectural form should be thought of as an instrument capable of allowing for individual interpretation by its users rather than as an apparatus capable of single limited use. More recently he has published his widely acclaimed books on 'Lessons for Students in Architecture' which are already influencing the next generation of architects.

He has taught at many universities and was Dean of the Berlage Institute, which he originally set up in a section of Aldo van Eyck's famous orphanage in Amsterdam.

Or could it be an 'intelligence' in itself? In fact, Cross's abilities would seem to demand all six of the forms of intelligence that Gardner identified. This could mean that design is a broad, wide ranging human activity that possibly does not absolutely require extreme intelligence in any of the six varieties, but rather a special combination of these intelligences. This in itself could be an important difference if we compare design with many other professions that seem to lean more on one dominant kind of intelligence. The very broadness of the intelligence base could be the reason that people often feel that there is something obscure about the design ability. Rather requiring a special intelligence of its own design is a complex brew of traits.

This could also help to explain the many species of designers that we see in practice. Designers are an extremely diverse bunch of people, there are those who could be characterised as 'entrepreneur', 'artist', 'rationalist', 'pragmatist', etc. Designers tend to take on these various roles in design teams—the combination of different strands of design intelligence could indeed be a reason to prefer designing in teams. In general, one could state that you need all kinds of design abilities and possibly all of Gardner's intelligences to achieve design quality.

In fact, there have been experiments at several design schools to maximise the personality differences when assembling a design team (some using a Meyers–Briggs-type indicator to test the students; others prefer the Kirton adaptor–innovator test (Kirton, 1989)). These experiments have also been taken up in some design practices (Sutton and Hargardon, 1996; Hirshberg, 1998). When each of the team members is innovative or extreme in one or more of the six forms of intelligence, and if they nonetheless share a broad understanding based on their education (Valkenburg, 2000), rather special things can happen. Case studies do suggest that teams that are put together to form this kind of 'collective design intelligence' are very successful indeed.

INTELLIGENCE AND DESIGN EXPERTISE

So what levels of which kinds of intelligence are needed in order to have the potential to create design expertise?

We are, apparently, getting more intelligent. The so-called 'Flynn Effect' shows that the average level of intelligence as measured by these tests is generally rising over time. The effect is named after James Flynn who first identified the phenomenon and later demonstrated it more widely (Flynn, 1987). These results give us a problem. IQ tests are re-normalised on a regular basis

to ensure that the average score is always 100. This means that if our grand-parents were to take today's tests, about half of them would be classified as mentally retarded and our great-grandparents would have been collectively stupid. It seems unlikely that the scientific and economic progress we have seen throughout the twentieth century could have been achieved by such a collection of morons. Something is wrong here.

There are many arguments as to what is causing this effect. Possible factors include improved nutrition, better education, and both students and teachers learning how to do the tests. Our modern scientific and technocratic society seems to reward the IQ test skills more than earlier more practical societies. The advent of personal computing means that most of us do far more daily problem solving than earlier generations did.

Overall too, the scores achieved by students taking national school qualifica-tions seem to be rising. The UK 'A' level score (the last pre-university qualifi-cation for most) has been rising for 25 years in succession with now around 95% passing compared with barely 50% at one time. The purely anecdotal evidence of university design school staff produces a commonly expressed perception that there may be some rise in intelligence among their intake but that this is not accompanied by an overall rise in design ability. Indeed, selecting students for university design courses remains a notoriously tricky business since none of the standard school results appear to be good pre-dictors. A study of a decade of intake at the Sheffield University School of Architecture showed no correlation between total 'A' level scores and perfor-mance in design studio at degree level.

Why should this be? Perhaps they simply do not measure the kinds of abili-ties that designers most depend upon. We can see from the typical IQ test question shown here that the real ability required is a perceptual and analyti-cal one. To succeed you need to be able to find patterns and work with a logi-cal system to find a correct answer. On the other hand, the typical creativity test requires a flight of ideas. It measures your ability to come up with many alternative possibilities.

Now clearly both these abilities are useful in designing. This dichotomy between creativity and intelligence does not tend to help us much either, nor did the divide between convergent and divergent production upon which it is based. Perhaps a more interesting question is how we tend to look at events around us and learn from them. A clue to this is given by an example used by James Flynn himself in a lecture in Cambridge in 2006. He suggested that, if in 1900 you had asked children what dogs and rabbits have in common, they might have replied with a concrete answer like, 'dogs are used to hunt

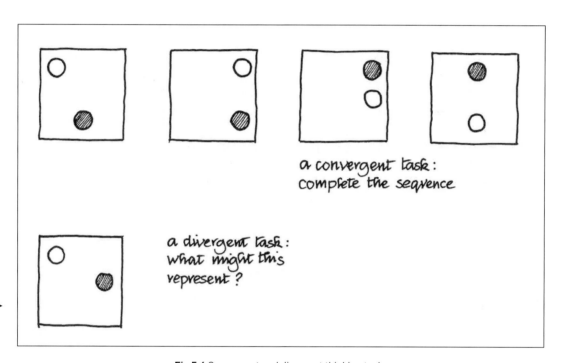

Fig 5.4 Convergent and divergent thinking tasks

rabbits'. By contrast, Flynn suggested, today's children would be more likely to say, 'They're both mammals'. Flynn is putting forward the idea that the tendency on average is to move towards the latter way of learning and understanding the world which he believes has taken place over time.

Perhaps the designer remains an exception to this trend. In looking at things around us, designers are seeking out not just one correct classification but instead searching for ideas that might be useful in the future. The whole idea of precedent collecting, which we discussed in detail in Chapter 4, is based upon this notion. Designers are essentially mental collectors of apparent garbage that might just come in useful when tackling some yet unforeseen problem. In this sense, they are not so much interested in the classificatory properties of an object as what Gibson would call its 'affordances' (Gibson, 1986).

Gibson saw perception as an active process devoted primarily towards action. He claimed that we look at the world not so much to understand it as to operate in and on it. So we see the possibility not just of sitting on a chair but also of standing on it. For us then, the chair has the affordability of climbing to reach high up. This seems very like what designers must be doing when looking at existing design solutions and gathering them for possible future use. This could explain why intelligence, as measured by classical IQ tests, is a poor predictor of the potential to develop design expertise. Whether a predisposition to think and perceive in this kind of way is innate or learned, remains another question. However, it must surely be the job of design education to encourage and develop it. We shall return to that later.

MASTERING MULTIPLE WAYS OF SEEING

So how does all this pan out in terms of real design activity? A characteristic of master designers seems to be their willingness to engage with multiple ideas.

Sometimes this may be expressed in the form of deliberate searches for alternative solutions; even in some cases apparently trying to map out the territory of possibilities as it were. This appears to be what Michael Wilford is describing when he talks of 'development on several fronts simultaneously' and 'having a full spectrum available'.

It must be said that there are other masterly designers who argue equally strongly against a strategy of deliberately generating alternatives. Richard MacCormac describes such an approach as 'needing a terrific amount of nerve'. Eva Jiricna though seems to support Michael Wilford in the way she

GENERATING ALTERNATIVES
MICHAEL WILFORD

People in the office will come up with a series of ideas, if it seems to us (James Stirling and Michael Wilford) from the ideas that are generated in the office that say for example for one building, three or four different strategies have a validity and potential architecturally then we will take those three or four examples and go and discuss them with the client. We'll show all the possibilities that we think are appropriate to their requirements in an architectural potential, I mean that's the key issue. If it's a dog we wouldn't develop it anyway. We are quite prepared to open up and discuss with the client...

My experience as a teacher is that I think it's a skill which has to be developed, it's not a sequential process. There's a sequential development but I think it's a development on several fronts simultaneously. But students also have a reluctance or in most cases, a lack of ability of conceiving of two ways of doing something or even more than two ways of doing something. They actually kind of do it and then they think that's it and they can't actually shake themselves out of it, they can't detach themselves from that particular solution or design to look at others. My personal experience is that it takes a long time actually to develop that kind of detached facility, to sketch and say well it could be done this way, it could be done that way or it could be done that way, what are the merits of this, what are the merits of that... Students get locked into a solution without having a kind of full spectrum available to judge whether that is an appropriate solution, in fact it's like clutching at straws and they are straws in the wind. The process becomes ephemeral really, it needs to be rooted in what becomes a very systematic process of investigations of options and selection.

talks of working alternatives up 'to the point where they can stand on their own feet'. This presumably means suspending judgement on each alternative until it has been given a chance to develop. It is often all too easy to critically evaluate a design idea that is at a very early stage of development.

Another way of looking at design alternatives is by emphasising the problem over the solution. Implicit in the Jiricna and Wilford strategies is a generation of a range of solutions. As we have repeatedly seen throughout this book, design situations are made up of problems and solutions. Inevitably, different solutions tend to be differentially good at satisfying different parts of the problem. Reframing problems and seeing them in different ways thus provides another strategy for generating different situations.

So far, this discussion has tended to focus on the idea of generating alternatives to map out the range of possible designs. However, a further way of allowing alternative ideas to develop is what Lawson has called 'Parallel Lines of Thought' (Lawson, 1993). Whereas the design alternatives discussed above are really multiple views of solutions, parallel lines of thought are more alternative views of problems. Lawson gives two examples both resulting from the analysis of drawings and interviews with master architects.

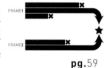

pg.59

In one case, Santiago Calatrava is seen working on a competition design for the Cathedral of St John the Divine in New York. Two series of sketches are identified from different sketchbooks worked on in parallel. In one set the investigation is clearly of the building as structure. The drawings are almost exclusively in section and show almost no details of the potential building skin or envelope. The problem is thus seen as one of structural support, though typically with Calatrava the solutions all have highly expressive and dynamic qualities. By comparison, the second set of sketches investigates the building as climate modifier. Here the structure is only shown in very abstract terms as Calatrava investigates possible external envelope designs to control and admit light; even suggesting a solar powered ecological gallery in the roof void above the nave.

In the second case, Bob Venturi is seen working on his design for the extension to the National Gallery in Trafalgar Square in London (which was illustrated in Chapter 2). Again, one series of drawings shows an investigation of the building as sequence of space. Venturi explores possible arrangements enabling him to relate the new gallery spaces to the existing main axis of the original Wilkins building. This sequence begins with a set of doodles on the menu of the Savoy Hotel in London just down the Strand from the site.

GENERATING ALTERNATIVES
EVA JIRICNA

When a project starts we always look at all the options we can think of to see which one is the strongest one and most appropriate one, I don't think it has ever happened that we would say that's it straight away and there is always an alternative A, B, C, D, E, F and then it gets reduced to three and the three produce two more because...

We work them all up... up to the point where they can stand up on their feet, because at one point they just fall because they produce failure to go any further and to express it properly, but you have got let's say five, on the first morning when you start working on the scheme you have got let's say ten and they are all equally possible and then you go through a process of analysing it and develop each of them slightly further on, five of them.

Then of course the one alternative which you have chosen has got millions of little options, it comes down to the last point when you put the door handle in the middle of the door and make the door look symmetrical, or whether it's a knob or whether it's a push plate or whatever, whether it's a pivot or hinge. There is always an option, there is hardly ever any solution which is the only one... but if you want to do it properly you can go on endlessly.

The second set of sketches—computer-aided drawings, montages and models—shows Venturi exploring the exterior form and appearance of the building as it impacts on one of London's most important spaces. Interestingly, this sequence also begins with doodles on a menu; this time on the plane returning back to Philadelphia. Perhaps in both cases the original graphics of the menu aid the process of initiating design thinking by removing that most terrifying of all obstacles, the blank sheet of paper!

We can see a similar strategy in product design. Some designers use the trick of developing several conceptual designs, each optimised from the standpoint of a different stakeholder. This then results in a collection of very different designs that help the designer understand the complexities and paradoxical nature of the complete design situation that needs to be resolved.

The same can be done while not taking the different stakeholders, but different aspects of the design problem as a starting point—for instance, creating a design that completely optimises the technical efficiency of a product: one that is pretty much ideal ergonomically, one that is most efficient from a business standpoint, one for aesthetics, and so on. It is important to note that none of these 'design concepts' is ever meant to be a complete resolution of the design situation. Thus, these designs are pure thought experiments, to help the designer attain a deeper understanding of the design situation through the development of design concepts that are deliberately skewed and un-integrated. Of course, some of the ideas that are generated in this process, and used in these design concepts, could end up in the final design— but the creation of the final integrated design is a creative design process in itself, informed by these thought experiments.

These examples show a number of common characteristics, all of them important to understanding this high level of design. In both cases, the designers explore problems through solutions. In both cases, they show alternative sets of problems being explored. We could see these as different frames in Schön's terminology. They are views on the problem, focusing on selected issues as if through a frame that temporarily blanks out other matters. Both Calatrava and Venturi explore their multiple frames in parallel lines of thought that allow them to mature unfettered by any consideration of resolving them into a single proposition. This can be seen to have a similar quality to the explorations of Stirling/Wilford and Eva Jiricna; allowing alternatives to mature until they are robust enough for more evaluative examination.

Clearly in these cases we see situation-based thinking determining the frames or lines of thought to be decided. We also see strategic-based

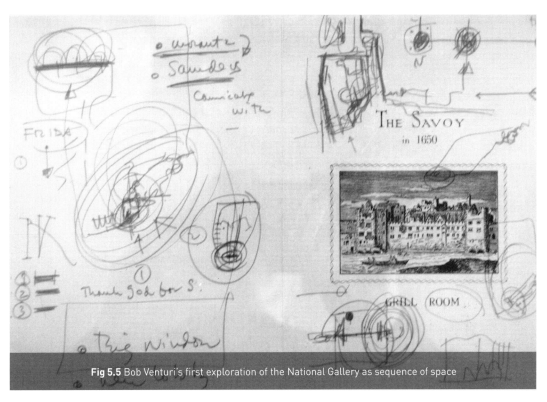

Fig 5.5 Bob Venturi's first exploration of the National Gallery as sequence of space

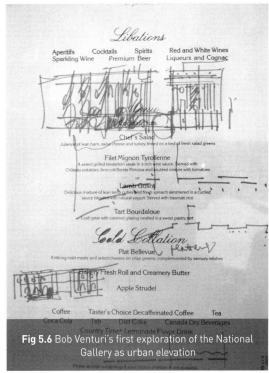

Fig 5.6 Bob Venturi's first exploration of the National Gallery as urban elevation

thinking allowing the designer's own sets of guiding principles to be brought to bear on the problem. Most importantly, we see a process that simultaneously allows for high levels of ambiguity and uncertainty and yet doggedly follows ideas through in considerable detail. Taken together, all these characteristics of 'parallel lines of thought' reveal a very sophisticated process. This is not simply generating loads of ideas as in much trumpeted techniques, such as 'brainstorming'. This is a very controlled development of solutions in a strategic and situated manner that obviously requires enormous experience and confidence to practice well.

pg.*69*

pg.*181*

VISIONARY DESIGN

The visionary takes the design process to another level but with an interesting twist. This mode of design breaks the mould and aspires to change the world. However, in doing so it may sacrifice competence to some degree. Also, this may not always be seen to be in the service of clients or users but rather as a focus on its revolutionary qualities. It could seem as if the process is so dominated by frame shifting or changing the paradigm, that other design activity is subjugated. Interestingly, this is effectively what is often recommended in some populist creativity books. Suspending judgement, for example, is one of the cornerstones of some stages of 'brainstorming; although the normal full brainstorming process also then involves later stages of evaluation and testing of ideas. In visionary mode, however, work in the hands of great designers reaches such heights that we seem prepared to accept some fairly fundamental functional deficiencies in the results.

Examples of such designs could be thought of as including Philippe Starck's famous Juicy Saleph lemon squeezer and Jørn Utzon's Sydney Opera House. Starck has sold an extraordinary number of this iconic product, and yet probably most owners are unlikely to have ever tried to use it. But this whimsical, mock 1950s science fiction rocket does appeal to the playful kid inside otherwise very serious grownups (Lloyd and Snelders, 2003). It actually captured the spirit of the day amazingly well, demonstrating the feeling of freedom that creative people felt as they shook off the yoke of an all-too-restrictive modernism. And it was one of the harbingers of a whole host of playful products for a new generation of grownups who wanted to hold on to their childhood (which later came to include terrifically expensive statuettes of old cartoon characters). Its utter simplicity helps it achieve a timeless quality.

Utzon's great building in Sydney Harbour must surely be one of the most admired, loved and famous pieces of architecture of the twentieth century. It not only seems so right in its location, as it has transformed the image

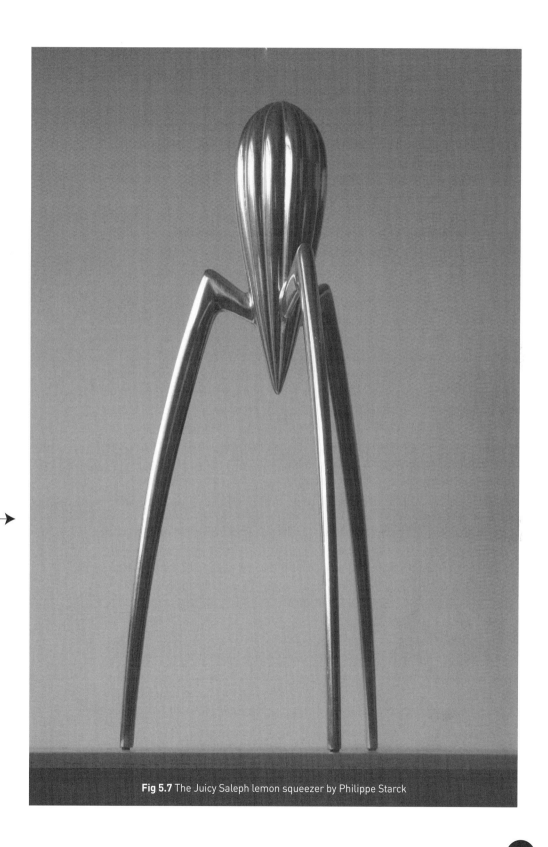

Fig 5.7 The Juicy Saleph lemon squeezer by Philippe Starck

of Australian culture, it now stands as a visual symbol for not just the city but the whole nation. It changed our understanding of what buildings could do, predating by many years the Bilbao effect named after Frank Gehry's extraordinary gallery. This effect is now well-documented as an impact on business and activity stimulated by a visionary piece of architecture.

We have already seen Richard MacCormac referring to this building earlier in this chapter. It is interesting here that this reference was not to the building as an opera house. It is probably fair to say that, although this incredible building broke new ground in many ways, it did not do so in the technical functional arena. MacCormac refers to a simple idea of form here; the floating sculptural forms sitting on a very firm base. This is surely an example of an architectural design gambit. It is identifiable as an idea that can be applied in a wide range of contexts.

pg.175

Of course we can see that the sailing boats in Sydney Harbour that are supposed to have inspired Utzon also have this characteristic. One of Utzon's many visionary ideas in this building was to take a fundamental form out of one context and use it in another. It certainly required some situation-based thinking to be done. Not only did Utzon create the athletic overlapping shell forms but he managed to incorporate the normally problematic fly towers of a theatre inside them without us noticing. Such masterly strokes of genius in design often look obvious in retrospect; a little like the way the tightrope walkers at the circus make the high-wire act seem easy.

pg.69

Almost as famous as the successes are the technical and functional deficiencies of Utzon's design. It has been well-documented that even the architect had little idea of how to actually construct the building once the competition was won. One very basic problem was that, at that time, no one knew how to calculate the location in space of all the points on the irregularly curved surfaces of the great sails. The famous solution to this conundrum was in itself a remarkable piece of creative thinking. The earlier irregularly curved surfaces were rendered as parts of the same imaginary sphere. This not only solved the mathematical problem of how to plot the points of the roof in space but also gave a perceptual orderliness to the design that seems to be part of its enduring attraction. In fact, we now have the mathematics and computer software to construct the irregular surfaces of the original design. Interestingly, in a personal communication the architect has said that, even given this, he still prefers the rationalised design as constructed.

At the time that the competition prize was awarded there was no guarantee that such a solution could be found. The history has been well-documented; companies were going bankrupt, people were losing their jobs, the

Fig 5.8 Sydney Opera House by Jørn Utzon

architect left the project and the whole business became something of a cause célèbre. The total cost of the building and time taken to construct escalated so many times that new funding sources were needed. Lotteries were created, new contractors employed and other architects completed the interior.

Even now the building has serious acoustical deficiencies especially in the concert hall, problems of access, and inadequate backstage space and circulation. These matters are hardly peripheral to an opera house and concert hall, and yet the building is seen as a huge success. Why? Perhaps only the very greatest vision can be enough to compensate for such deep-rooted flaws. The fundamental form of the building, sitting as it does jutting out into Sydney Harbour, still takes away the breath of hordes of first-time tourists and draws many others back to admire the bravery of this extraordinary building.

pg.175

In product design, the big visionary breakthroughs tend to be less obviously identifiable because they give rise to a new series of developments. Unlike buildings, they do not always stand still to be admired. We can think here of the Moulton folding bicycle that solved many problems inherent in earlier folding bikes in a quite revolutionary way. The Brompton and others have followed in its path. The Sony Walkman is another one, and the first mobile personal sound system which really revolutionised the way we listen to music in our daily lives. The iPod and other digital MP3 devices have taken over since then. Although Alec Issigonis is forever associated with the Mini, the names of the visionaries behind many of these products will never reach the general public (oddly enough, CEOs like Steve Jobs are the figureheads of these developments). Because product design is such an intensely collaborative effort these days the 'star' designers who everybody knows often concern themselves with comparatively simple products, like furniture, where an individual can still have an overriding impact.

In order to understand our love affair with visionary design and the inconsistency of many attitudes towards competence in design it is useful to explore the notion of risk. Perhaps we admire such great pieces of design precisely because they were simultaneously more pioneering and more risky than is normally expected. Would we admire a brain surgeon for taking high level risks in order to pioneer a new method of operating on the brain? Almost certainly we would expect the innovations in such an area to be brought in much more gradually and cautiously. Would Herman Hertzberger see the outcomes here as 'real' or only 'fake' creativity? This kind of visionary work is undoubtedly of huge value to the field in progressing ideas. It can perhaps be seen to be analogous to a chess master inventing a wholly new gambit. The knowledge created will be analysed and discussed. Whether it actually worked in detail, or won the game, in this pioneering case seems almost immaterial. Clients of such visionary design may feel ambivalent about the outcome.

It is clear that Utzon's work in Sydney is much loved by people all over the world and of huge value to the Sydney Opera House (Watson, 2006). Although the financial problems may be largely behind them, the operators continue to struggle with the poor acoustics and circulation problems. A new set of interiors have been proposed but such work would be enormously expensive not just in capital cost terms but in lost revenue as the house is closed for several seasons. This visionary building continues to delight and infuriate at the same time!

REFERENCES

Adelson, B. (1981). **Problem solving and the development of abstract categories in programming languages.** Memory and Cognition 9(4): 422–433.

Ahmed, S., Wallace, K.M. and Blessing, L.T.M. (2003). **Understanding the differences between how novices and experienced designers approach design tasks.** Research in Engineering Design 14(1): 1–11.

Brand, S. (1995). **How Buildings Learn: What happens after they're built.** Harmondsworth, Penguin.

Chase, W.G. and Simon, H.A. (1973). **Perception in chess.** Cognitive Psychology 4: 55–81.

Chi, M.T.H., Feltovich, P.J. and Glaser, R. (1981). **Categorization and representation of physics problems by experts and novices.** Cognitive Science 5: 121–152.

Chi, M.T.H. and Koeske, R. (1983). **Network representation of a child's dinosaur knowledge.** Developmental Psychology 19: 29–39.

Cross, N. (1990). **The nature and nurture of the design ability.** Design Studies 11(3): 127–140.

De Groot, A.D. (1965). **Thought and Choice in Chess.** The Hague, Mouton.

Durling, D., Cross, N. and Johnson, J.H. (1996). **Personality and learning preferences of students in design and design-related disciplines.** International Conference on Design and Technology Educational Research, IDATER96, Loughborough University.

Eckert, C. and Stacey, M. (2000). **Sources of Inspiration: A language of design.** Design Studies 21(5): 523–538.

Flynn, J.R. (1987). **Massive IQ Gains in 14 Nations: What IQ tests really measure.** Psychological Bulletin 101: 177–191.

Gardner, H. (1983). **Frames of Mind: The theory of multiple intelligences.** London, Heinemann.

Getzels, J.W. and Jackson, P.W. (1962). **Creativity and Intelligence: Explorations with gifted children.** New York, John Wiley.

Gibson, J.J. (1986). **An Ecological Approach to Visual Perception.** Hillsdale, N.J., Lawrence Erlbaum.

Hinsley, D.A., Hayes, J.R. and Simon, H.A. (1978). **From words to equations: meaning and representation in algebra word problems.** Cognitive Processes in Comprehension. P.A. Carpenter and M.A. Just. Hillsdale, N.J., Erlbaum.

Hirshberg, J. (1998). **The Creative Priority.** New York, Harper Business.

Hudson, L. (1966). **Contrary Imaginations: A psychological study of the English schoolboy.** London, Methuen.

Khaidzir, K.A.M. (2007). **An expertise study of cognitive interactions between tutors and students in design tutorial conversations.** Architecture. Sheffield, University of Sheffield. PhD.

Kirton, M., ed. (1989). **Adaptors and Innovators: Styles of creativity and problem solving.** New York, Routledge.

Lawson, B.R. (1993). **Parallel Lines of Thought.** Languages of Design 1(4): 357–366.

Lawson, B.R. (2001). **The context of mind. Designing in Context.** P. Lloyd and H. Christiaans. Delft, DUP Science: 133–148.

Lawson, B.R. (2006). **How Designers Think** (4th Edition). Oxford, Architectural Press (an imprint of Elsevier).

Lloyd, P.A. and Snelders, H.M.J.J. (2003). **What was Philipe Starck thinking of**. Design Studies 23: 237–253.

Loewy, R. (2000). **Industrial Design**. London, Laurence King Publishing.

MacKinnon, D.W. (1962). **The nature and nurture of creative talent**, Yale University.

Maguire, R. (1971). **Nearness to need**. RIBA Journal 78(4).

Miller, G.A. (1956). **The magic number seven, plus or minus two**. Psychological Review 63: 81–97.

Schön, D.A. and Wiggins, G. (1992). **Kinds of seeing and their function in designing**. Design Studies 13(2): 135–156.

Sutton, R.I. and Hargardon, A. (1996). **Brainstorming groups in context: effectiveness in a product design firm**. Administrative Science Quarterly 41: 685–718.

Tovey, M. (1992). **Automotive stylists' design thinking**. Research in Design Thinking. N. Cross, K. Dorst and N. Roozenburg. Delft, Delft University Press: 87–98.

Valkenburg, R.C. (2000). **The Reflective Practice in product design teams**. Delt, Technical University of Delft.

Watson, A., ed. (2006). **Building a Masterpiece: the Sydney Opera House**. Sydney, Lund Humphries.

6

EDUCATING
DESIGNERS

 To make this painting took me 10
minutes and 80 years.
SENGAI (JAPANESE MASTER-PAINTER)

Learning is finding out what you already know.
Doing is demonstrating that you know it. Teaching
is reminding others that they know it as well as
you. We are all learners, doers, and teachers.
RICHARD DAVID BACH

THE LIMITS OF FORMAL EDUCATION

A common misconception about design education is that it is actually some form of training for practice. The excerpts from employers' letters complaining about the capability of graduates clearly suggest that they see the university as a training ground for their practice. They expect the graduate to have reached a level of expertise that guarantees competence. But it can never be that way for several reasons.

Firstly, the design fields are so wide that such a training could never be specialised enough to satisfy every employer. For example, within architecture alone there is a huge range of special expertise needed among individual practitioners. Some might concentrate on small-scale buildings and others on huge complexes such as hospitals or airports. Some might be more concerned with the preservation, conservation or adaptive re-use of fine old buildings; some might be experts in sustainable design, some more technical and some more managerial and so one. Industrial designers deal with everything from small-scale environments right down to hand-held devices. Some of their work might be almost manufacturing engineering, others working on the interfaces of electronic devices, and others may be form stylists.

Secondly, we have a problem of expectation. Our exploration of design expertise in this book suggests that there are many layers of expertise to develop well beyond that which can be attained by the graduate. We saw right at the start of this book how the design professions themselves recognise 'young' designers as being much older than their counterparts in the sciences and engineering.

Thirdly, the university is hardly an ideal location in which to train people for practice. Actually, by far the best place to do that is in practice. There are just so many features of the commercial, legal and technical world of practice that cannot easily be simulated in academia. Getting things made is often extremely difficult and even finding real clients and users is highly problematic.

Timing also makes it impractical to train designers to be completely competent professional practitioners in university degree courses. We live in such a rapidly changing world that this simply is not feasible. Imagine training a first year architecture student to use a particular piece of CAD software. By the time this student finally qualifies some six years later, not only will the software be out-of-date but industry will most likely have taken to a new generation of computing technology.

STUDENTS ARE NOT WHAT THEY WERE
EMPLOYERS' COMPLAINING LETTERS

The following are extracted from letters
by employers of design graduates:

(I ask) whether the basics are being taught properly in
order that the products of our schools of architecture are
equipped adequately to progress in whichever facet of
modern professional practice they choose to work in. Key
subjects now include accurate cost forecasting, reducing
operating costs... For a large variety of reasons architectural
education has let slip some of these (basic subjects) and
this, accompanied by a growing belief that we do not need to
design to suit the material any more but we use or develop
materials which do what we want them to do, has led to
the development of the 'concept' which can be anything
from what somebody thinks the building might actually
look like to what somebody would like the building to look
like. This trend is not particular to architectural training
but is noticeable also in product design and fashion.

The student of today needs extensive supervision. I have to
check all his drawings. It is all very well encouraging students
to come up with wacky ideas but the universities really need to
concentrate on covering the basic competencies first. Without
that their graduates are increasingly unemployable by practice.

Finally, what students really need from their university education is some sort of foundation or platform upon which they can build their lifelong learning and expertise development. If they are expected to perform to the timetables and commercial demands of practice too soon they are likely to be unable to see past the very conventions that creative designers delight in challenging.

So for the remainder of this chapter we shall discuss design education rather than design training. The two models that teachers and students might have in their minds about what happens in a university design degree course offer a useful way of thinking about this.

MOVING THROUGH LAYERS OF EXPERTISE

So far in this book we have argued that expertise is not acquired in some continuous seamless manner but that there appear to be more or less distinct layers of expertise. Moreover, we have argued that those layers characteristically enable quite different modes of thinking and action. The transitions between the layers are of particular interest to us in this chapter; they must be key points in the journey towards becoming a designer. If this is so then one of the most important functions of an educational system must surely be to facilitate transition from one layer of expertise to the next. But this may be no easy challenge.

VISIONARY VISION/
MASTER MASTERMA!
EXPERT EXPERTEXPER1
COMPETENT COMPETENT
ADVANCED BEGINNER ADVA
BEGINNER BEGINNERBEGINN
NOVICE NOVICENOVICENOVICEN

pg. 101

From our study of expertise we might reasonably expect novice students to use largely rule-based and convention-based thinking. We might hope that, as they progress, students would learn to use situation-based thinking and by the time they graduate they will have added strategy-based thinking to their range of cognitive approaches. Each of these layers represents a different way of problem solving, a specific layer of abstraction (in analysis and synthesis), and a specific kind of reflection. They could hardly be more different. Formal university education is clearly expected to facilitate this development but often, we suspect, this is hardly made explicit.

pg. 69

The distinct and different nature of the expertise layers must make the transitions between them a challenging time for the student. How can one let go of one way of thinking, and adopt a new one? What happens at these transition moments? Or are the transitions just a figment of our own theoretical imagination, brought about by an expertise model that posits distinct layers of expertise while, in practice, there is no such thing? If the 'layers of expertise' were to intermingle, the whole transition from one layer to another could be a very smooth process, to the point of being unobservable.

MODELS OF DESIGN EDUCATION

I ask my fresher students to imagine two
models of design education.

In the first they are effectively some kind of raw
material and the university is a production line that
somehow turns them into a finished product.

In the second they see the university as a secret cave,
the walls of which are encrusted with precious jewels.
The degree course they are on will provide them
with the tools they need to dig out those jewels.

From our own practice, and observations made by our colleagues in design schools, we would hold that these transitions do indeed exist in reality, and that they can be quite dramatic events that are crucial in the growth of a designer. We see our students go through periods of absolute confusion when an old and cherished way of working is being undermined, and moments of exhilaration when they find and grasp a new handle on design reality. Tutoring this transition process is a subtle art. However, we are getting ahead of ourselves. Just as earlier in the book we reviewed what is known about the design process, now we must explore design education as it is currently practiced.

THE NATURE OF DESIGN EDUCATION

There is a very odd thing about design education that we need to address. The two authors of this book come from different design fields (industrial design and architecture); we are natives of different countries (Netherlands and UK) and thus were educated in different languages. Between us we have taught in design departments in many fields and in many countries. The odd thing is this. When we go into a design department in a university anywhere in the world we immediately feel 'at home' to a considerable extent. We understand a lot about what is going on, how things are being organised, about the way students are progressed and staff are teaching. And yet if we go into a different kind of department in our own universities we often feel in a strange and foreign world. Why is this? Why are there so many shared features of design departments? What can this tell us?

One thing it might seem to tell us is that design education is really pretty well sorted out. Surely such a common system is unlikely collectively to be wrong or badly adapted to its situation? Indeed there is often a feeling around in design education circles that it is ahead of the game as it were. After all, it relies heavily on project work, appears student-led, takes place in a social context and explores and develops individual talent and creativity. Are these not all very modern educational ideas?

And yet there is now a growing feeling that all is not as well as it might be. A particularly reflective and articulate architectural graduate, Laura Willenbrock, describes her own emerging doubts 'Architectural education, I sensed, was deemed nobler than other areas of study because of its bimodality of technical skill balanced with design artistry. I suspected an elitism among architecture professionals, and perhaps even higher echelon upon which architecture academics posed' (Willenbrock, 1991). Now while it is entirely possible that Laura was a thoroughly lazy and truculent

THE DESIGN 'TEACHING HOSPITAL'

Some have proposed that we should have design practices associated with our universities paralleling the role a teaching hospital plays in medical education. Sadly this is impractical. The average medical school hospital probably has at least 300 beds and hundreds of day patients. Each of these effectively offers a kind of project. Thus a medical student can, at any time, see a pretty comprehensive range of syndromes and stages of treatment. The average design practice may have perhaps half a dozen projects on the go at once and each may last for months or years.

student, it seems more likely from her subsequent analysis that her perceptions were initially sensitised by transferring onto the course from a liberal arts degree in International Studies. Her concerns began to develop about the 'way we were being directed towards knowledge' but she trusted her tutors sufficiently to continue with her studies. We shall return to her observations later; first we need to review the system of which she, like so many design students, was part.

THE BEGINNINGS OF FORMAL DESIGN EDUCATION

Design education as we see it today is a relative newcomer to our university systems. Most of the design fields as we know them today grew out of the business of making things and were thus craft-based until relatively recently. In earlier times people who created buildings were stonemasons rather than architects, and the makers of products were blacksmiths and carpenters rather than industrial designers. These craftsmen trained their apprentices in their own workshops. They literally learned by doing, and they did it on the job.

In the early days of formal education the association of design and particularly architecture with the art schools took us in something of a different direction. The famous original École des Beaux-Arts, founded in Paris back in the seventeenth century, gave rise to a model of teaching fine art and architecture based around a highly conventional pattern of progressive exercises.

The most significant restructuring of design education came with the revolutionary school of art, design and architecture at the Bauhaus. Formed in 1919 at Weimar, though later moved to Dessau and eventually Berlin, this one school was to set the scene for much of our contemporary design curricula. It elevated design to sit alongside fine art as an equal intellectual activity. The agenda was very much informed by an ideological ambition to connect art and industry. The modern art of that time was moving towards abstraction and industry was moving towards simplification. The same intellectual agenda (connecting art and industry) would probably now lead to very different results.

In addition to this ideological position about design, the most revolutionary pedagogical change was to move away from the single pupil-teacher relationship of the École to a community working and learning together environment. One of the key features of today's design schools, the studio, was born. Originally the Bauhaus under Gropius and Meyer also had an

THE BAUHAUS
WIM BROENEBOOM

The philosophy of the Bauhaus is for me soberness, demureness, those are the terms that describe it best for me... Of course we know it was not meant that way. But still, this is an important inspiration for me. It is just that those statements can become a dogma, like much in life, if you take them too seriously. You have to be able to let go... I have always considered the Bauhaus to be a basis. I can still work with it very well. I never felt it as a limitation. I am still inspired by the issues that were made explicit there.

explicitly social mission. It believed in designing for the ordinary citizen and was essentially a fraternal organisation. The influence spread throughout Europe with many teachers moving into the Soviet Union, at least partly on political grounds. In turn, the influence spread from the United Kingdom throughout the old British Empire particularly to Australasia and South Africa but also later to the newer countries of Singapore and Malaysia. Many of the early Bauhaus scholars moved west to the USA. Not only did Moholgy-Nagy open the New Bauhaus in Chicago but Albers went to Yale and Gropius to Harvard and later Mies van der Rohe arrived at the Illinois Institute of Technology.

Another German school, the relatively short-lived but highly influential HfG Ulm, took things on in Europe during the late fifties and sixties. It particularly focused on mass production and a re-statement of social objectives which had perhaps become overtaken by more stylistic concerns in the later years of the Bauhaus. It too was to be associated with a style before long. Manufacturers such as Braun and Krupps, with their rejection of ornament and use of simple geometric lines, took up the thinking of the Ulm school and have influenced much contemporary industrial design through the internationalisation of markets so characteristic of the late twentieth century.

DESIGN EDUCATION TODAY

So we can see how the tentacles of the Bauhaus and Ulm originally reached around the world, but more than this the influence has lasted and persisted in many aspects of our design schools. In parallel we can see the rise of Modernism and thus a view developing across the educational system that being a good designer meant being a Modernist. While many would argue that we have moved on from this global approval of Modernism, it could be that the educational systems we have inherited still have Modernist assumptions embedded in them.

Although Modernism was rather viewed at the time as being a full stop at the end of design history, it has in fact turned out to be just another stylistic period. That period, they would argue, has now passed and that while there may no longer be a single dominant ideology, stylistic belief systems still pervade much design education. Bond argues that the profession of architecture has undergone enormous change since the Bauhaus but that the architectural curriculum is still based on the same assumptions (Dutton, 1991a). Beyond the idea of a style of form we can certainly identify a number of huge changes in western ideas and values that might be thought to require adjustments in the skills and knowledge needed by the designers of today.

Among the most significant of these would be the advent of the computer and Internet changing working practices, access to knowledge, communications systems and shifting power from centralised to personalised sources. The development of the application of social sciences to our understanding not just of the way designed objects are used but also of the impact of them on our quality of life leading to the new challenges of evidence-based design. The massive changes taking place in our attitudes to resources and sustainability impacting not just on manufacturing methods but on the very way in which designed objects consume resources during their life; ideas about the empowerment of users and the potential participatory role of users in the creation of large-scale design such as public and social architecture. All of these can be seen to impact on some parts of the curricula of design courses, but usually only on the periphery rather than at the core. We shall return to this point in a later section of this chapter.

So what are the common features of our contemporary design schools; why have they survived in so many places and how well do they really work? There are at least four features we want to identify here and explore. They are the *Studio*, the *Design Tutorial*, the *Crit* and the use of the *Library*. We are going to suggest that these are such strong and common features that they are embodiments of the nature of design as a cognitive activity. However, we shall also find that, for the very same reason, they can easily become 'sacred cows'. As a result, these fundamental features of design education are often not reviewed critically and can eventually become counter-productive. Analysing them in terms of our model of design expertise may give us the opportunity to identify both the undoubted strengths and possible weaknesses of these features and move towards a refreshed view of design education.

THE STUDIO

The studio is perhaps simultaneously the most important and yet most confusing of these 'big four' design education features. When an academic calls for 'more computers in the studio' this is almost certainly a plea about facilities in the physical space. A colleague may also express concern about 'whether year 2 Studio C is functioning as creatively as usual'. This is likely to be a question about a much more abstract concept. The design studio then is not just a physical place but also a social and cultural one. Indeed, these very social and cultural features of it are amongst its most important and precious characteristics. There are perhaps five major features of the design studio that we need to explore here. They are 'co-location', 'learning by doing', 'unrestricted timetable', 'integration' and 'mimicking practice'.

THE STUDIO
CO-LOCATION

The studio is usually a physical place that becomes a hive of activity. One might also see it as a marketplace for ideas. The fact that both students and, for periods of time, tutors are co-located is one of the most important characteristics. Referring back to the images of university studios in Chapter 1 makes this very clear. The clothes and some social norms may have changed over the years but the place remains essentially the same.

Students know that this is a place where things happen, where knowledge can be found and advice given, where like minds will meet and share reasonably common values. Usually, but not always, students have personal places to work in the studio allowing them to work both privately and publicly. Often though, students report the need, at times, to be more private than this arrangement allows and to retire to working in their own entirely private world. This combination of private and public seems extremely important in the development of design ideas and progression of design learning. The nature of design is such that early ideas can be fragile and easily demolished by robust debate. However, the student also often wants to test those very ideas out on others to get feedback. Being able to control the private and public domain of their work is thus vital to the learning environment.

Often the students will have far more contact with each other than directly with staff and may expect to exchange ideas extensively with their peers. In this sense the studio is a delightful example of the social community that was introduced so powerfully by the Bauhaus. It inherits the quality of a 'community of scholars' out of which so many of our oldest and most distinguished universities grew. Students may even teach each other quite specific skills such as computing, drawing and so on which they inevitably begin with unequally and may acquire at a different rate. Without the physical location such learning is likely to be far less effective. Universities often want to save money on the space devoted to studios since the senior non-design-based staff cannot see the formal timetabled activity that demands such accommodation. It is of course the totally informal and open quality of the studio that makes it such a valuable resource in a design school.

In the studio, students work very much on their own approaches to shared problem situations. They support each other in learning how to find solutions that lie inside the value system of the studio or unit. Because of the iconoclastic culture of design schools, they also compete to find the extreme edges of this in order to give their work identity. This might be seen to be a process similar to the MAYA notion already discussed earlier in this book, though in

BOUNDARIES OF ACCEPTABILITY
INDUSTRIAL DESIGN STUDENT

I do not know my own style, although the tutors seem to agree: I do not see it. What I do see is that it is nothing like the trendy 'style of the day'. That looks nice but I just cannot do it, and people take it against you...as if you are wearing clothes of 10 years ago.

DUTCH INDUSTRIAL DESIGN STUDENTS' REFLECTIONS
Industrial design students at the Design Academy of Eindhoven were asked to write reflective short pieces on their own experience of learning to design. These comments are excerpts from them.

the hands of students it is likely to be far more adventurous. Indeed, design students often seem like naughty children, pushing back the boundaries of acceptable behaviour to find out just how far they can go. Education must surely encourage such an attitude which may then need to be constrained by a little more discipline in professional practice. The Dutch industrial design student quoted here seems to be struggling with this very difficulty while trying to understand and develop a personal voice inside the studio.

An interesting question here is the extent to which the physical co-location of people in a studio can be augmented or even replaced by virtual worlds. In recent times a number of what are effectively chat rooms or discussion forums have sprung up in the design community. Some more formal work has been developed by researchers such as Mary Lou Maher on the use of virtual worlds (Maher et al., 2006). These virtual studios offer a number of apparent benefits such as anonymity, privacy from tutors, ability to work in multiple time zones, both asynchronous and synchronous forms of communication and many other more minor differences. The concomitant features of loss of non-verbal communication, cumbersome interfaces and unreliability of respondents are obvious major concerns. We are probably only at the very beginning of developing these ideas and are yet to see how such media might really work alongside the physical studio. Already though it is clear that such virtual studios can take on their own sub-cultures and, if they are to be useful devices organised within the curriculum, there are many questions about how they can be shaped and managed without losing many of their other advantages.

We must be careful not to adopt rose-coloured spectacles when it comes to the society of the studio. This whole notion is effectively based on the idea of a community of scholars, all working with a common set of values and objectives. However, Dutton has questioned this. In his view the studio often turns out to be hierarchical in its social structure and to have a competitive culture rather than a collaborative one (Dutton, 1991b).

Dutton's concern about hierarchy is that while modern educationalists tend to argue in favour of dialogue as a key tool, dominance by one party leads to much less good results. The axiomatic sets of theoretical ideas that are often found in the studio, especially in unit versions of the studio, create a huge imbalance of power. Here the tutor effectively owns the intellectual agenda and controls the language and concepts deemed to be useful in the discussion. The quote from a Dutch industrial design student reflects exactly this problem. This is hardly the ideal circumstance for a dialogue to take place.

IMBALANCE OF STUDIO POWER
INDUSTRIAL DESIGN STUDENT

As a student you sometimes see that assignments are dominated by the tutor. The tutor then clearly lets you know where his preferences lie, and limits you as a student in developing your own way. But you do want to deliver a result that will give you good marks.

Dutton also argues that academic staff often regard competition 'as indispensable to studio culture'. This argument holds that the competitive element is what really motivates students to produce better work not through collaboration but by pitting the students against each other. This certainly seems to match much experience of studios all over the world and can be seen as having both positive and negative aspects. While it may indeed drive students to work harder it also implicitly views design ideas as the personal property of individuals. It certainly seems that students are often unwilling to take and build on each other's ideas for exactly this reason and thus may do far less interacting about their work during projects than is somewhat fancifully assumed. It may also not help to prepare students for the skills of collaborative working that they must inevitably acquire to be successful in practice; more of that in the next chapter.

THE STUDIO
UNTIMETABLED ACTIVITY

The main use of the studio is usually in large blocks of otherwise unstructured time. Undoubtedly, there are both scheduled and unscheduled events happening in studios. These may be tutorials, crits, meetings, and so on. There may also be visits, trips and other activities taking place away from the physical space of the studio itself. More importantly though the bulk of studio time is not scheduled at all but free for design activity. Again it is this very freedom that is valuable here. We have seen that design is not an activity that can be scheduled. We cannot predict how long any particular phase of designing will take and indeed different students will require varying lengths of time. Again this apparent lack of structure often puzzles uninformed senior university management who, not surprisingly, question the value piece of real estate sitting apparently waiting for something to happen. Important and influential visitors, often ones holding budgets, seem to have a knack of arriving to look around studios at the very time the students are not there!

Along with this apparently unstructured timetable we frequently find a culture of using time that is quite distinctive. Students are often to be found working late at night in the studio, particularly towards the end of projects. They are after all learning the skill of managing their time here. This is a much more difficult skill to acquire in design than in subjects where activities can be scheduled and give allocated time slots. Managing an academic design department often leads one into battles with estates offices, safety offices, porters, cleaners and other service staff who are both puzzled by this erratic behaviour and frustrated by being unable to timetable their own

STUDENT ACCESS TO THE STUDIOS

In a university that one of the authors worked at, the students were not allowed into the building housing the studio after 6 pm. This was deemed to be for security reasons. Of course they cheated and copied keys, propped doors open and creatively entered through fire escapes. There were even instructions on how to get in during the night posted on the Internet. After much argument, the authorities partially relented and allowed the post-graduates in until 9 pm. Thus access to the studios was seen as some sort of privilege of seniority rather than an essential educational need.

activities. Long and unpredictable hours are quite common and universities struggle to provide the physical place on a twenty-four-seven basis as is often seen desirable.

In the UK, while women comprise nearly 40% of the intake of university architecture courses they only comprise 13% of the profession; in the USA, 20% of architects are women but in Australia this is only 10%. It seems that the relatively high drop-out begins at university, and in a number of studies respondents have cited the studio culture and hours as a major contributory factor (Morrow, 2000). However, this distortion in the gender balance is not really seen on other design courses and this suggests that the rather male-dominated construction industry and the length of architecture degrees may also be playing roles here.

Ismail bin Samsuddin has been studying this studio culture and its role in design education (Samsuddin, 2008). Common characteristics of the studio as identified by him include a rather free and relaxed atmosphere in general. The unrestricted timetable is often favoured with events being organised as required and on demand rather than planned well in advance. Adherence to deadlines is often seen as secondary to producing good results. In other words to be good and late is often a more successful and admired strategy than being poor and punctual.

Because the studio is largely based around design projects it also has the potential to develop an all embracing timeless set of demands on the student. Unlike the kind of work done in apparently parallel settings such as the engineering laboratory class, the studio cannot be realistically timetabled. We have seen that there is no definitive moment when a design can be said to be finished. University projects finish because the tutors have imposed a submission deadline rather like a design competition. But work on such projects cannot be restricted to timetabled periods. Students who undergo a degree course that has access to the studio available throughout the course thus hardly ever experience periods when they are free of design projects. In many cases, these design projects will also be the longest major pieces of work encountered so far in their lives and thus they have little experience of managing them.

The Dutch industrial design student quoted here surely reflects this problem of the studio project dominating not just time and effort but emotion and motivation. This can easily lead to a failure to attend other more formal parts of their course such as lectures; an experience common towards the end of major design projects. Even more likely is that design students will

THE ALL-EMBRACING PROJECT
INDUSTRIAL DESIGN STUDENT

The period of two weeks before the crit (assessment) until the crit itself I find the most captivating. Everybody is busy, and when you work in a group you find out that now is the time to take decisions. In these moments you really get to know each other and that is when we are, I think, most immersed in design.

After having worked with each other intensely for weeks on end, and after everybody has worked the last three days and nights, then you get to the crit. You present, you wait all day and at the end of the day you get the word, whether you made it or not... But then!

Then you get to the really awful period when everybody has had enough of design school and you hardly see each other for three to four weeks. Deadly for your motivation, because of the rush you were in the weeks before means that you loose all energy for a couple of weeks. Back to the sluggish tempo in which you started the semester.

How does this happen? Design should be captivating without the design school assignments and assessments? It would be great to be able to just work on. Why can't we do it?

neglect other untimetabled activities such as reading. Whether such a pattern offers a sound educational environment must surely be open to debate.

THE STUDIO
INTEGRATION

When Sheffield University first developed a dual degree in structural engineering and architecture the two groups of staff had to learn a little about the pedagogical practices of their new colleagues. For a while the engineers struggled to understand the idea of studio. It was tempting for them to see it as a parallel with what they called lab classes. At first sight they seemed similar. Both were highly practical and involved student-led problem solving. However, the lab classes were usually inside modules, whereas the studios were modules in themselves. This very important difference showed that in engineering a lab class is a practical exploration of some theoretical principles probably first developed in the lecture theatre. There would be lab classes accompanying many of the lecture courses. The design studio, however, is not inside a theoretical subject but rather a way of integrating the ideas from many subjects. Indeed it introduces many ideas of its own.

pg.127

It is this very integrative quality of the studio that probably is one of the major reasons for its success and persistence. In Chapter 2 we saw how design problems and solutions map onto each other in very confusing ways. So much so that in this book we really prefer to talk of 'design situations' rather than always distinguish between and separate the two. We saw how design solutions are often integrated responses to multiple complex sets of requirements, specifications, demands, needs and feelings. The studio is exquisitely designed to promote an atmosphere in which so many factors are considered at once and in which creative innovation is valued.

pg.51

However, it is this very central characteristic of integration that our model of design expertise may lead us to question. There can be no doubt that integration is not just desirable but absolutely essential. The ability to integrate must surely be one of the most difficult design skills that we have identified here. For many students it probably does not just happen. So the question is this. How much integration should be required and in what way in each studio design project? The answer to that is it must frame much of the pedagogical pattern for the course.

We have seen many instances of design courses where this issue is left virtually unexplored. It is somehow assumed that we must set projects demanding integration and that somehow students will achieve it. Perhaps we should

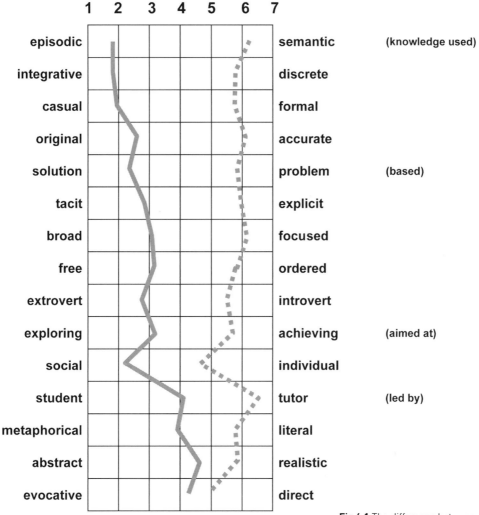

	1	2	3	4	5	6	7		
episodic								semantic	(knowledge used)
integrative								discrete	
casual								formal	
original								accurate	
solution								problem	(based)
tacit								explicit	
broad								focused	
free								ordered	
extrovert								introvert	
exploring								achieving	(aimed at)
social								individual	
student								tutor	(led by)
metaphorical								literal	
abstract								realistic	
evocative								direct	

Fig 6.1 The difference between a design studio (solid line) and an engineering lab class (dashed line)

THE STUDIO AND THE LAB CLASS
ISHMAIL BIN SAMSUDDIN

Ismail bin Samsuddin studied students taking a dual degree course in structural engineering and architecture. After running a series of focus group workshops with the students he drew up a series of semantic differential adjectival scales that reflected the topics of their conversations. He then asked the students to use these scales to describe their experience of the design studio in architecture and the lab class in engineering. The scales have been shuffled to show the greatest psychological gap between the two at the top and the smallest at the bottom. It is interesting to note that the integrative-discrete scale exhibits the second largest difference. The greatest difference is about episodic versus semantic knowledge, a theme we have often returned to throughout this book.

more carefully target design exercises, constructing an agenda behind them that emphasises the building of one particular bridge between different domains within the design situation. Multiple targeted design challenges could add up to giving the student a better feeling for what is needed to attain complete integration.

THE STUDIO
LEARNING BY DOING

The studio is usually associated with both teaching styles and learning styles. The teaching styles used still very much adhere to the pattern set down in the École Des Beaux-Arts and reinforced by both the Bauhaus and Ulm Schools. Students are generally set a series of design projects that are seen by the tutors as getting progressively more difficult. This degree of difficulty is often associated with the extent to which integration is expected. Thus more difficult projects are often those that require resolutions between conflicting demands of quite unrelated constraints.

The learning style is thus dominated by the idea of learning by doing. Students may be given extensive formal education in a whole series of specialist subjects and this is usually done outside the studio. Design history, technologies, legal and managerial subjects are often taught this way. Some specific skills such as graphics, use of computers, physical modelling and so on may be taught in concentrated workshop sessions. However, most design schools still teach relatively little material in terms of the essential and central skills of designing that we have identified here. Students are simply expected to pick these up through a process of learning on the job as it were. This was literally the case in the apprenticeship model of design education. In academia the studio has become a substitute for that real-world design apprenticeship. The question is: has it really improved upon it?

There is then a paradox here that Ken Yeang is clearly referring to. Probably the most important thing for a student is to acquire the expertise needed for designing. We have also seen that experts generally operate apparently intuitively, and certainly much less self-consciously than their more novice counterparts. Because leading designers are not normally articulate about their processes, this may seem to make design somehow unteachable. However, there are many other fields requiring sophisticated skills where experts work unselfconsciously in which it is normal to teach by breaking them down into subcomponents. Is it the very integrated nature of design that makes us less willing to teach design in this deconstructed manner? Our concern that

WHICH PROBLEM TO SOLVE FIRST?
KEN YEANG

You can't teach a student to design but you can teach him to develop a sense of intuition, what he feels is right. I agree with Charles Chorea. In any project there are so many problems you can solve. You can solve squatter problems, you can solve accommodation problems, you can solve points of view but which problems you are to solve first is a gut feeling, and so you have to develop intuition. The best designers have got the best intuition in the world and I sort of sympathise with that because when you are teaching you are really developing intuition and confidence.

students must learn to integrate perhaps blinds us to other possible routes through the earlier phases of education.

Herman Hertzberger's comments would suggest an alternative view on this. He clearly articulates a position about students having differential levels of expertise in analysis and synthesis. This would be hardly surprising and a research project at Delft University adds some hard evidence to support this. In any case, we surely all know some excellent design critics who have taken appraisal to a far higher level than their own design solution output suggests.

THE PROBLEM OF ASSESSMENT

A problem associated with these learning styles is that of assessment. Most design degree courses use continuous assessment methods. This means that the major activity used for learning, the design project, is simultaneously the major vehicle for assessment. The studios often call for experimental work and admire iconoclastic work. Thus the student has to balance learning, discovering and experimenting with performing for assessment in the same pieces of work. This is hardly an ideal learning scenario.

But it is not just that each project is simultaneously a vehicle both for learning and performing; it is the very way the marks are assembled together. There are a variety of systems in use here and they are often associated with different countries. The UK generally uses the degree classification system in which all marks are assembled to give the student a simple category of degree ranging from the excellent 'first' down to the very basic 'unclassified pass'. Usually, universities using such a system only rely on marks from the later years of the course to calculate this result. Probably the most aggressive system in its relentless insistence on assessment must be the US-inspired GPA system. The GPA or Grade Point Average is often calculated right from the first project completed in the first year of the course. This has a terrible demotivating effect on those students who enter their final year with an already low GPA. Built into this system is a notion that our model of design expertise enables us to challenge. The assumption is that progress in learning is a steady, risk-free process. It takes no account of the need to go through transition periods between expertise layers that may temporarily cause a dip in performance while learning is very intense.

There are potential solutions to some of these problems. What we might call the 'Formula 1' approach to design projects is just one possible way of tackling this difficulty by creating space for experimentation.

PROBLEMS AND SOLUTIONS
HERMAN HERTZBERGER

I try to say that to all the students, to all the people in my office and it seems to be very difficult to not mix up the questions, what is the problem and what is the solution to the problem. People have somewhere in their brains, the idea that this must be done at once which is not true. Students have a very rotten analysis most of the time. First there must be this question and then you must do the analysis.

FORMULA 1
APPROACH TO ASSESSMENT

Until 2003, the Formula 1 motor racing season consisted of more Grand Prix races than were used in calculating the result of the drivers' championship. This allowed for, and probably encouraged, some experimentation in the design of cars, the risk-taking of the drivers and the teams' management of the race in terms of pit stops. You could have a failure and still not necessarily lose your standing in the championship.

Such an approach could be taken to the overall mark awarded for studio in a semester or academic year. So a number of projects could be set with students counting only the marks from a predetermined smaller number towards their degree result. This might have a very different impact on the students' willingness to explore, learn and develop than the GPA system.

LINKING EXPERTISE IN DIFFERENT FIELDS

A further problem with the studio remains the link between the learning of design skills and the other more formal material. We have seen how design depends greatly on episodic rather than semantic or theoretical knowledge. This has always proved problematic in design degree curriculum development. Some subjects that we may want students to study may have theoretical structures that we wish them to learn or at least appreciate. In such structures, knowledge often builds on previous knowledge in complex ways. Quite simply, until some simpler concepts are studied, the more sophisticated concepts cannot be taught. In such cases pedagogical environments that are not studio-like may be favoured both for reasons to do with the structure of the subject and for efficiency. It might be thought a risky educational strategy to rely on the whole of a theoretical subject being learned through studio projects. Lectures, seminars, lab-classes and many other similar events may be used. A problem here then is that the student is learning highly theoretical material and highly episodic material in different contexts and may find it difficult to integrate these. For example, in schools of architecture it has long been recognised that students can be taught to pass examinations in environmental science with excellent marks but still produce studio designs for highly unsustainable architecture.

SYMBOLIC   EPISODIC

pg.127

Design schools have characteristically battled with this problem. Often the call can be heard to integrate the lecture courses with the design studios, but this is not an easy task. One problem here is that the way some of the more theoretical subjects develop in terms of their knowledge structures is not necessarily sympathetic to the episodic knowledge structure being learned in the studio. An example here would be that of mass housing—one of the most complex projects that can be set in architectural design terms. However, such a project could easily be designed relying only on very simple forms of building construction. Thus the pace of the design and technical construction subjects is not easily resolved in one integrated pedagogical pattern.

One way of moving towards some reconciliation of these styles of learning and kinds of knowledge is to use a case-study approach for at least part of the theoretical subject material. Architects as designers are very reliant on a whole slew of technical consultants to realise their work. Among these, structural engineers are normally far more theory-based than their architectural colleagues. One of the structural engineers most admired by architects of his generation is Tony Hunt. He has successfully collaborated with many of the most well-known architects to produce a huge portfolio of admired buildings. His books show how to present the theoretical knowledge he uses in his work in a case-based approach more useful to architects (Hunt, 1999;

DIFFERENT LEVELS OF EXPERTISE

A design assignment was given to 12 second and 12 final year students of Industrial Design. They had 2.5 hours to come to a design proposal. Each student worked individually, and they were asked to think aloud while designing. The sessions were video recorded for analysis of the design processes and the student's design thinking. They had to develop a litter system for a new Dutch train (see also Chapter 2). The resulting designs were all redrawn on a standard format and judged by a panel of design specialists.

The designs of the 2nd year students were actually judged to be significantly better than those of the final year students! This of course spurned further analysis—it cannot be the goal of a design school to deliver designers to the job market that are worse than when they come in... On further analysis of the tapes a pattern emerged; the 2nd year students worked quite fluently and easily on the design task because they saw a much simpler problem than the final year students. Happily unaware of many complications, they playfully created quite imaginative solutions. Not so the final year students. They all started out on a long analysis of the design situation, actually taking onboard many more of the relevant issues in the problem arena. They made long lists of specifications. But they then apparently lacked the skills to get to a design of sufficient quality within the time available to them. There was an imbalance between their analytic and synthetic skills, and that resulted in particularly poor results.

2003). Perhaps many years of collaborating with architects has given him an intuitive feel for the way they think and know about his own more mathematical subject.

MOVING THROUGH THE EXPERTISE LAYERS AGAIN

There is a silent assumption behind many design curricula that designers by and large develop in a linear way. You learn to become a designer by gradually building up your design knowledge, skills and experience. Even the modern, competency-based learning models of design education in which the student's development is monitored on an individual basis expect students to show a steady progress at every assessment point. But looking at the development of design expertise as it was described in the earlier chapters of this book, we would expect this linear development to be interrupted by dips and leaps-and-bounds. These interruptions are the transitions between the layers of design expertise, and these crucial moments warrant further analysis.

VISIONARY VISION/
MASTER MASTERMA!
EXPERT EXPERTEXPER1
COMPETENT COMPETENT
ADVANCED BEGINNER ADVA
BEGINNER BEGINNERBEGINN
NOVICE NOVICENOVICENOVICEN

pg.101

So our questions here must be 'what is it that provokes these leaps and bounds?' 'What can the studio system do to facilitate both progressive linear development and the more sudden turmoil of expertise layer transitions?'. One obvious answer would be to enable penetrative reflection by students on both their current cognitive actions and the implicit agenda that accompanies each layer of expertise. When this development is seen not to be taking place, we find that academics in design schools often instinctively react in an understandable but probably counter-effective way. They add in more projects. Such a response simply clutters up the curriculum. There is sometimes an argument that says students must have experience of every major design typology in their field. In architecture this might mean at least one building with a major space such as an auditorium, at least one housing project, at least one high rise building and so on. In industrial design it might be designing the complicated bodyshell of a small electronic appliance, or the creating, building and testing of a small human-powered cart.

In effect, all of this might be to enable the students to gather more experience, albeit in a condensed form, but it is also likely to reduce the time and encouragement for reflection. When every studio project leads inevitably to an end product of some kind, the emphasis naturally falls on the quality of the end product rather than on the learning experience. Combined with the problems we have also seen to do with design projects being Parkinsonian with regard to time (expanding to fill the time available) and the assessment

problem (applying a disincentive to creative experimentation) the end result can easily be more experience but less learning.

An alternative to just adding in more projects must surely be to study the kinds of cognitive transitions we expect the students to be making. To lure novice students from their initial convention-based design thinking into a more situated view of design, the students do indeed need to experience many fundamentally different design situations. These should be designed in such a way that they lead to absurdities in the application of the convention-based approach. When students are wrong-footed a number of times, they are likely to see that the 'rules of the game' are not rules at all, but just tools that should be applied in the appropriate situations to help designers. In other words, they begin to look for exceptions and exceptional design solutions. More often design courses seem to demand that students make the transition very abruptly and pretty much at the start of the course. Laura Willenbrock again expresses this so clearly based on her own experience (Willenbrock, 1991): 'One of the earliest addresses we received, and one often repeated, was that we were being taught to think; an important goal, I agreed, but what this meant was that we were expected to *unlearn* everything we absorbed in high school and before'.

pg.69

The next transition, from the situation-based way of thinking towards a strategy-based approach, requires a different kind of challenge. This is the moment when students should really learn to interpret the design challenge, and do so in a way that helps mould the design project. This is a moment of real empowerment; students are encouraged to make their own design situations, and reflect upon the appropriateness of their approach. So, while the transition from rule-based to situation-based requires the design school to confront the student with many very different concrete design situations, this transition from situation-based to strategy-based requires the school to open up the design challenges, and allow many different interpretations. Students should be provided with something like a context in which they effectively have to make their own problems, and be able to defend the choices they make on this level. Some students just cannot wait to get at the helm of their design projects, but for others the challenge to engage in this framing activity can be quite a shock. The unsuspecting student might feel disoriented and wonder why the design school has suddenly become very vague in its criteria ('What do you want me to do?'). This is a considerable change in learning style.

Indeed, in general this is just what we tend to see in design studio courses with final year projects very much defined by the students; whereas the first year projects have heavily constrained projects defined by the tutors.

A RIGHT TO KNOW WHAT THE PROBLEM IS

A Norwegian colleague of one of the authors teaches engineering design within the framework of a classic engineering curriculum. By the time he sees the students, in the third year, they are well on their way towards becoming engineers. Being a designer, he tends to give them very open problems. This apparently can come as quite a shock. A very angry student came up to him one day, three weeks into the project, and said 'I am an engineering student; I have a right to know what the problem is!'

In general, this makes sense in terms of our model. Unfortunately though, this final project almost invariably counts most in the overall assessment of the student. Indeed it is often referred to as the 'thesis' project and is thus seen very much as a 'magnum opus' or 'tour de force' demonstration of the students' capability. This creates even more concentrated tension between learning and performing in a way that inevitably leads to many anxious, puzzled and worried students as they are challenged to excel at something they have never really done before.

THE STUDIO
MIMICKING PRACTICE

Wilson showed that architectural design schools produce students with closely associated sets of stylistic preferences. This process of 'joining' the studio is a well understood phenomenon in social psychology. The members of such strongly bound social groups develop not only shared intellectual territory but also behavioural norms and common sets of values and preferences. An advanced version of this was delightfully documented by Tracey Kidder observing the design team for the famous Data General Eagle computer (Kidder, 1982). Such behaviour undoubtedly has some significant advantages in design practice. The various groups involved had names like 'Micro-kids' and could be identified through their dress codes and showed different sets of attitudes towards authority and deadlines.

We have seen how successful designers often have a set of guiding principles, which include values and preferences. In highly pressured design teams, it is obviously of considerable advantage to have the members sufficiently signed up to understand this shared territory without holding things up by arguing or contesting too much of the common ground. In an earlier example the architect John Outram talked explicitly about the need for his staff to either work this way or leave.

We could then see the studio as having the advantage of preparing the student for working in such circumstances. Indeed, it does have such a potential. But the studio is never likely to offer a realistic imitation of the design practice. In professional design practice, timescales for projects are often longer than in the academic studio. This can be due to issues like obtaining budgets, technical evaluations, legal permissions and all sorts of other outside delays. Paradoxically, the student may have the luxury of more actual design time on a project. The academic studio though most lacks the contact with clients, manufacturers, consultants and so on. This can induce a tendency among students to rely more on their own personal experience than

is the case when real clients and users are involved. Bringing clients and users into the academic studio can be difficult to achieve with real interest and motivation. Sheffield University Architecture Department tackles this through having a limited number of 'live projects' where clients actually want the project completing rather than pretending to. Finding such projects in sufficient numbers, and with the right learning opportunities to fill the whole curriculum, is a huge task. Even so, Eindhoven University manages to use this as the central feature of its Industrial Design course.

The very axiomatic lack of questioning that may be useful in highly pressured practice is perhaps just what students do not need during their education. In a popular model of studio teaching, parallel, almost competitive groups are set up under the tutelage of different members of staff; they are often referred to as 'units'. This lack of questioning can often be observed to extend to disrespect for the ideas of competing studios or 'units'. In such patterns, what distinguishes the studios or 'units' from each other is often something very similar to guiding principles and these are often set by one, or a small number, of tutors. These tutors may indeed also be in practice themselves and thus studio may well be an intellectual extension of the practice guiding principles.

While such guiding principles may well be extremely valuable devices in design practice they may have some other less desirable effects in an educational setting. This is particularly dangerous when they represent sets of values and attitudes which are largely axiomatic within the studio setting. The danger here must surely be that the goal of developing an independent questioning attitude in the student is subverted by the need to remain loyal to the studio position. A pattern of education in which students join a number of such studios in succession may remedy this to some extent but this could be an extraordinarily confusing educational experience. Whether this is the kind of intellectual atmosphere that we really want to engender in higher education must surely be a matter for debate.

THE STUDIO
THE HIDDEN CURRICULUM

Dutton rehearses a far more fundamental critique of the studio by applying the ideas of modern educational theory (Dutton, 1991b). He argues that there is what educationalists now regard as the 'hidden curriculum' at work in the design studio. This idea explored by Snyder suggests that there are a set of influences at work at least as strong in their impact as the declared explicit curriculum (Snyder, 1973). These influences are all the more effective due

NOT USING PRIOR EXPERIENCE

Bryan Lawson was once teaching a second year architecture student who was designing multi-occupancy residential accommodation. In one drawing-board tutorial the student presented plans showing the entrance to an upper level apartment with the door at the top of an approach staircase having no landing. Thus a resident would have had to stand perhaps two or three steps down to find their keys and then reach up to unlock and open the door. This was pointed out to the student who had amazingly lived with this design for several days apparently without noticing the problem. The student readily agreed that it would be a most inconvenient arrangement. He was then asked if he had ever seen such a situation in his life. There was quite a pause while the student thought this through. Finally, he admitted that this did indeed stand outside his real-world experience. However, the puzzled expression on his face revealed the real problem here. The whole approach of his tutors had of course not encouraged him to consider that his own personal experience prior to university was of any value at all. Now here was a tutor asking him to use this experience. It was hardly surprising that he was puzzled.

Our Norwegian colleague referred to earlier put this problem rather nicely by saying that: 'it takes a couple of years for our students to find out that they are also human'.

to their implicit rather than explicit nature. They include not so much what must be learned as how it must be learned and they often deal with values as much as knowledge. They include the way assignments are set and framed as well as the kinds of performances that are recognised and approved of.

More alarming seems to be a commonly recognised tendency of first year design courses to assume that students begin with no knowledge of value to their development. This is often actually made clear by the hidden curriculum, but can even be made totally explicit. Willenbrock, reflecting on her own experience, describes this phenomenon quite clearly: 'Essentially we were asked to forget most things in our past, to come to the studio "naked", to allow ourselves to be directed by the professor who claimed unquestionable authority in our focused world' (Willenbrock, 1991). While it may be mistaken, such an approach to the development of design skills is understandable. Clearly those who have already acquired more expertise are only too well aware of the cognitive shifts they experienced in moving through the transitions between expertise levels. Appreciating this they understandably want to ensure their students make these transitions and thus try to create worlds for them in which they cannot rely on their past experiences. It seems much more likely that students will successfully transition between expertise levels when they recognise for themselves, even if unconsciously, that they are ready to shift. Then perhaps they can also usefully take with them all their prior knowledge instead of having to reject it. The second year architecture student 'not using prior experience' demonstrates the problem.

THE DESIGN TUTORIAL

Design projects by their very nature do not have single, optimal or correct solutions. Inevitably this means that students working in the studio are developing individual approaches and this makes it difficult to tutor them in groups. The individual design tutorial is commonplace in university design schools right from the beginning of the first year. Academics teaching many other subjects would not contemplate this and would delay the personal tutorial until the third or final year of an undergraduate degree.

Marcia Pereira has studied these tutorials and concluded that the tutor actually plays a complex series of roles in such a context (Pereira, 2000). Even more confusingly these roles may merge or may slide one into another at various times during the discussion without this being made explicit. Because of the unique student-led problem solving nature of most studio design exercises, the tutor inevitably becomes involved in helping to progress the design.

THE TUTOR AS TEACHER
A DESIGN STUDENT TUTORIAL

TUTOR

Well, you can make sections work for you. So that they're not all, you know, it's not just one simple cut line through the building. You can actually manipulate the section so that it's revealing...

STUDENT

You'll go like that and... (gestures imaginary line along plan)

TUTOR

Yeah, you usually step in parallel. So if you're taking a section through, say, the building here and you get to that point and you want to show the staircase, you can bring the section back show it through the lift and step it back again and bring it through this space so that you have a series of sections...

You can only see that from the section. That's just not available on plan. So, yeah, it's one of the... it's a hard drawing to think about because it doesn't come naturally. You've got to kind of practice.

THE TUTOR AS CONSULTANT
A DESIGN STUDENT TUTORIAL

TUTOR

So I think I would just examine those spaces and see whether they could be brought down to say 2.4 as a single height, floor to ceiling height... which pushes, well it takes a metre and a half off, doesn't it... 4.8? And that might just help to bring this down. And simply doing that will have an impact. So, remodeling this bit might push things to a different kind of perspective

STUDENT

Do you think that the single floor one, 3.3, is too much?

TUTOR

I think when it's only one floor and... so it's fairly small-scale accommodation, isn't it? I think you can afford to bring that height down. So I think the whole thing might shrink. Oh! Having said that I would look at the public spaces at ground level because you've got much larger volumes... These large kind of, almost an auditorium-type spaces. But it could be used as an auditorium. You could have conferences, meetings, all kinds of things happening here. And these are larger spaces, practice rooms... and I think you can afford to push that floor to ceiling height up in at ground floor level.

The most obvious role the tutor can play here is indeed that of 'teacher'. In this sense the tutor is genuinely and directly teaching the student. The discussion is likely to feature suggestions about emphasis, use of time, focus and, in general, aspects of design that are admired as opposed to those that are not.

The tutorial discussion is also likely to feature suggested improvements and ways forward not just about process but, more often, about product. In this sense the tutor plays the role of 'consultant'. Here the emphasis is mostly on making a good design. As consultant the tutor is cast in a role more like the one played by senior colleagues in a professional design practice.

The sensitive tutor may also, from time to time, pick up the student's own growing sets of guiding principles. Because of the tutor's more extensive knowledge, this may cause some discussion about new sources of information that the student may find rewarding. Marcia Pereira described this as 'Parrot' mode after a quotation from the architect Ian Ritchie who imagined he had some exotic parrot sitting on his shoulder as he drew, which would occasionally squawk and remind him of something (Lawson, 1994). This role may be one of the most important and yet difficult to manage. The tutor may sense that the student is within sight of some transition between layers of expertise, ready to accept a bigger challenge and move on. Encouraging the student to accept that challenge may well result in a less well-resolved design on this particular occasion.

A well-connected tutor may appreciate that students can and do learn a great deal from each other. Here the discussion may feature suggestions about how to get together and enable that process more deliberately. Such an idea, of course, deliberately exploits the notion of the studio in which the tutor is really a 'facilitator'. It concentrates on encouraging exploration and learning rather than performing.

We now suggest yet another role; that of 'master'. The very expert tutor may be so used to working with members of a design practice and leading them, that this behaviour is transferred into the academy. In this role the tutor is not so much interested in developing the student's own line of thought as in imposing his or her own. This may lead to a distinguished result for the project in hand, but not necessarily a great deal of learning on the part of the student. Often too, we see the more confident student trying to battle against the master's ideas and probably losing in some confusion and possible damage to confidence.

THE TUTOR IN 'PARROT' MODE
A DESIGN STUDENT TUTORIAL

TUTOR

Have you got any kind of precedent examples, have you looked at the ones that might be relevant?

STUDENT

I looked at Laban and there's one in America by, I can't remember. It's quite new. It was in the AR last month and then, there's the Scottish dance-based and...

TUTOR

I mean, have you looked at them in depth at all as to what defines their characters in the way they are?

STUDENT

Yeah, well each of them has got their own kind of key, about their sort of façade or maybe like a key sort of idea like the dance space is all about relation to site, lighting and things like that... And then Laban is all about sort of the transparency and the material, skin

TUTOR

Right, so what's yours about, you've identified them very clearly. If I said to you what's yours about, what's your project about?

What is interesting about these modes is the variable range they have. Some are focused directly on the project, and even on the student's own particular solution, while others are not even restricted to the curriculum of the school. Such a range may be seen as providing a very rich educational experience. On the other hand, it may also seem confusing to a struggling student. Indeed, the confusion of objectives here can easily spread to tutors. Design schools live in the design world of prizes and awards. Design schools, and indeed sometimes individual tutors, can become focused on winning such awards. Since the tutor is clearly a consultant on a student project, in reality it must be seen as a team effort to some extent. This may lead tutors to expand the consultant mode to the possible deficit of the more learning oriented roles. Those tutors who teach part-time and are also in practice may easily be confused by the similarity between a school tutorial and a session with junior staff in the design office. This might lead the tutor away from recognising and supporting the student's own tentative guiding principles.

We cannot say how widespread these effects are and whether they are as undesirable as they may seem. Certainly we have personal experience of real problems like this. Our analysis would suggest that tutoring a student without having some understanding of where that student is in terms of their own expertise development may be a dangerous thing to do. And yet it is commonplace in design schools for distinguished visiting critics to be employed from outside the system to play an important tutorial role. An interesting question here is whether tutoring is more helpful from a nearby expertise layer or one far above the student's current layer. The answer is likely to be that a combination of the two is probably desirable, but there does not seem to have been a systematic investigation of this issue.

The tutorial conversations used as examples here were systematically collected by Khairul Khaidzir in a study mentioned in earlier chapters. His analysis of these conversations showed some remarkably strong differences in the characteristics of the two participants in the conversation. Firstly, tutors tended to dominate the conversation with a clear hierarchy evident, just as Dutton has suggested. In fact, tutors spoke for about one and a half times as long as students. The comments made were all classified as being 'formulations', 'moves' or 'evaluations', as defined in Chapter 2. Interestingly, both tutors and students spent longer formulating than they did on either of the other two design skills. That is to say the dominant tone of the conversation is about finding, expressing, structuring and framing problems rather than about suggesting solutions. While tutors spent virtually a third of their time discussing 'moves', students only did this for about a tenth of their time. The additional expertise of the tutors clearly allowed them to come up with

A STUDENT-LED CRIT

One of many ways to run a design review with the students in charge. Twelve students are divided into 3 panels of 4. All pin up their work. There are then 3 panels each kept rigidly to time. In each panel:

- The 4 students present their work to the other 8 students for 5 minutes each (20 minutes)

- The presenters leave and review what they said. During this time the other 2 panels discuss the presentations and formulate questions (20 minutes)

- The presenters return and the spokespeople for the other 2 panels put the questions, give feedback and chair discussion (15 minutes)

- The 4 presenters summarise what they feel they have learned and how they might proceed with their designs (5 minutes)

- The same procedure is then followed for each of the other 2 panels

- Tutors are allowed to make general concluding observations.

more ideas about solutions and to elaborate and develop them further. In fact, tutors talked about moves for seven times the length of time that students did; this in spite of the fact that they were reviewing a student design. It is clear from all these results that tutors could read more into the situation from the students' own drawings and models than they were able to themselves. Importantly Khairul saw a huge discrepancy between students and tutors in terms of what he classified as 'process-based move actions'. This is where the comment is about moving towards a solution but in terms of how to do so rather than in terms of the content of the design itself. Tutors talked about such matters for twelve times longer than students.

We can now connect these various studies and suggest that during the design tutorial the tutor is not only acting in 'consultant' mode by suggesting new ways of moving the design forward, but also effectively 'teaching' the student how to understand design situations and furthermore to develop their own sets of ideas about design beyond the project. We can see, in terms of another concept we introduced in Chapter 2, that the tutorial is simultaneously a vehicle for the development of the 'project', of the student 'process' and also effectively of the student 'practice'. This is an extraordinarily complex and rich learning and teaching situation. While on the one hand this is clearly a very powerful pedagogical tool, it is also likely to require enormous skill to manage in a way that avoids imbalance and confusion. And yet, probably a very large proportion of such tutorials are given by part-time academic staff who mainly practice and who are unlikely to have had much, if any, pedagogical training.

PROFESSION
PRACTICE
PROCESS
PROJECT
pg.61

THE DESIGN CRIT

The crit is a curious beast in educational terms. Often known as the 'design jury' or 'review', especially in the USA, the very name implies something negative and rather frightening. The full-blown version seems more common in architecture than design, particularly in English speaking countries. The idea is simple. Students display their design work and a number of staff sit around and criticise this in a public forum with other students listening in. One could see it as a parallel to the master–class that might take place in a music school. However, a key difference there is that the performance of the music student is constantly interrupted and constructively moved forward. Usually the design crit takes place at the end of a project when it is more difficult to be constructive.

This idea has become so embedded in design education that it has in fact taken on many roles. It clearly has the potential to be a device for teaching

and learning. However, since most design schools use continuous assessment on the very same work, it is also used for assessment. Clearly these two roles can be confusing and the student's need to defend in order to achieve a high mark is clearly in conflict with the learning role. Laura Willenbrock summarises her feelings about exactly this problem (Willenbrock, 1991). 'My struggle with grades was frustrated by the critique or jury review system used to discuss the merit of student work. To me the relationship between the grade and the review is vague and nearly mysterious.'

The crit is also used as a kind of ceremonial end to a project which may have lasted for some weeks and is thus a way of rounding up and getting general feedback in both directions. Often the crit is supported by external, visiting and sometimes distinguished critics. They may have other agendas in terms of their personal promotion to a new generation of students and may not be aware of all the learning objectives and educational context of the project.

Several studies of the crit, or design jury, have now been published and do indeed suggest that it has many pedagogical problems hitherto unnoticed. The first major hint that all might not be as well as was assumed was raised now some years ago (Anthony, 1991). More recently, a book has been published suggesting ways forward both for staff and students (Doidge et al., 2000). One of the key educational lessons here seems to be that the various roles of the crit need to be separated out in order for each of them to work well. Revolutionary ideas of student-led crits have shown that learning may well be increased if tutors play a greatly reduced role. In such a model all the students have a role and responsibilities to the group for the complete duration of the session rather than just when their own work is being reviewed. To be successful though, such events need extraordinarily careful choreography and some cultural shifts.

THE DESIGN LIBRARY

It is common to find libraries in professional design practices. They may contain technical information on products and manufacturing processes. They often hold legal information about planning law, contractual agreements, consumer protection legislation and regulations. They will often contain drawings and other images of work done by the practice in the past. However, they also often hold magazines and design journals as well as books. More often than not these are sources not just of hard information but of design ideas. Quite simply they are part of the precedent store available to those working in the practice.

In universities, libraries are often assumed to be places where theory is studied but, in the case of some subjects, libraries are also depositories of experience. For example, the law library normally contains massive chunks of case histories. These precedent repositories are both studied in their own right and later referred back to in order to develop particular arguments. So it is with design libraries (Lawson, 2002). We have seen that expert chess players can gain what we might call 'accelerated experience' through studying recorded games of the masters. In the case of designers this accelerated experience probably plays a far greater role since the timescales of a game of chess and a design project are vastly different. Thus designers relying solely on their own experience would probably gain knowledge too slowly to reach the more advanced layers of expertise. This provides more understanding for us about why gaining 'precedent' through magazines, exhibitions and so on is so important in the design world. It also suggests a very particular set of needs in terms of library provision for design education.

For example, one would not expect a psychology undergraduate to read the latest issues of all the major journals in the field. A design student, however, would lap these up as being sources of the latest ideas. Conventionally many university libraries actually separate out the journals from the books they hold. Often journals are relegated to unpleasant unlit dungeon-like stacks where only dusty academics are expected to tread. Universities do not expect their undergraduates to make extensive use of such places. In the design departments though there is little point in making a distinction between journals and books. A tutor might refer a student to a project which could be illustrated in either and often in both.

In the course of a design tutorial both tutor and student might like to browse this material together. There is a common feeling in design schools that the library should be either in the design studio or at least very close to it so this creative work can go on more or less without interruption. Not surprisingly, design students therefore may want to take their sketchbooks into the library, often copying or tracing images and ideas and perhaps doing some design development thinking. Just as the studio is on demand throughout the late hours, so is the library.

Thus the design library in a university is rather an oddball. The University of Sheffield now has a library largely intended solely for undergraduate student use. As is the way these days, we are not allowed to refer to it as that; it is instead known as the 'Information Commons'. This change of title is presumably intended to reflect the changing pattern of modern information sources. Although this suggests some creative thinking, the university was quite unable to apply the same level of consideration to its architecture

library. An attempt was made not only to divide the books from the journals, with the latter of course being located in the post-graduate library, but also to divide the books into those suitable for undergraduates and those only expected to be used by staff and post-graduates. Such an idea is clearly nonsensical in the design library. Knowledge is simply not divided that way. There is no advanced body of highly sophisticated theory that might be deemed too difficult for the undergraduate design student. The current journals are just as likely to be interesting to any level of student as any of the books.

Resistance to this idea was demonstrated when a librarian produced figures from the computer loans system to show that students of architecture borrowed fewer books than students of most other subjects and that these books could be identified from the records. Of course this data did not reveal the multitude of books and journals that had been browsed by the students in the library. That is the pattern of their working; they are much more likely to refer to an apparently unpredictable mass of books and journals all together in one session in a library than they are to take one book home and read it cover to cover.

So the location, opening hours, layout and pattern of use of the design library are all rather problematic for many university librarians. These are not just perverse and unreasonable demands placed on them by truculent academics but a pattern of behaviour that shows sensible adaptation to the way design skills and knowledge are acquired. Getting all this wrong is likely to be seriously damaging to the effectiveness of the learning that can take place on design courses. Unsurprisingly we see this pattern of usage of libraries as a very direct demonstration of the nature of design knowledge and the way designers create expertise.

QUO VADIS?

Where next indeed? We have seen that the period of formal education in universities is only a relatively small part of learning to become a designer. It is not that we need longer courses; indeed some might argue that we need shorter ones. It is quite simply that the process of creating design expertise is a lengthy one and that in most cases this cannot be significantly shortened. We still have several stages of expertise acquisition to come and the next chapter will deal with the way this process continues in practice.

Formal design education then faces challenges at both ends of the process. At the beginning it needs to address the question of continuity of learning. At

DEVELOPING YOUR OWN PRACTICE
INDUSTRIAL DESIGN STUDENT

It is strange to see that you gradually get to know your own manual as you study design. When you work the best, and that that depends on the assignment... One of the most important things I have learned during my study is to constantly question what you want. Not just what you want to achieve in a certain project, but especially what you want to achieve in the general scheme of things, with your education and your qualities. You constantly have to question yourself on this because the picture keeps changing, like you are changing yourself during your education.

the end it needs to have prepared the student for continued learning. Design education frequently seems to fail to connect students' prior knowledge and learning with their formal knowledge. This can only lead to confusion and the isolation of design knowledge from everyday knowledge. We have several times relied on quotations from the writings of Laura Willenbrock who has shown us how an obviously well-educated and intelligent person is distressed by such a process. Design education can, and must do better than offer the isolating and unsettling experience she describes.

At the end of the process, design education must enable students to continue the learning process on into practice in a more or less self-sufficient sort of way. Perhaps then the main challenge in design education is to give students the tools with which to continue developing their expertise.

While they are at university most design students will undergo enormous cognitive development and change. On arrival most will have not been prepared well for acquiring knowledge through precedent and practice. As they pass from practicing everyday design through their novice and graduate phases they will learn to think in new ways. They will add the more sophisticated situation-based and strategy-based styles to their prior rule-based and convention-based thinking approaches. They will learn to be both reflective in practice and reflective on practice. Perhaps most distinctively they will develop a strong tendency to think in an integrated way, choosing to include and combine ideas rather than to separate and divide knowledge. Above all they will learn to be intensely self-critical and demanding. They will learn how to create their own crises in projects and be prepared to throw ideas away and look for more satisfying and satisfactory concepts. They will learn to learn from all this project-based experience and begin to develop their own practice-based approach. The Dutch industrial design student quoted here has obviously discovered this important truth.

All of this suggests a tumultuous time in the minds of our student designers. They will pass through many transitions as they re-engineer their very minds. The real role of education then is surely to challenge them to recognise when they are ready to move on to another phase. Such a transition is usually painful and confusing. For a while it may be very ineffective and produce poor or immature results. The role of education then is to support them at these times and create an environment that rewards such creative exploration of their expertise.

REFERENCES

Anthony, K.H. (1991). **Design Juries on Trial: The renaissance of the design studio**. New York, Van Nostrand Reinhold.

Doidge, C., Sara, R. and Parnell, R. (2000). **The Crit**. Oxford, Architectural Press.

Dutton, T.A. (1991a). **Architectural Education and Society: An interview with J. Max Bond, Jr**. Voices in Architectural Education. T. A. Dutton. New York, Bergin and Garvey: 83–95.

Dutton, T.A. (1991b). **The hidden curriculum and the design studio: toward a critical studio pedagogy**. Voices in Architectural Education. T. A. Dutton. New York, Bergin and Garvey: 165–194.

Hunt, T. (1999). **Tony Hunt's Sketch Book**. Oxford, Architectural Press.

Hunt, T. (2003). **Tony Hunt's Second Sketchbook**. Oxford, Architectural Press.

Kidder, T. (1982). **The Soul of a New Machine**. Harmondsworth, Penguin.

Lawson, B.R. (1994). **Design in Mind**. Oxford, Butterworth Architecture.

Lawson, B.R. (2002). **Architecture libraries from a university perspective**. ARCLIB Bulletin 11: 1–4.

Maher, M.L., Bilda, Z. and Gul, F.L. (2006). **Impact of collaborative virtual environments on design behaviour**. Design Computing. J. S. Gero. Dordrecht, Springer: 305–321.

Morrow, R. (2000). **Architectural assumptions and environmental discrimination: the case for more inclusive design in schools of architecture**. Changing Architectural Education. D. Nichol and S. Pilling. London, E & FN Spon.

Pereira, M.A. (2000). **ArchCal : a conceptual basis for the application of information technology into learning and teaching technical subjects in architectural education**. PhD, Sheffield, University of Sheffield.

Samsuddin, I.b. (2008). **Architectural Education: peer culture in design studio and its relationship with designing interest**. Architecture. PhD, Sheffield, University of Sheffield.

Snyder, B. (1973). **The Hidden Curriculum**. Cambridge, Mass, MIT Press.

Willenbrock, L.L. (1991). **An undergraduate voice in architectural education**. Voices in Architectural Education. T. A. Dutton. New York, Bergin and Garvey: 97–119.

7 THE CONTINUING JOURNEY

I have always been occupied by design, even before I knew it was a profession, something you could do for a living.

FRANS DE LA HAYE

Allow me to say that I find it beautiful to be as misunderstood at age sixty as at age thirty.

FRANCIS POULENC
(IN A LETTER TO IGOR STRAVINSKY)

INTRODUCTION

Way back in Chapter 3 we showed that designers are relative late developers compared with many other professions. Chapter 5 suggested that the creation of design expertise continues long after the period of formal education is complete. Indeed it seems to be a continuing and lifelong journey for many designers.

pg.101

This final chapter offers a sketch of how this continuing journey might look. Where possible, we will base ourselves on the ideas from the expertise and design process models, as they have been developed in the previous chapters, and extend them into design practice as far as we can. But more than in other chapters we will also rely directly on the ideas and messages we get from practicing designers in the field. They are the real specialists, living their own design journeys.

In Chapter 2 we looked at design in terms of project, process, practice and profession. Since then we have implicitly concentrated on the development of expertise inside a single mind. But, because a large proportion of professional design is done collaboratively, we should also explore how expertise is created in a design practice. Inevitably now we need also to look at the way expertise is developed at the level of the design professions themselves.

pg.51

Just as the university was the setting for the learning we looked at in Chapter 6, for professional designers it is the design practice. Just as the studio project was the main vehicle for learning at university it will be the commercial project that will be the main vehicle here. Of course, such commercial projects usually have real clients with particular circumstances, pressures, budgets, timescales, reputations and problems. Inevitably this makes learning through professional practice a rather different business to learning in the academic studio.

PERSONAL DEVELOPMENT

In Chapter 3 we asked why it is that although professional sportspeople and musicians have a trainer to coach them in their development (even when they are star performers), designers on the whole do not seem to feel they need this. By now, we hope to have made the point that creating design expertise is a serious matter, and a complicated one at that. So why do designers not continue to go to their teachers? Have they learned all they need to at University? Well most professional designs do not feel this to be the case when they employ graduates. So is this a question of oversight, or are there good reasons for it? How do designers in practice develop their expertise,

FAMILIAR AND NOVEL PROBLEMS
THEO GROOTHUIZEN

When you have a lot of knowledge in a field, that is comfortable but is also limiting. I notice that when I design telephone booths. I know so much about telephone booths that designing one becomes more and more difficult. Because if you did a good job on the last one, then that contains many of the optimal solutions, or the optimal choices, or the choices that fit me as a designer... this reminds me of playing chess; it always surprises me how easily a beginner can play. We call that beginner's luck, they are not hampered by too much knowledge. The more you know about chess, it does not become easier or more difficult, but you are able to make many more combinations...

anyway? A clue to the answer here comes in the delightful quotation (which we also saw in Chapter 2) from Theo Groothuizen who highlights the difference between designing something new and something unfamiliar.

In this book we have tried to discern some of the general patterns in this journey, using general models of design and expertise development as the backbone for our story. But apart from these general patterns we should not forget that design is a personal journey too. People build up their identity and self-image in various ways. When asked to describe their identity ('Who are you? What do you associate most closely with?'), some people base their answer on a particular ability or skill that they possess that might be unusual or even unique. Others most closely associate themselves with possessing some knowledge, with the practice of their profession or the way they connect to the world (their own personal style of doing things).

PROFESSION
PRACTICE
PROCESS
PROJECT
pg.61

The quotes of the most experienced designers in this book suggest that they are their practices (as opposed to their projects, processes and professions), and that they identify very closely with their development; their journey. Each of them talks of this journey in a curiously non-goal-directed way; it is more about weaving an original pattern than achieving a pre-set goal. Unless asked directly about their process most designers seem to feel easier describing themselves through the projects that, taken together, make up their practice.

People who have adopted one of the designing disciplines as their profession often describe themselves as 'designers' and usually quite proudly. Apparently, designing is not just something you do, or that you take lightly when you practice it, but rather it helps to form your identity. The many quotes from designers that are sprinkled throughout this book portray an enthusiastic almost loving tone in which many designers speak about their profession. It is not difficult to see where this love affair might come from; design becomes a part of one's being because it involves so much that is personal, like your creativity, way of approaching the world's problems, your own history, learning style and view of the world (see Chapter 2). It is a deeply human thing to do. The buildings, environments and products we design are expressions of their designers as much as their clients and users.

But it is not just the end products of design that captivate us. The design activity itself is often so intense that it tends to eat up huge chunks of your life. Students quickly learn this; often working late at night towards the end of projects and, for many, this will last throughout their professional lives. Designers inhabit their projects, and they are emotionally attached to their success or failure in a manner almost akin to an addiction.

MASTER DESIGNERS DESCRIBE THEMSELVES THROUGH THEIR PROJECTS

When interviewing masterful designers we are repeatedly struck how they tell the story of their own development, and that they really like to talk about it. In fact, many of the more well-known designers, who have illuminated this text with wonderful insights, originally declared themselves only able to talk about their products rather than their process. Of course this was not true, but they were more used to talking about their designs and, in most cases, no one had either tried or been able to ask them the questions that would unlock their tacit knowledge about process rather than product. Usually such designers asked to give a lecture at a university design school will describe a series of projects drawing out the way their work has developed or moved on with time.

THE IDENTITY OF DESIGN

The word 'design' has always been both a verb and a noun. Today the word 'designer' is both a noun and an adjective. Designers have an increasingly strong identity in a consumerist society. But just how do a group of people like industrial designers or architects develop and manage their collective identity? Many design practices are known by the name of a single person and yet in reality they depend on the collective expertise of all their members rather than just one.

But we now need to explore beyond the 'practice' layer of designing where there is yet another 'professional' layer of activity. Although the profession as a whole does not actually design, nevertheless it plays an important role in the creation and development of expertise. In some design fields the professional body may go as far as publishing conditions for the engagement of designers, setting rules for design competitions, lobbying and even advising government and so on. Most professional bodies will hold exhibitions and lectures and some may offer a simple introductory design advice service.

THE FORMULATION OF DESIGN PROFESSIONS

The various design professions we are interested in here have not all reached the same stage of development and sophistication. The existence of a body of people recognised professionally as designers is a relatively recent phenomenon.

The initial push in the nineteenth century was a period in which many of our modern professional bodies were formed, recognised and given some legal status. In design terms this could be seen to some extent as a logical outcome of the industrial revolution leading to the separation of designing from making. But many current design professions were not formed until late in the twentieth century. In the wider scheme of things then, the formal organisation and professional recognition of designers is still at an early stage of development.

Thinking about learning and development in design, as we are here, the existence of professional bodies has proved to be something of a mixed blessing. On the plus side, these bodies are essential in promoting the idea and value of design and creating a collective identity for their members. The professional body is one that the media or governments can turn to when they want comment or advice.

THE DEVELOPMENT OF DESIGN PROFESSIONS

Architects were probably the first to become members of a professionally recognised body. Although there had been clubs and societies for architects earlier, it was not until 1837 that architects in Britain became formally chartered by royal assent. But they were hardly pioneers, lagging some years behind their engineering colleagues who had formed the Institute of Civil Engineers in 1828.

By comparison, the Institute of Landscape Architects was not formed until nearly a century later in 1929, while interior and product designers in the UK still only have associations and institutes that have little legal status. Urban Designers still congregate in something called a 'Group'. Web designers have an association that is totally unregulated and even free to join.

Professional bodies can also set standards and regulate membership, set rules of conduct and discipline members. These are surely signs of a maturing profession that is becoming reliable and consistent; protecting clients and users from sub-standard work. However, the outcome of design is so unpredictable and so wide ranging that setting any meaningful standards of quality of work has proved extremely difficult. What discipline the professional bodies do operate is thus focused on the conduct of the service rather than the quality of design. For example, British architects are required to hold professional indemnity insurance. This cannot guarantee design quality but does ensure that there will be money available to compensate clients who can legally prove negligence.

Professional bodies can control admission to their membership by approving university courses and examining their standards, but this leads to the risk of conservative ideas and attitudes dominating. In a rapidly developing and changing field this might easily be in conflict with more adventurous and progressive ideas within universities. This is where the set identity offered by the professional body can be something of a burden. A well-developed identity in the minds of the public can become static and old-fashioned. Often professional bodies are run by older and more conservative members. For a collection of professionals in a creative field these bodies display a surprising amount of rule-based behaviour.

Even more problematical here is when the profession becomes regulated through some legislative power. For example, the European Union has set standards for universities running architecture courses, but the definitions of curriculum and syllabus have lagged well behind progressive thinking in the field itself. In the UK the architectural schools have been buffeted for a number of years now by what can only be described as outright war between the professional body and the regulation council, each trying to assert its authority over education.

A PLURALIST VIEW OF PROFESSIONAL DESIGN EXPERTISE

In the early chapters of this book we saw that there are many ways of being a designer. The expertise in design could actually be seen as developing roughly in the shape of an egg timer. It begins fairly widely as the university schools accept students with many different nationalities, backgrounds and experience. In general the trend at university seems to be the sharing of a common basic expertise. Professionally then we might all start out fairly uniformly, living under the pressures of having to survive as a designer. But

VISIONARY VISIONA
MASTER MASTERMAS
EXPERT EXPERTEXPERT
COMPETENT COMPETENT
ADVANCED BEGINNER ADVA
BEGINNER BEGINNERBEGINN
NOVICE NOVICENOVICENOVICEN

pg.101

THE IMPACT OF PROFESSIONAL REGULATION

The Architects Registration Board (ARB) is required by an act of parliament to protect the title 'architect' in the UK. It maintains the legal list of individual people who are allowed to describe themselves as architects. It has no control over design practices, which are loosely controlled by the Royal Institute of British Architects. The ARB is supposed to protect the consumer and yet clients have a relationship not with an individual architect but with a practice often consisting of many members.

The ARB has claimed responsibility for controlling the university schools of architecture and regulates their performance on the basis that every graduating student must be capable of running a complete one-person practice.

once a basic level of expertise is attained, the field design opens up, becoming much more diverse in the higher layers of expertise.

And it keeps opening up; even very experienced designers report that they keep discovering new things. These higher level things are more subtle, based on an ever deeper insight into the subject and practice of design, and of the growing self-knowledge of the designer. These may not be great revolutionary lateral moves, but they have a different kind of quality, perhaps more detailed and often more personal. The quotes of older, more experienced designers convey a strong impression that design can be a satisfying and compulsive journey.

CREATING EXPERTISE COLLECTIVELY

We return now to a theme that has been mentioned a number of times throughout this book; the happy circumstance that we are not alone in developing our design expertise. The days of the lonely design practitioner are largely gone. Designers often work in teams, and they also develop their expertise in concert with others. This opens up the possibility for sharing inspiration and reflection in a more or less organised manner, and thus achieving a collective level of expertise that is higher than any individual could achieve alone.

Larger professional design practices have many ways of combining expertise. Among the ones that have yielded quotations for us in this book we can discern several patterns. Some divide up into federations of more or less similar little practices, each under one of the principle partners. Some have partners who specialise; perhaps one is more technical, one more concerned with concept development, perhaps one with the contractual and legal side of things. Among the staff these practices employ there are often many levels of experience, but also sometimes real specialisms; perhaps some who are particularly good at presentation, using computers, understanding sustainability issues, managing projects, relating to clients and so on.

So an issue central to this chapter is the way expertise is built not just by individuals but also by practices. Such a notion seems in direct conflict with the idea that all individuals must be general practitioners which underpins the outlook of some professional bodies. As design has developed and become more specialised, such a model is only likely to get progressively out of date. We can only ask whether such a state of affairs really helps to develop expertise at either the practice or professional levels.

CONTINUING PROFESSIONAL DEVELOPMENT

One of the most long-lived design professional bodies is the Royal Institute of British Architects (RIBA). It has imposed a set of continuing professional development conditions (CPD) on its members that requires them to attend a number of hours of formal educational events from a catalogue. This effectively sends architects back into a form of 'classroom' that they never really encountered even at university. The idea that such formal instruction guarantees continuing professional development in a design profession seems rather out of step with both modern educational theory and actual practice in design.

THE PROFESSIONAL BODIES AND CONTINUING DEVELOPMENT

Some of the professional bodies have become more formal in their demands on individual members by imposing continuous professional development requirements. Unfortunately, they have struggled to understand the normal way of professional learning that we shall explore in this chapter. Designers are puzzled by such approaches especially when coming from their own professional bodies. They think that they are part of what can be seen as a 'community of practice' not just in their own business level but at the professional level. Designers actually learn and develop best through their practice and principally through the projects they carry out in that practice.

Universities find it difficult to devise courses that seem useful to practicing designers and are frustrated at the poor take up and difficulty of marketing. These same universities may be flooded with applications to their undergraduate degree courses. Even more extraordinary is the demand made on academic members of these design professions to attend formal courses in order to complete the annual continuing professional development forms that are the prerequisite of renewing their membership. These are not only teachers but also researchers and often even practicing designers; their very business is learning but this it seems may not match the curious form of pedagogy adopted by their professional bodies.

The old-fashioned formal models of learning sit uncomfortably alongside the situated learning in practice that designers have become so used to. Many, of course, have not thought consciously about these pedagogical issues and just remain puzzled and sometimes infuriated by the lack of connection that their own bodies seem to have with their everyday continuing journey of creating design expertise through practice.

But we should not altogether abandon formal teaching methods for continuing education in design. What we lack is some enquiry into how this could usefully be linked into learning through practice. Curiously, many of the professional bodies came to understand some time ago that undergraduate students can benefit from periods of working in design practice as well as in the university. However, even here little has been done to link the two kinds of experience and many students report finding them almost totally disconnected.

USING THE PRACTICE PARADIGM IN EDUCATION

The new design department at Eindhoven University of Technology in The Netherlands is completely modelled on design practice. Students are considered to be 'junior employees', and work in design projects for real clients from day one. And the metaphor does not stop there; as with any design firm, all of their activities take place in design projects. There are no lectures but rather students have to seek the knowledge they need for their design challenges from a rich and knowledge-intensive environment provided within the school. Being junior employees, the students get no marks, but they have to defend their progress in 'performance reviews'. The progress of each student in developing their design competencies is coached and monitored individually. Every half-year they are assessed on their learning and design outcomes. The aim is to educate the students to become self-propelled learners, and create design expertise throughout their professional lives.

LEARNING FROM PRACTICE

The way in which designers learn from projects seems to us to offer an excellent example of what has recently come to be known as 'situated learning' (Lave and Wenger, 1991). This concept is a highly social, even anthropological, view of learning. It holds that learning takes place best not in the formal classroom but in the very context in which it is to be applied. This idea goes further than the traditional view of design education as 'learning by doing', which we explored in the previous chapter. It is not just the doing that is important here but also the context or situation in which it is done.

Traditionally, the apprenticeship was such a form of learning but it lacked formal elements and could thus be somewhat hit and miss. Some highly developed forms of an apprenticeship though have been shown to be remarkably effective. In their study of advanced apprenticeship systems Lave and Wenger examined such trades as midwifery, tailoring and butchery. These hardly offer close parallels to designing since they are characterised by repetition and application of physical craft rather than originality, cognition and imagination.

Nevertheless the situated learning idea seems particularly relevant to design which itself is now seen as an intrinsically situated activity. The importance of this might be glimpsed from Lave's remarkable demonstration that skills are learned to such a contextual degree that they may not always be generically transferable. For example, she showed that shoppers could perform quite advanced arithmetic operations when comparing prices and deciding on value for money. However, when asked to perform the same mathematics in the theoretically based classroom, they were quite unable to do so (Lave, 1988).

Even more useful to us here is the idea of 'communities of practice' through which situated learning is seen to develop (Wenger, 1998). Wenger argues that such communities define the context for learning and even determine much of the content of that learning. Apprentices then can be seen to join such a community and adopt its norms and values, which in turn influence and structure the learning that takes place.

We can now see new members of a design practice as what Lave and Wenger would call 'legitimate peripheral participants'. Such junior staff personnel are undoubtedly legitimate, since they have formally joined up to the practice and are recognised members of the community. They are probably, to begin with at least, peripheral rather than central to the functioning of the practice. They are unlikely to be given core responsibilities to begin with;

THE VALUE OF ROUTINE
WIM CROUWEL

The moment you have little time, you fall back on your routine, because you don't have the time or you don't take the time to really think about it. In my own practice I have had times that I was just too busy, so in much of my work, with the benefit of hindsight, routine has been important.

although if they do well, they may move rapidly from the edge to the centre. They are most certainly active participants rather than passive observers. They are expected to contribute and at the same time learn the ways of the community. These three characteristics seem to offer a beautifully constructed conjunction of good conditions for learning. This is learning through doing in a social context. The comments by Ken Yeang (throughout this book) show how he consciously adapts this process for staff of varying levels of experience.

The students joining a studio that we discussed in the previous chapter can equally be seen as 'legitimate peripheral participants'. In recent research we have found that tutors tend to think that the studio is much more student-led than the students themselves do (Samsuddin, 2008). Dutton's points about the unequal distribution of power showed the importance of the community (as run by a tutor) in determining the learning that would take place.

What we see in the design practice is much more than the simple transmission of expertise from the group to the individual. Rather we see the development of collective expertise. The guiding principles belong not to an individual but to the practice. They are developed progressively through a series of projects that enable the team as a whole to develop an appreciation of what they mean in future practice.

CONTINUOUS MULTI-LEVEL LEARNING

So if designers are really in lifelong learning it seems sensible to turn to existing models of experiential learning to understand this process. One popular and influential model of experiential learning was developed by Kolb in the 1980s. Kolb describes experiential learning as taking place in a cycle, consisting of four stages around which the learner loops continuously (Kolb and Fry, 1975).

HOW DOES THIS WORK IN DESIGN?

In order to understand how this experiential learning process might work in design practice we can turn back to one of the views of design we introduced in Chapter 2. In that view we saw design as involving activity at the four levels: project, process, practice and profession. Clearly the main vehicle for continuous professional learning in design is the project. Designers spend the vast majority of their professional lives inside projects. We shall return to the problems this might cause shortly, but for now we must just accept this phenomenon. It is through projects that designers get a very large proportion

PROFESSION
PRACTICE
PROCESS
PROJECT

pg.61

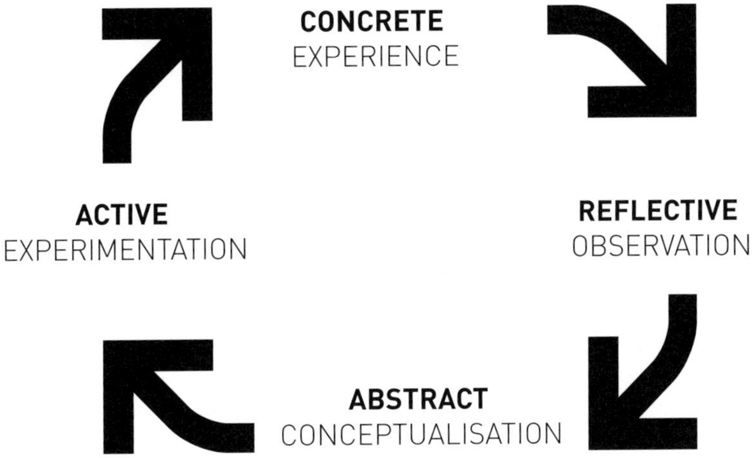

CONCRETE
EXPERIENCE

ACTIVE
EXPERIMENTATION

REFLECTIVE
OBSERVATION

ABSTRACT
CONCEPTUALISATION

Fig 7.1 Kolb's learning cycle

KOLB'S LEARNING CYCLE

Kolb suggests that we learn from what he calls concrete experience through a process of reflection and then abstraction to more generic ideas (creating an idea—theory, model, hypothesis). This has some resonances with Kelly's ideas introduced in Chapter 4 of humans as scientists. We look at the world and try to work out how to predict in future from our current experiences, said Kelly. For Kolb, this abstract idea can lead to a new experimental action, which in turn leads to a new experience that can be reflected upon; and so we go round the loop again. If we use this simple model to look at the extremely complex case of the development of design expertise, many questions arise. The main questions for practitioners centre around the place these four phases of the learning cycle have in their working lives, and what you are doing to support each step in the learning process.

of the experiences that offer learning opportunities and the further development of expertise.

It seems reasonable to examine the processes used by designers to see how these might maximise or inhibit learning opportunities. Are there some particular points during design projects when the process naturally offers learning and, if so, how can these be identified and exploited? Clearly, for designers a substantial amount of what Kolb would call their 'concrete experiences' comes in the form of projects. Designers tend to gather precedent voraciously. The vast majority of this gathering is not passive or aimless but done inside projects in order to tackle specific problems. Whichever way you look at it, the design project appears to be the start of Kolb's cycle for designers.

We turn now to the view of design as 'practice'. We can interpret this in two ways here. Firstly, there is the practice which forms the personal development of every individual designer. Secondly, there must inevitably be the practice of the professional grouping or organisation that the designer is working through; often literally referred to as a 'practice'.

This analysis allows us to see designing as a two-way process. On the one hand, the design project is apparently primarily aimed at solving some problems for clients and users. On the other hand, it is also a major vehicle for learning by the designers. In this way we can see design almost as a form of research (Lawson, 2002). In fact it goes further. Design is the very core of the way in which the whole profession learns. It is a major part of the discourse about the subject. If you want to know where a particular design field is going you might read some papers but equally you might study some recent design work. Normally of course you do both. However, our point is made here. In many fields the profession as a whole gathers and disseminates knowledge, and therefore expertise, through research leading to published articles. In design it is just as likely to be through the act of designing itself and looking at design solutions.

Indeed the formation and development of what in Chapter 5 we called 'guiding principles' is surely done through this process. Designers develop their own personal or practice agenda; a set of concerns or issues that interests them. They explore those ideas through their designs gradually understanding, advancing and developing them. In Chapter 2 we saw how the Malaysian architect Ken Yeang developed ideas on tropical sustainable high rise buildings in exactly this manner. Although he personally started this line of enquiry when he was studying in the UK, now it has to be carried out and developed with the help of all the staff of his practice. Here he talks about

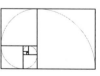

pg.181

DESIGN AS A FORM OF RESEARCH
BRYAN LAWSON

One clue to how we should answer this question (can design be seen as research?) lies in the fact that many good architects have been less active as writers, but remain well published. For example architects I have interviewed (Santiago Calatrava, Eva Jiricna and Michael Wilford) have all had many books and articles written about them and their work. George Bernard Shaw reports Richard Wagner as responding rather testily to a critic who asked him to explain The Ring. 'It is the explanation', Wagner is said to have replied! (Shaw, 1992).

Surely we would not regard the output of music critics as having greater value than that of Wagner himself. Similarly I have published material on the design process of Santiago Calatrava, but it would be absurd not to recognise that his contribution to knowledge is infinitely greater than mine. However his work is in the form of design and mine in the form of a book and papers in refereed journals. In conventional terms I have conducted research and he has not! Either this is nonsense or we must accept design as a form of research at least in our field.

how he assimilates new staff into the practice so that they become part of the programme of work. This accumulated experience is then analysed and published more conventionally (Yeang, 2006).

LEARNING FROM THE PROJECT

The project is clearly the most concrete and direct source of learning for designers. It is principally from looking at and analysing projects where designers gather the episodic knowledge that allows them to develop and share precedent and gambits. Simply doing projects does not guarantee that learning takes place and that expertise is created. A major study of the extent to which design organisations in the construction industry learned from their projects revealed some clues about this (Lawson et al., 2003). This study (LEAF–see below) taught us that two things must be in place and in harmony for learning to be maximised. There must be both skills and values.

SYMBOLIC   EPISODIC

pg.127

As we have seen throughout this book there are skills involved in abstracting generic lessons from particular cases. Identifying the points in the project of when reflection is valuable, and when not, is clearly one of those skills. Storing the knowledge gained, transferring it and making it accessible to others at other times is clearly another skill.

The second requirement is that such skills must be valued. For the individual this is a very simple matter. Either you have a set of values about development or you do not. For the team practice, however, this is a little more complex. In our study of learning in practices we found a major common obstacle to developing these values. Quite simply, most design practices use the project team as their main organisational structure. During the life of the project, it is a major source of income for the practice; so understandably you are not keen to have resource sitting outside project teams that is not obviously earning fees. In larger practices, members of teams often do not remain constant but are shuffled around according to the nature and size of the projects currently running. Typically a designer will finish working on a project and immediately move into a new team and begin another. It is all too easy therefore simply not to schedule in responsibilities to transfer knowledge from individual projects to the practice as a whole. This renders these design firms dangerously vulnerable to a loss of this knowledge, experiences and memory when a designer leaves the firm.

ASSIMILATING NEW STAFF INTO A DESIGN PRACTICE
KEN YEANG

If the person is not a mature designer you can't just let them wonder what you like, so if he's not a mature designer, if he's a training student then you have to work a little bit more, you teach them, you bring them out, the same way you are working with a student to bring out the best in them but if it's an experienced designer like (names several of his staff) very confident and they have very definite views of what they like and what they don't like and I try not to interfere with them and I try to respect them and I say 'well how do you feel about this' and they actually say 'Ken I think it's vile you know' even if it's my own idea and if they think it's vile they say they think it's vile. So that's where you bring out the best in other person you're working with. Otherwise you are doing it all yourself, you never get the best out of the other people.

REFLECTING AT THE RIGHT TIME

Actively managing and supporting your own development process empowers the practitioner to keep developing. But it is all too easy in a busy professional life to move on quickly to the next immediate task. More often than not, we only turn to these things when it is too late. That is why many therapies can start quite easily by asking the patient for some basic reflection and abstraction: they start with having to write your life story—and that already has great therapeutic value. In normal daily life, one would never take the time to reflect. That often is the weak link in the learning cycle.

So the question is: What do you do to support your reflection? There are parts of the design profession that potentially are more reflective in nature. In the course of any design project you give presentations, and judge the developing design numerous times. Another point might be when you write a new job description, or talk to new staff members who have just come into the design team. But those opportunities are few and far between and these activities can be done without much evaluation. Other reflection might be limited to telling a story over a couple of drinks but that may not be accurate enough to serve as a basis for the all-important process of developing yourself as a designer!

The logical application of Kolb's experiential learning model to design would suggest that when a project is finished we should reflect on it in order to create generic ideas. We found many organisations used extensive post-project analysis but still failed to transfer knowledge. In this scenario reports are written by the project team at the end of the project. The comments about 'post-project depression' suggest that psychologically the designer or design team is hardly in the right frame of mind to do this. In any case this is a dull and unrewarding chore. Even worse those performing it suffer more disincentives than benefits. Who wants to document their own mistakes or inadequacies?

One possible way forward here is to require teams to perform a review of recent relevant projects at the beginning of each new project. This at least has the advantage that those who are doing the work stand to benefit from it and also have some reasons for looking critically. This is rather like reading a book or visiting a building. If you have no particular context it is amazing how little you can get out of the process. Have a particular current problem in mind and the book or the place suddenly reveal all sorts of useful ideas.

Another technique is to involve the whole practice in some communal activities. This can be either outside projects altogether, such as lectures or field

POST-PROJECT DEPRESSION

Design projects are quite an experience. Often they involve a great creative challenge, high stakes for all involved and project dynamics that are really unpredictable. This puts an enormous pressure on the designer. These are the kinds of situations that can bring out the best in you. Intense emotions of hope, fear, enthusiasm and uncertainty follow each other in quick succession; a roller-coaster ride.

This requires huge personal involvement by the designer. The intensity can be such that the design project becomes an absorbing world in itself, leaving the designer lost to the rest of the world. Relationships get stale, houses run down, gardens become wildernesses: the project is the only thing that counts.

Surely, the successful ending of such a project would be a cause for celebration. But somehow designers find it difficult to do this. They tend to dive into the next project. There is no time to look back, we need to move on—the grass in the future is always greener. Many design projects do not even have a clear ending. There are always a couple of things that need some follow-up so projects tend to peter out, ending in silence, in nothingness.

Psychologically speaking, this is not good for us at all. A project is a world that you have inhabited for weeks or months, maybe even years. And now that world is gone. It can leave an uncanny hollow feeling, a real psychological and physical hangover.

All the attention, commitment and momentum that kept you going through the hard times evaporate. The goals that were all-important a couple of weeks ago are now irrelevant. This sudden shock of relativity makes you feel a fool, desperately asking yourself 'Why did I let myself be dragged into it again?'. Dejection can easily lead to a full-blown post-project depression; feelings of loss, emptiness, and vague discontent accompanied by a monumental dip in energy levels. It will take a while before you are back on your feet. If we want to avoid this, we really should learn to celebrate our successes.

trips. It can also be inside projects. The English architect John Outram's idea of running a whole practice esquisse, or rough sketch design competition, is one way of achieving this. Ken Yeang talked of similar benefits in Chapter 2.

FORMALISED MODELS OF GATHERING KNOWLEDGE

One useful way to build expertise through projects is to apply a common and formal set of structured questions. Many design projects are so complex that they are likely to contain lessons of quite different types. A number of design project analysis formats have been published and some are required within certain procurement routes. An advantage of such techniques is that the common structure encourages a concentration on generic issues. On the other hand, over-formalised methods of project knowledge transfer can easily become routine and uncreative. One apparently popular structure is to see design as a sequence of activities. Examples of this abound in the construction industry largely sponsored either by client organisations or professional bodies. Sadly many of these seem to have been created not by designers but by those perhaps on the periphery of the process. As a result, they often demonstrate a lack of understanding about design by creating structures that simply do not match the real experience of designers. Product designers who have had to work under the inflexible whip of the ISO 9000 series of standards for design projects will recognise this phenomenon.

The typical comment from a design team member in the LEAF (Learning from Experience and Applying Feedback) study suggests that, even when similar projects are run, mistakes are being repeated (Lawson et al., 2003). Clearly, some form of formal learning tool is needed. However, the comments by the project manager warn us that imposing unrealistic structures on design simply is unlikely to be effective.

The LEAF model suggests an alternative kind of structure for gathering and recording knowledge about projects. LEAF suggests that projects can go well or badly in at least three importantly different ways. The structure refers to these as 'product', 'process', and 'performance'.

The product issues are all of those to do with the materiality of the components and systems in the designed object. Questions here would include those about how well all of these physical elements worked and met the specifications laid down for them, how easy, reliable and cost effective they were to operate and maintain.

DESIGN COMPETITIONS
JOHN OUTRAM

We tend to do a few big projects, we virtually do no small projects and the way it's been working more and more is when a project comes in we hold an esquisse, everybody in the office does a design, competitively. For the one we are negotiating now, my three associates and I, each presented our design to the client. Now this I thought was quite dangerous, Max Fordham who was there, thought it was quite unprecedented, he'd never known anybody expose themselves like this you see. But, in fact it had a very good effect on the client because it winkled out of the client what he was somehow looking for which meant that we could identify much better what the client was thinking about and therefore relate it to what we could offer.

REALISTIC STRUCTURES TO DESCRIBE DESIGN
LEAF

DESIGN TEAM MEMBER
Despite carrying out relatively similar projects yet the same mistakes are repeated over and over again on every project, every time!

IN-HOUSE PROJECT MANAGER
These procedures have to be simplified to be more effective. They ought to be designed to be used as guidance through the main critical stages of the project, but in their current state many have been left on the shelf.

IN-HOUSE PROJECT MANAGER
There is not enough time given for the organisation to prepare for, set up and run evaluations. We would like to have more time at the early stage of the project.

LEAF
LEARNING FROM EXPERIENCE APPLYING FEEDBACK
LEAF was a four-year research project to study the extent to which the construction industry learned from building design projects. It was funded by the British Government and EPSRC Research Council. It worked by reviewing a series of projects carried out by three major national client bodies in the transport industry.

The process issues are all of those to do with the procuring, designing, manufacturing, and constructing of the object. Questions here would include how well this went in relation to time schedules and budgets.

The performance issues concern the impact of the designed object on the client's primary business. Questions here would include the extent to which it has made money, expanded business, increased throughput, enhanced quality of life, or added value.

Interestingly, these three dimensions appear to be more independent than one might expect. It is, for example, quite possible to design and deliver a building early and under budget and yet for it to obstruct the users' everyday life infuriatingly.

The LEAF model also used another dimension known as IPA; or 'intentions', 'practices' and 'aspirations'. This enables us to see a project in terms of what was intended to happen, what actually happened and what those closely involved would like to happen. Learning can then take place around the relationship between these three views of the project. Are there frequent and recurring mismatches between what was intended and the actual outcomes? Are the aspirations of the clients and users really being heard in the process? Is the design practice managed in a very top-down manner with intentions absolutely adhered to but the knowledge of the job designers not being utilised?

This also enables us to analyse where a design practice is in terms of the way it makes use of knowledge in the creation of its collective expertise. It is, of course, entirely possible that the practice is in the apparently virtuous state of having its intentions, practices and aspirations all lined up or synchronised. Alternatively, and much more likely, is the situation where one of these three is out of synch with the other two. Since the world is always changing, the state of complete synchrony can only be maintained by an organisation that is not learning and adapting. So the interesting question here for a design practice is how it moves itself around and constantly attempts synchrony.

Such a pattern of questions allows for great flexibility in the nature of projects and yet structures knowledge in a way that offers the potential of learning generic lessons and adding to the total expertise of the practice. This precisely addresses the issue we have found to be a recurring theme in this book: designerly ways of knowing tend to be focused on experiential knowledge rather than theoretical knowledge. The trick though lies in the ability to transfer experiences from one situation and be able to reframe them into apparently different situations.

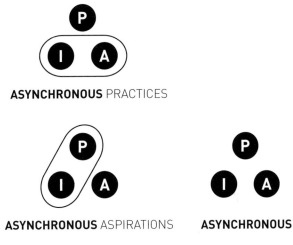

ASYNCHRONOUS PRACTICES

SYNCHRONOUS ASYNCHRONOUS ASPIRATIONS ASYNCHRONOUS

ASYNCHRONOUS INTENTIONS

Fig 7.2 The LEAF Intentions, Practices and Aspirations model

THE REALITY OF DESIGN PRACTICE

In Figure 7.2 the middle column of situations is very commonly found. In each case the letter outside the line represents a view that is out of synchrony with the other two inside the line. In the top case the designers have a set of Intentions (I) that are exactly what they all Aspire (A) to. However in practice they actually do something else, probably in response to external circumstances. This might be pragmatic but is confusing for their collaborators and clients. The middle case shows designers with perhaps humble Intentions (I) that are carried into Practice (P) but leaving those involved unhappy and wanting much more (A). The bottom case shows designers Practising (P) as they Aspire to (A) but declaring something else altogether. Many clients have told us that they feel this way about their architects who seem to have a hidden agenda.

These learning cycles actually take place on all of the levels of design practice that were described in Chapter 2. They are nested, with the project level being the most concrete and direct. But on the basis of the accumulated experiences within the project, a designer develops his or her own process, and the processes make up a design practice. We could add here that the design practices together inform the personality and identity of the designer. This complex system of multiple learning cycles on four different levels is not easy to manage. It takes a lot of effort to get this right. Yet we tend to take our own development for granted. It is hugely important, and difficult to see because we are too close to it.

THE DARKER SIDE OF CREATING DESIGN EXPERTISE

Designing seems to be addictive. Designers feel the need to be designing.

Architects and designers are one of the first professions to be hit by economic recessions since they work right at the beginning of the development cycle. When this happens many continue to work inventing projects, doing competitions, working speculatively for little or no fees just to keep designing. Those that do leave the profession often find ways of getting back into design, working for themselves or breaking into new fields such as web design.

Good practicing designers joining the staff of an academic department to teach often express feelings and demonstrate symptoms that suggest withdrawal. Often academics want to set up consulting practices within schools of design to retain their connection with practice. We find academics changing perfectly good studio projects for no other reason that they want novelty—effectively complaining that they have seen most of the answers already and they are bored. This suggests that, although they are not actually doing designs here, even when tutoring, they feel unrewarded unless new challenges are being put in front of them.

There is no doubt then that designing is both exhilarating and exhausting. The exhilaration comes mainly from achieving an outcome when you had no idea where you were going at the beginning. The exhaustion comes from this perpetual need to create new things and have original ideas. To add to this the need to develop and get better as a designer poses a huge challenge. There are several possible reasons for an arrested development of design expertise. Designers themselves may settle for working comfortably at a certain level; they may tend to lose the admiration of their peers and paradoxically this is perhaps what many designers crave most! This approach also

HEARING THE ASPIRATIONS OF USERS?
LEAF

The following were fairly typical comments from the users of buildings designed in projects studied for the LEAF project.

 At the end of a project, we normally land up with a product that costs us more to run. Because the people who design and build projects are only interested in the capital figure to meet their budget requirements as the major factor of success which in order to achieve, they would have made a lot of compromises while the cost of running the building will be much more over a much longer time period.

As end users, we feel that we are generally ignored, we do have a very small voice and little involvement, the times we have got involved, we tend to feel ignored, because we are perceived to be low priority and less important.

 There was no feedback at the post-project stage. We wish to have follow-up meetings after going operational.

seems to run the risk of actually losing expertise. Jan Lucassen summarised this nicely in his quote seen in Chapter 5 when he talked of 'raising the bar' in each project.

Other designers may lose their self-confidence and impose self-inflicted barriers to progress, based on a low self-image. Within a fast-moving and sometimes exhausting profession, it is sometimes hard to muster the energy to keep valuing yourself. Many of the designers' quotes we use here show an acute ability for self-criticism. This raises one of many paradoxes about designing. You must be your own severest critic as usually it is you who can see most clearly the failings of your work. On the other hand such repeated self-criticism can be destructive. We find some designers like Jeroen van Oyen actually saying that they should be more positive in their attitude; even criticising their self-criticism!

Another cause for arrested development of design expertise can be found in the environment. Sometimes the circumstances in which we practice just stop any potential learning from happening. The environment might be completely over-stimulating to a designer, providing an abundance of fascinating challenges that are way out of one's zone of proximal development. Deadlines and circumstances may prevent the reflection that allows the learning from rapidly passing sets of events. These can be the conditions for the 'burn-out' we have already identified and which is not that uncommon.

pg.175

Alternatively, we can be forced into a corner where there is not that much to learn; for instance, in a design practice where the gambits and guiding principles are very much set. Once you have mastered them, there can be some satisfaction in applying them appropriately and wisely, but there is nowhere to go from there. There may be reasons to stay in a job like that for a while, but it might also be a golden cage.

Sometimes though, a stable sequence of development comes to a natural end, offering little further potential for development. Perhaps at this point some revolution or paradigm shift is needed. It is possible to look back over the careers of some famous designers and find such a pattern. For example, the architect Frank Gehry was known for a certain geometric regularity in many projects done well and consistently over a lengthy period; then suddenly there was a revolution into the irregular forms for which he has more latterly become famous. Again that set of ideas has now been explored over a series of projects. Similarly, one could see that the work of James Stirling went through a number of sudden changes followed by evolutionary exploration and development.

Fig 7.3 Bookshelves—Jeroen van Oyen—originally developed for a public library, to encourage browsing and serendipity (finding what you are not looking for). Their design marks the transition in Jeroen van Oyen's work from product design towards the design of (contexts for) communication.

SELF-CRITICISM JEROEN VAN OYEN

I have noticed that, the better I have grown to know myself, the better I have been designing. I have not changed my way of designing, but there is a different feeling. I am not embarrassed anymore for designing in the way that I do... I have the feeling that I can be myself in this, and that I do not need to make a design that looks like something else. I do not have to deal with that any more.

This daring to trust that all will be well and that a solution will present itself, that grows with self-confidence and the development of a better form of self-critique. I used to have a lot of negative self-criticism. I always had to design something incredibly beautiful. And that never happened. Now, I am not pressuring myself about this anymore. Whether it looks good or not, it has to be right!... Letting go is an important part of the process.

JEROEN VAN OYEN
Jeroen van Oyen (1966) worked as a design engineer at General Electric Plastics. There he has developed plastic products for train interiors, football stadiums, bathrooms and the like. In 1992 he started his own design firm, now called KAO, that has moved away from product design and is largely concentrating on the design of communication.

STABILITY AND UNCERTAINTY

As usual with design though, we must be careful not to develop rigid rules here. What works for one designer may well not work for another. Some are more at home in a stable environment and others crave change and innovation at every turn. What this does suggest is that for the creation of design expertise we need some balance. In our rapidly changing world, there is a lot of wisdom in being able to change your practice continuously, while still maintaining a stable foothold. As Wim Crouwel suggests, keeping some sort of routine may be helpful.

The immediate fascination of design must also make it hard to keep your balance all the time. 'Balance' might be the wrong word in the context of design; you need challenges, a certain measure of imbalance, to be able to grow as a designer. Managing a dynamic equilibrium is perhaps the fine art of creating design expertise. The gambits and guiding principles we have described in Chapter 5 are an important basis for the work of a designer, but they can never be quite static. In Chapter 4 we have argued that design education is just the start of the design journey. That point was reinforced in Chapter 6, when we described design education as being relatively limited, almost primitive in comparison to the delightful complexity and richness of the design professions. It is absolutely crucial for any designer to build up an ability to keep developing further. Through this prolonged, intense development, the journey we have been describing as a professional quest in this book becomes an ever more personal one. In moving through the levels of expertise, the identity of the designer changes, too.

pg.175

pg.181

The art of creating design expertise then has as much to do with oscillating between the healthy tension needed to deliver good work and the taking on of too much of a challenge, and having to struggle to survive. This is particularly true in times of growth; there are distinctive growing pains and intense anxieties that accompany the phase when one leaves one way of working, without having yet attained mastery on the next level (e.g. when students of design move from a rule-based to a strategy-based way of working). The anxieties that are always just around the corner in design practice never go away. Even experienced and expert designers can easily get it wrong in any one project.

pg.69

Every design project from the beginning of university to the end of a professional career demands both performance by the designer and yet offers opportunities for learning and exploration; a unique and exquisite tension. Our final quotation from Frans de la Haye sums this up beautifully: 'There is so much continuous development going on in the life of every

MANAGING CHANGE
FRANS DE LA HAYE

 If all goes well you will have changed after every project, you will have developed yourself further. If you manage to deal with change in this manner it energises you. I think this can be taught. If you confront students with this in design school, you are just in time. Later in life it gets harder. But when they are 18, 19, you can still touch them, you can still get them in a complete panic... I still have moments of complete panic, and to be honest, I seek them.

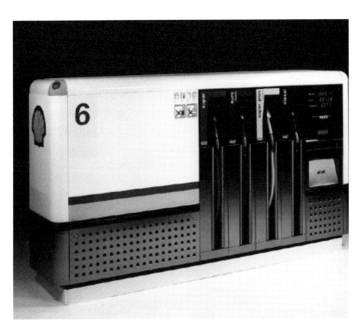

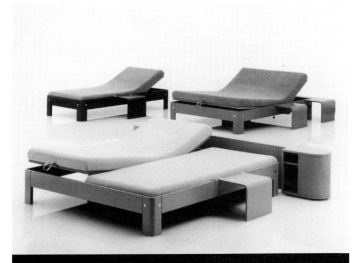

Fig 7.4 The Auronde line of beds for Auping, and the Shell petrol stations exemplify Frans de la Haye's drive for coherent forms and functional integration. The resulting shapes are simple, rounded and friendly—no matter how complicated the mechanisms that they hide

FRANS DE LA HAYE

Frans de la Haye (1943) started his own Industrial Design studio upon graduating and later became one of the partners at Tel Design, one of the most innovative European graphic and product design firms in the 1970s. A classic design from that period was the 'Auronde' a range of beds for Auping (1972). The hugely successful 'Auronde' range responded to the trend of bedrooms becoming more part of living spaces due to the introduction of central heating. It is a clear illustration of Frans' view that the core of the Industrial Design profession is to be sensitive to developments in society, and to translate these trends into commercially successful products.

From 1982 on he has again worked as an independent product designer, working on projects like the 'spanfiets' (a revolutionary lightweight racing bike with a frame that gets its strength from cables under high tension) and a line of petrol stations for the Shell oil company that was the first to integrate all the different functionalities within a clear and logical simple square form. This design, completely revolutionary in its time, has become the iconic example for designing new generations of petrol stations around the world.

committed designer that design might be better described as a journey, rather than a job. You are forever creating design expertise; you are forever becoming a designer…'

REFERENCES

Kolb, D.A. and Fry, R. (1975). **Toward an applied theory of experiential learning**. Theories of Group Processes. C. Cooper. London, John Wiley.

Lave, J. (1988). **Cognition in Practice: Mind, mathematics and culture in everyday life**. Cambridge, Cambridge University Press.

Lave, J. and Wenger, E. (1991). **Situated Learning: Legitimate peripheral participation**. Cambridge, Cambridge University Press.

Lawson, B.R. (2002). **Design as Research**. Architectural Research Quarterly 6(2): 109–114.

Lawson, B.R., Bassanino, M., Phiri, M. and Worthington, J. (2003). **Intentions, practices and aspirations: Understanding learning in design**. Design Studies 24(4): 327–339.

Samsuddin, I.b. (2008). **Architectural Education: peer culture in design studio and its relationship with designing interest**. Architecture. PhD, Sheffield, University of Sheffield.

Shaw, B. (1922). **The Perfect Wagnerite**. New York, Dover.

Wenger, E. (1998). **Communities of Practice**. Cambridge, Cambridge University Press.

Yeang, K. (2006). **Ecodesign: A manual for ecological design**. London, John Wiley.

BIBLIOGRAPHY

Adelson, B. (1981). "Problem solving and the development of abstract categories in programming languages." **Memory and Cognition** 9(4): 422–433.

Ahmed, S., K. M. Wallace, et al. (2003). "Understanding the differences between how novices and experienced designers approach design tasks." **Research in Engineering Design** 14(1): 1–11.

Anthony, K. H. (1991). **Design Juries on Trial: the renaissance of the design studio**. New York, Van Nostrand Reinhold.

Bannister, D. (1966). "A new theory of personality." **New Horizons in Psychology**. B. M. Foss. Harmondsworth, Penguin: 361–380.

Bartlett, F. C. (1958). **Thinking**. London, George Allen and Unwin.

Boden, M. (1990). **The Creative Mind: Myths and Mechanisms**. London, Weidenfeld and Nicolson.

Brand, S. (1995). **How Buildings Learn: what happens after they're built**. Harmondsworth, Penguin.

Broadbent, G. and A. Ward, eds. (1969). **Design methods in Architecture**. London, Lund Humphries.

Bruner, J. S., J. J. Goodnow, et al. (1956). **A Study of Thinking**. New York, Wiley.

Chase, W. G. and H. A. Simon (1973). "Perception in chess." **Cognitive Psychology** 4: 55–81.

Chi, M. T. H., P. J. Feltovich, et al. (1981). "Categorization and representation of physics problems by experts and novices." **Cognitive Science** 5: 121–152.

Chi, M. T. H. and R. Koeske (1983). "Network representation of a child's dinosaur knowledge." **Developmental Psychology** 19: 29–39.

Christiaans, H. H. C. M. and C. H. Dorst (1992a). "Cognitive models in industrial design engineering: a protocol study." **Proceedings of the fourth international conference on Design Theory and Methodology**. D. L. Taylor and L. A. Stauffer. New York, ASME Press: 131–137.

Christiaans, H. H. C. M. and C. H. Dorst (1992b). "An empirical study into design thinking." **Research in Design Thinking**. N. Cross, C. H. Dorst and N. Roozenburg. Delft, Delft University Press: 119–125.

Cross, N. (1982). "Designerly ways of knowing." **Design Studies** 3(4): 221–227.

Cross, N., ed. (1984). **Developments in Design Methodology**. Chichester, John Wiley.

Cross, N. (1990). "The nature and nurture of the design ability." **Design Studies** 11(3): 127–140

Cross, N. (1996). **The Method in Their Madness: Understanding how designers think**. Delft, Delft University Press.

Cross, N., H. H. C. M. Christiaans, et al., eds. (1996). **Analysing Design Activity**. Chichester, Wiley.

Cross, N., H. H. C. M. Christiaans, et al. (1994). "Design expertise amongst student designers." **Journal of Art and Design Education** 13: 39–56.

Cross, N. and E. Edmonds, eds. (2003). **Expertise in Design: design thinking research symposium 6**. Sydney, Creativity and Cognition Studios Press.

Darke, J. (1978). "The primary generator and the design process." **New Directions in Environmental Design Research: proceedings of EDRA 9**. W. E. Rogers and W. H. Ittleson. Washington, EDRA: 325–337.

de Bono, E. (1969). **The Mechanism of Mind**. London, Jonathan Cape.

de Bono, E. (1976). **Teaching Thinking**. London, Temple Smith.

de Bono, E. (1991). **Six Action Shoes**. London, Fontana.

De Groot, A. D. (1965). **Thought and Choice in Chess**. The Hague, Mouton.

Doidge, C., R. Sara, et al. (2000). **The Crit**. Oxford, Architectural Press.

Dorst, C. H. (1995). "Analysing design activity: new directions in protocol analysis." **Design Studies** 16(2): 139–142.

Dorst, C. H. (2003). **Understanding Design**. Amsterdam, BIS Publishers.

Dorst, C. H. (2006). **Understanding Design**. Amsterdam, BIS Publishers.

Dorst, C. H. and N. Cross (2001). "Creativity in the design process: co-evolution of the problem-solution." **Design Studies** 22(5): 425–437.

Dreyfus, H. L. (1992). **What Computers Still Can't Do: a critique of artificial reason**. Cambridge, MA, MIT Press.

Dreyfus, H. L. (2002). "Intelligence without representation- Merleau-Ponty's critique of mental representation." **Phenomenology and the Cognitive Sciences** 1: 367–383.

Dreyfus, H. L. (2003). The Spinoza Lectures, University of Amsterdam.

Dreyfus, H. L. and S. Dreyfus (2005). "Expertise in real world contexts." **Organization Studies** 26(5): 779–792.

Durling, D., N. Cross, et al. (1996). **Personality and learning preferences of students in design and design-related disciplines**. International Conference on Design and Technology Educational Research, IDATER96, Loughborough University.

Dutton, T. A. (1991a). "Architectural Education and Society: An interview with J. Max Bond, Jr." **Voices in Architectural Education**. T. A. Dutton. New York, Bergin and Garvey: 83–95.

Dutton, T. A. (1991b). "The hidden curriculum and the design studio: toward a critical studio pedagogy." **Voices in Architectural Education**. T. A. Dutton. New York, Bergin and Garvey: 165–194.

Eckert, C. and M. Stacey (2000). "Sources of inspiration: a language of design." **Design Studies** 21(5): 523–538.

Flynn, J. R. (1987). "Massive IQ gains in 14 nations: What IQ tests really measure." **Psychological Bulletin** 101: 171–191.

Galway, J. (1990). **Flute**. London, Kahn and Averill.

Gardner, H. (1983). **Frames of Mind: the theory of multiple intelligences**. London, Heinemann.

Gero, J. (1998). "Conceptual designing as a sequence of situated acts." **Artificial Intelligence in Structural Engineering**. I. Smith. Berlin, Springer-Verlag: 165–177.

Gero, J. S. and M. A. Rosenman (1990). "A conceptual framework for knowledge-based design research at Sydney University." **Artificial Intelligence in Engineering** 5(2): 65–77.

Getzels, J. W. and Jackson, P.W. (1962). **Creativity and Intelligence: Explorations with gifted children**. New York, John Wiley.

Gibson, J. J. (1986). **An ecological approach to visual perception**. Hillsdale, N.J., Lawrence Erlbaum.

Goel, V. (1995). **Sketches of Thought**. Cambridge, Mass, MIT Press.

Goldschmidt, G. (1998). "Creative architectural design: reference versus precedence." **Journal of Architectural and Planning Research** 15(3): 258–270.

Gordon, W. J. J. (1961). **Synectics: The development of creative capacity**. New York, Harper and Row.

Gould, S. J. (1992). **The Panda's Thumb: more reflections on natural history**. New York, W.W. Norton and Co.

Groeneveld, R. (2006), **De innerlijke kracht van de ontwerper** ("The Inner Strength of the Designer" (in Dutch, with English summary)). PhD Thesis TU Delft.

Hatchuel, A. (2002). "Towards design theory and expandable rationality: the unfinished program of Herbert Simon." **Journal of Management and Governance** 5(3): 260–273.

Heylighen, A. and I. M. Verstijnen (2003). "Close encounters of the architectural kind." **Design Studies** 24(4): 313–326.

Hinsley, D. A., J. R. Hayes, et al. (1978). "From words to equations: meaning and representation in algebra word problems." **Cognitive Processes in Comprehension**. P. A. Carpenter and M. A. Just. Hillsdale, N.J. Erlbaum.

Hirshberg, J. (1998). **The Creative Priority**. New York, Harper Business.

Hudson, L. (1966). **Contrary Imaginations: a psychological study of the English schoolboy**. London, Methuen.

Hunt, T. (1999). **Tony Hunt's Sketch Book**. Oxford, Architectural Press.

Hunt, T. (2003). **Tony Hunt's Second Sketchbook**. Oxford, Architectural Press.

Kelly, G. A. (1955). **The Psychology of Personal Constructs**. New York, Norton.

Kelly, G. A. (1963). **A Theory of Personality**. New York, W.W. Norton and Co.

Khaidzir, K. A. M. (2007). "An expertise study of cognitive interactions between tutors and students in design tutorial conversations." **Architecture**. Sheffield, University of Sheffield. PhD.

Kidder, T. (1982). **The Soul of a New machine**. Harmondsworth, Penguin.

Kirton, M., ed. (1989). **Adaptors and Innovators: styles of creativity and problem solving**. New York, Routledge.

Kolb, D. A. and R. Fry (1975). **Toward an applied theory of experiential learning. Theories of Group Processes**. C. Cooper. London, John Wiley.

Kuhn, T. S. (1962). **The Structure of Scientific Revolutions**. Chicago, University of Chicago Press.

Lakoff, G. and M. Johnson (1980). **Metaphors We Live By**. Chicago, University of Chicago Press.

Lave, J. (1988). **Cognition in Practice: mind, mathematics and culture in everyday life**. Cambridge, Cambridge University Press.

Lave, J. and E. Wenger (1991). **Situated Learning: legitimate peripheral participation**. Cambridge, Cambridge University Press.

Lawson, B. R. (1979). "Cognitive strategies in architectural design." **Ergonomics** 22(1): 59–68.

Lawson, B. R. (1993). "Parallel Lines of Thought." **Languages of Design** 1(4): 357–366.

Lawson, B. R. (1994). **Design in Mind**. Oxford, Butterworth Architecture.

Lawson, B. R. (1997). **How Designers Think**. Oxford, Architectural Press.

Lawson, B. R. (2001). "The context of mind." **Designing in Context**. P. Lloyd and H. Christiaans. Delft, DUP Science: 133–148.

Lawson, B. R. (2002a). "CAD and creativity: does the computer really help?" **Leonardo** 35(3): 327–331.

Lawson, B. R. (2002b). "Architecture libraries from a university perspective." **ARCLIB Bulletin** 11: 1–4.

Lawson, B. R. (2002c). "Design as Research." **Architectural Research Quarterly** 6(2): 109–114.

Lawson, B.R. (2006). **How Designers Think** (4th Edition). Oxford, Architectural Press (an imprint of Elsevier).

Lawson, B. R. (2004a). "Schemata, gambits and precedent: some factors in design expertise." **Design Studies** 25(5): 443–457.

Lawson, B. R. (2004b). **What Designers Know**. Oxford, Elsevier-Architectural Press.

Lawson, B. R., M. Bassanino, et al. (2003). "Intentions, practices and aspirations: Understanding learning in design." **Design Studies** 24(4): 327–339.

Le Corbusier (1951). **The Modulor**. London, Faber and Faber.

Lloyd, P., B. Lawson, et al. (1996). "Can concurrent verbalisation reveal design cognition?" **Analysing Design Activity**. N. Cross, H. Christiaans and K. Dorst. Chichester, Wiley: 437–463.

Lloyd, P. A. and H. M. J. J. Snelders (2003). "What was Philipe Starck thinking of." **Design Studies** 23: 237–253.

Loewy, R. (2000). **Industrial Design**. London, Laurence King Publishing.

Mackinnon, D. W. (1962). **The Nature and Nurture of Creative Talent**, Yale University.

Maguire, R. (1971). "Nearness to need." **RIBA Journal** 78(4).

Maher, M. L., Z. Bilda, et al. (2006). "Impact of collaborative virtual environments on design behaviour." **Design Computing**. J. S. Gero. Dordrecht, Springer: 305–321.

Menezes, A. and B. R. Lawson (2006). "How designers perceive sketches." **Design Studies** 27(5): 571–585.

Miller, G. A. (1956). "The magic number seven plus or minus two." **Psychological Review** 63.

Minsky, M. (1975). "A framework for representing knowledge." **The Psychology of Computer Vision**. P. H. Winston. New York, McGraw Hill.

Morrow, R. (2000). "Architectural assumptions and environmental discrimination: the case for more inclusive design in schools of architecture." **Changing Architectural Education**. D. Nichol and S. Pilling. London, E & FN Spon.

Pearman, H. (2005). "A river of talent?" **The Sunday Times**. London. 9434: 24–25.

Pereira, M. A. (2000). **ArchCal : a conceptual basis for the application of information technology into learning and teaching technical subjects in architectural education.** Sheffield, University of Sheffield. PhD.

Pirsig, R.M. (1991). **Lila**. New York, Bantam.

Postgate, J. (1991). "Bring in the Long-service commission - Science should follow the army's example." **New Scientist** 1753(26 January): forum.

Rittel, H. W. J. and M. M. Webber (1973). "Dilemmas in a general theory of planning." **Policy Sciences** 4.

Ryle, G. (1949). **The Concept of Mind**. London, Hutchinson.

Samsuddin, I. b. (2008). "Architectural Education: peer culture in design studio and its relationship with designing interest." **Architecture**. Sheffield, University of Sheffield. PhD.

Schank, R. C. (1982). **Dynamic Memory**. Cambridge, Cambridge University Press.

Schön, D. A. (1983). **The Reflective Practitioner: How professionals think in action**. London, Temple Smith.

Schön, D. A. and G. Wiggins (1992). "Kinds of seeing and their function in designing." **Design Studies** 13(2): 135–56.

Shaw, B. (1922). **The Perfect Wagnerite**. New York, Dover.

Simon, H. A. (1973). "The structure of ill-formed problems." **Artificial Intelligence** 4: 181–201.

Snyder, B. (1973). **The Hidden Curriculum**. Cambridge, Mass, MIT Press.

Sturt, G. (1923). **The Wheelwright's Shop**. Cambridge, Cambridge University Press.

Sutton, R. I. and A. Hargardon (1996). "Brainstorming groups in context: effectiveness in a product design firm." **Administrative Science Quarterly** 41: 685–718.

Tham, K. W., H. S. Lee, et al. (1990). "Building envelope design using design prototypes." **ASHRAE Trans** 96: 508–520.

Tovey, M. (1992). "Automotive stylists' design thinking." **Research in Design Thinking**. N. Cross, K. Dorst and N. Roozenburg. Delft, Delft University Press: 87– 98.

URA (2004). **20 Under 45**. Singapore, Urban Redevelopment Authority.

Valkenburg, R. C. (2000). **The Reflective Practice in product design teams**. Delt, Technical University of Delft.

Vermaas, P. E. and C. H. Dorst (2007). "On the conceptual framework of John Gero's FBS model of designing and the prescriptive aims of design methodology." **Design Studies** 28(22): 133–157.

Visser, W. (1995). "Use of episodic knowledge and information in design problem solving." **Design Studies** 16(2): 171–187.

Watson, A., ed. (2006). **Building a Masterpiece: the Sydney Opera House**. Sydney, Lund Humphries.

Wenger, E. (1998). **Communities of Practice**. Cambridge, Cambridge University Press.

Willenbrock, L. L. (1991). "An undergraduate voice in architectural education." **Voices in Architectural Education**. T. A. Dutton. New York, Bergin and Garvey: 97–119.

Wilson, C. S. J. (1986). "The play of use and use of play." **Architectural Review** 180(1073): 15–18.

Wilson, M. A. (1996). "The socialization of architectural preference." **Journal of Environmental Psychology** 16: 33–44

Wittgenstein, L. (1953). **Philosophical Investigations**. Oxford, Basil Blackwell.

Yeang, K. (2006). **Ecodesign: a manual for ecological design**. London, John Wiley.

SUBJECT INDEX

Notes: Page numbers in **bold** refer to figures/illustrations